ACCOUNTING
FOR GROWTH

For
Katy and Emily

ACCOUNTING FOR GROWTH

*Stripping the Camouflage
from Company Accounts*

Terry Smith

C
CENTURY
BUSINESS

First published in 1992 in Great Britain by
Century Business
An imprint of Random House UK Limited
20 Vauxhall Bridge Road, London SW1V 2SA

Random House Australia (Pty) Limited
20 Alfred Street, Milsons Point, Sydney
New South Wales 2061, Australia

Random House New Zealand Limited
18 Poland Road, Glenfield
Auckland 10, New Zealand

Random House South Africa (Pty) Limited
PO Box 337, Bergvlei, South Africa

Typeset in Bembo by SX Composing Ltd, Rayleigh, Essex
Printed and bound in Great Britain by
Mackays of Chatham PLC, Chatham, Kent

British Library Cataloguing in Publication Data
A catalogue record for this book is available from the British Library

ISBN 0–7126–5764–9

Companies, institutions and other organizations wishing to make bulk purchases of this title or any other Century Business publication should contact:

Direct Sales Manager
Century Business
Random House
20 Vauxhall Bridge Road
London SW1V 2SA

Fax: 071–828 6681

Contents

Acknowledgements

Without engaging in wordy platitudes, it is necessary for me to express my indebtedness to my colleagues in the UK Company Research Department of UBS Phillips & Drew for their help in compiling the information for this book. Apart from widespread help in compiling the examples and completing the Major Companies Accounting Health Check, special mention should go to Richard Hannah, the Shipping and Transport analyst, who co-authored the original Accounting for Growth research report. The other individual who must be singled out for mention is my assistant Sally Dell who prepared the manuscript, and patiently accepted my corrections, changes and handwriting. I fully acknowledge that the comments expressed in this book are my opinions, and I am not suggesting that the practices analysed are illegal, or that they even contravene Generally Accepted Accounting Practice (also known as 'GAAP') or that the various companies and accountants mentioned did not have valid reasons for using these techniques. I am more interested in the impact of these practices upon the clarity of financial information than in whether or not they satisfy the letter of the law or regulation. I believe that it is in the public interest for these issues to be discussed. Finally, I wish to acknowledge the help of all those companies who gave permission for reproduction of parts of their Annual Report and Accounts to illustrate this book.

TCS
May 1992

Part I

1

INTRODUCTION

Definition of a recession: A time when money is returned to its rightful owners
Anon

Why write another book on accounting? A visit to the Business section of any bookshop reveals a wealth of textbooks on the subject. There are several reasons for writing this particular book:

Since I began working in finance during the Secondary Banking Crisis and recession of 1973–75 I have continually been challenged by friends outside the City with a question which goes something like 'XYZ company went bust last week, but it was making profits. How can that happen?' The first example of such questions I can recall was the collapse of a retailer called Brentford Nylons in February 1976. The company had a high profile as a cut-price high street retailer whose TV advertising featured a well-known disc jockey, Alan Freeman, so its collapse attracted attention from many people outside the financial services industry. It is to those people in part that this book is directed – to help answer the question so often posed of how a company reporting profits can still go bust. Brentford Nylons was a private company. Its last accounts prior to going into receivership were for 1974, when profits of £130,000 were recorded, but only after a special credit of £550,000 in respect of a claim against a supplier, and receipt of a regional development grant of £180,000. There is nothing new about creative accounting. Incidentally, for antiquarians amongst you, Brentford Nylons was ultimately taken over by Lonrho.

Secondly, it became apparent that the recession of 1990–91 was producing a similar effect in that some companies reporting record profits were almost simultaneously going into administration. Probably the most dramatic example from the point of view of the speed of the collapse is Polly Peck, which is dealt with in the following section, 'How could it happen?' and in more detail in Appendix III. And there are plenty of other examples of companies going bust in this recession which reported 'profits' in their last results announcements and accounts – British & Commonwealth, BCCI, Maxwell Communications. To deal with some of the issues of accounting which were being raised by the events of the 1990/92 recession Richard Hannah, the Transport analyst at UBS Phillips & Drew, and I co-authored a report entitled *Accounting for Growth* at the beginning of 1991.

The title *Accounting for Growth* was a deliberate pun. We felt that much of the apparent growth in profits which had occurred in the 1980s was the result of accounting sleight of hand rather than genuine economic growth, and we set out to expose the main techniques involved, and to give live examples of companies using those techniques.

Accounting for Growth was sent to UBS Phillips & Drew's institutional clients and we presented the report to more than 60 of them. We found a surprising thirst for information in this area, particularly when it is allied to live examples. So much so that the original report was voted the best piece of research published during 1991 in the Extel survey of institutional investors. What this volume attempts to do is expand on the original work and in particular to go further into each company example, where possible reproducing the relevant section from Annual Report and Accounts so that readers can see where to find the information and how to perform the calculations needed to spot creative accounting techniques.

Is *Accounting for Growth* intended to help you make money? I start from the standpoint that few, if any, of us would read books on finance without this aim in mind, although it is probably fairer to say that this book is intended to prevent you from losing money in investment. The original research publication had a chapter entitled Major Companies Accounting Health Check, which is reproduced and updated in Chapter 16. This looked at over 200 UK companies listed on the International Stock Exchange and indicated where they were using one of the accounting/financial engineering techniques identified in the report. This checklist became affectionately known as the 'blob guide' because a blob or mark was placed in the appropriate column for each technique used by a company. Unfortunately no method of ranking the degree of a company's use of a particular technique could be found despite some heroic failures in the attempt to compute a scoring system. It always came down to a matter of judgement whether one company's change in depreciation policy was more or less serious than another's currency mismatching. We were therefore left with the simplest guide of all: the number of techniques (or number of blobs) used by each company. Since the publication of the original report this remarkably simple technique has proved to be an amazingly accurate guide to the companies to avoid as the following table shows:

Table 1.1 Share price performance of the high scorers in Accounting for
Growth Mk. I

	Number of 'Blobs'	Relative share price performance in 1991%
LEP	5	−90
Maxwell	7	−100 (suspended)
ASDA	5	−66
British Aerospace	7	−44
Burton	7	−43
Ultramar★	5	−16
Blue Circle	5	−10
Cable & Wireless	6	−5
Granada	5	−4
Sears	5	−4
Laporte	5	+6
Dixons	6	+40
Next	5	+234

★*After* bid from Lasmo

The table shows all the companies with five or more blobs i.e. using five or
more of the 11 accounting and financing techniques surveyed in *Accounting
for Growth*. With the notable exceptions of Dixons and Next, which
performed well in 1991, the share price performance of the other companies
has ranged from indifferent to disastrous, with Maxwell Communications
Corporation representing a near certain total loss to shareholders.

SO IF IN DOUBT ABOUT THE ACCOUNTING DON'T HOLD THE SHARES

Which brings us to practical advice on the layout of this book and how to
read it. Parts II and III details the techniques of accounting and financial
engineering which have proved most frequent and pernicious. Part IV is the
Major Companies Accounting Health Check (or 'blob guide') updated for
current events and also has a chapter entitled Survival Techniques in the
Accounting Jungle. For company accounting, like the investment industry
or the dealing room of a major securities firm, is a jungle with many species
of animal – some benign, some carnivorous – and its own rules. Anyone
who believes this is an exaggeration should read one of the entertaining

studies of the securities industry, perhaps most notably Michael Lewis's *Liar's Poker* (Hodder & Stoughton, 1989) about events and personalities at Salomon Brothers, including John Gutfreund and John Meriwether, the Chairman and head of bond trading who both left Salomons after the revelations about bids at US Government bond auctions.

The Survival Techniques chapter is intended to give some simple, and some unorthodox rules about reading a set of company annual accounts which might ensure that the reader is not caught up in the gloss of the annual accounts and can separate 'profit' from cash. Reverting to the Brentford Nylons example with which this Introduction began, this is the key distinction. The word 'profit' has been placed in inverted commas for good reasons – it's the result of the accountants' 'true and fair view' or, to give it its less polite name, a guess. What we would call 'an opinion' in plain English. Whereas cash is a fact. And cash is ultimately what makes or breaks a business, and this distinction is the one that my questioners could not grasp back in the recession of 1973, but which you must now learn if you are to survive in the Accounting Jungle. Good luck and good hunting.

2

HOW COULD IT HAPPEN?

POLLY PECK

On Monday 3 September 1990, Polly Peck International, the food and consumer electronics group, reported its Interim profit figures for the half year to 30 June 1990. Pre-tax profits were £110.5m, well up from £64.4m in the first half of 1989, as were Earnings Per Share of 22.4p (17.8p) and the Interim dividend of 5.5p net (4.5p). At this point Polly Peck was capitalized by the London stock market at £1.05bn. It had interests in quoted subsidiaries, Sansui and Vestel, electronics companies listed in Tokyo and Istanbul, valued at £660m, and had recently acquired the fresh food interests of Del Monte. The Interim balance sheet showed shareholders' funds of £932.7m – nearly one billion pounds.

The only cloud on the horizon was a strange episode in which Asil Nadir, Polly Peck's high profile Chairman, had recently made an approach aimed at acquiring the company's shares from other shareholders in a bid to 'take it private'. This was just the sort of move which had been seen across the Atlantic in the Management Buy-Out (MBO)/Leveraged Buy-Out (LBO) boom of recent years. But Nadir had decided not to proceed with his bid approach and had attracted some speculation on the reasons why, and why he had launched it, not to mention criticism from the Quotations Panel of the International Stock Exchange about the manner of his approach and its announcement.

How could it be that just over two weeks later at 2.21pm on Thursday 20 September, trading in Polly Peck's shares was suspended after the share price plunged by 135p to 108p?. The immediate cause was a search hours earlier of the offices of South Audley Management, a company connected with Asil Nadir, by members of the Serious Fraud Office (SFO). In August 1990, Polly Peck's shares had peaked at 457p, valuing the company at £1784m. They were now on their way to becoming worthless.

On Thursday 25 October, one month later, partners of Cork Gully and Coopers & Lybrand were appointed as administrators for Polly Peck. During a High Court hearing, the results of an insolvency study by

Coopers & Lybrand were revealed allegedly showing that an immediate liquidation of Polly Peck would produce a deficit for shareholders of £384m.

How could it happen? There are many explanations which can be proffered: obviously liquidation values are not the same as going concern values in a balance sheet and so on. But the fact is that in a period of about six months Polly Peck had changed from a darling of the stock market, reporting record profits, with Shareholders' funds of nearly £1bn and a market value which peaked a month earlier at £1.75 billion, into an insolvent company whose shareholders' investment has probably been wiped out. It is this sort of contradiction, and the inability of investors to understand what happened, which brings accounting and stock markets into disrepute.

The UK entered into a recession in the third quarter of 1990, and many public companies have since gone bust, but Polly Peck's demise should not be lost in this welter of failures. Its interests were mostly outside the UK, so it was not caught in the dramatic slowdown induced in the UK economy as an antidote to the Lawson boom.

Polly Peck is probably the most dramatic example of the large company collapses of this period, partly because of the legal proceedings against Chairman Asil Nadir, but also because of the sheer speed of its demise. (A longer review of Polly Peck's rise and fall is given in Appendix III.) But it is not the only large company to suffer this apparently inexplicable fate at this time . . .

BRITISH & COMMONWEALTH

British & Commonwealth's (B&C's) demise was not as rapid or so apparently unexpected as that of Polly Peck, but if anything, it fell from a greater height. At the peak of its share price in July 1987, B&C was valued at £1853m, making it the 46th largest company in the UK by market value, and the second largest financial company after the venerable Prudential.

By the time B&C's last set of results were announced on 27 September 1989, problems were already apparent. Not only were profits (before goodwill amortisation) down from £82.9m to £60.3m, but B&C was also experiencing difficulty disposing of some of the superfluous businesses it had acquired with Mercantile House in 1987, such as MW Marshal & Co. the money brokers, and fatefully it had acquired Atlantic Computers a year earlier in September 1988.

On 17 April 1990, the first day back to work for the City after a Bank holiday, B&C's shares were suspended at 53p. At a hastily convened analysts' meeting at the Waldorf Hotel, new Chairman Sir Peter Thompson, who had been brought in from the highly successful NFC (the flotation of National Freight Consortium which had been an MBO from BR) attempted to explain what had gone wrong. At this point the main problem was identified as the liabilities of B&C's computer leasing subsidiary Atlantic Computers, which was to be 'ring fenced' or, less politely, B&C was to rely upon the principle of limited liability by allowing its subsidiary to go into administration.

Unfortunately, or fortunately depending upon your point of view, this ploy did not work and B&C itself went into administration on 3 June 1990.

(A more detailed study of B&C's complex life and times is included in Appendix II.)

COLOROLL

Coloroll was not as big as B&C, nor was its end as speedy and unexpected as Polly Peck's. But it is still worth studying as one of the major failures of this era of the late 1980s. At its peak in June 1988, Coloroll had been valued at £424m.

Coloroll's last profit announcement was on 16 November 1989 and, once again, it was already apparent that everything was not well. Pre-tax profits fell from £20.55m to £10.01m. Factory closures and redundancies characterised the results statement, and as *Marketing Magazine* put it 'when Coloroll, the notoriously bullish home products group, starts talking about "organic consolidation" times are getting tough'. Gearing was stated at 75 per cent, although this was much less than the reality (see Appendix 1).

The shares were suspended and administrative receivers were appointed on 7 June 1990.

HOW COULD IT HAPPEN?

These three large corporate collapses all owe their occurrence in some respects to techniques of creative accounting or financial engineering. The relevant chapters for analysing the techniques they used in the section on Accounting Techniques which follows are:

Polly Peck – Currency Mismatching (Chapter 15)
British & Commonwealth – Acquisition and disposal techniques
(Chapters 3–6)
Contingent liabilities (Chapter 9)
Coloroll – Acquisition and disposal techniques (Chapters 3–6)

MAXWELL

But probably the greatest puzzle is how events at the late Robert Maxwell's empire were allowed to develop to the point where the two quoted companies in Maxwell's control were in the following (estimated) position after his demise:

Maxwell Communications Corporation (MCC)

MCC had net debts of around £1.5bn against net assets of under £1bn. It has already filed for Chapter 11 bankruptcy protection in the United States, and an administrator has been appointed in the UK. MCC's shares are almost certainly worthless, having fallen from a peak of 241p in 1991 to a price of 77½p at which they were suspended.

Figure 2.1   MCC share price chart 1991

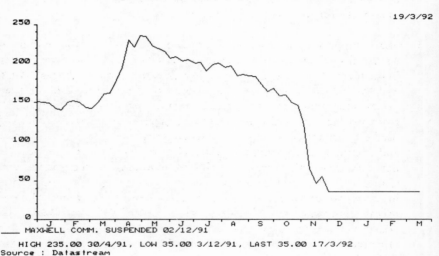

HIGH 235.00 30/4/91, LOW 35.00 3/12/91, LAST 35.00 17/3/92
Source : Datastream

Mirror Group Newspapers (MGN)

Some £97m has disappeared from MGN's bank account and was transferred to Maxwell's private companies, and £350m is missing from its pension fund, turning a £150m surplus into a £110m deficit.

But despite the enormity of the sums involved, and the complex daisy chain of 400 companies involved in the Maxwell group, Maxwell's action was 'not sophisticated fraud' (*Financial Times* 7.12.91). The methods by which Maxwell misappropriated hundreds of millions of pounds were:

1. Pledging assets and then selling them rather than delivering them to the lender as security – this occurred more than once in Maxwell's empire:
   i) the 'sale' of the Berlitz language school to Fukutake, a Japanese

publishing company, when the shares had already been pledged as security for loans by Swiss Volksbank and Lehman Brothers to Robert Maxwell Group, and ii) a £57.5m loan from Swiss Bank Corporation to a private Maxwell Company to finance a bid for First Tokyo Index Trust, which was to be secured by the Japanese shares held by the Trust. But the shares were sold, and the proceeds diverted elsewhere.

2. Plundering the pension funds – Maxwell diverted shares and cash held by Mirror Group Newspapers' £400m pension fund from outside advisers such as Lazards, Capel Cure Myers and Lloyds Investment Managers to Bishopsgate Investment Management, a privately owned Maxwell company. The assets of the pension funds were then pledged as security for loans to other Maxwell companies.

3. Share support operations – part of the collateral for the lending to Maxwell's private interests was the security which he gave the bankers in the form of a mortgage over his shares in the quoted vehicles – MCC and MGN. But when his empire began to run into trouble the share prices came under pressure and he faced the possibility of margin calls from his bankers which he could not meet. Consequently, Maxwell used the cash raised by other methods to purchase more shares in MCC and MGN, so supporting the price. The problem here is twofold: i) he never disclosed the increase in his shareholding in accordance with Companies Act and Stock Exchange requirements, so misleading investors about the reasons for the rise in share price. Thus, Maxwell private companies had a disclosed interest of 67.7 per cent in MCC, but actually controlled more than 80 per cent and ii) the companies were effectively funding the purchase of their own shares – a practice forbidden by the Companies Acts, except in certain limited circumstances, and the offence which was at the centre of the Guinness trials.

Funds of £130m from Maxwell Group, Bishopsgate Investment Trust and London and Bishopsgate Group, private Maxwell companies, were used to buy MCC shares in April and July 1991.

Perhaps the most sophisticated element of the operation was that in which Maxwell sold put options in MCC shares to investment bankers Goldman Sachs in August 1990 and July 1991 at prices higher than those then ruling in the market. This meant that Goldman had the right to sell the shares to Maxwell under the put option and could they buy in the market at lower prices, thereby showing a profit. Maxwell thereby indirectly supported the price, and increased his stake in MCC.

4. Simply taking the cash – in the months after MGN's flotation, MGN 'lent' £43m to private Maxwell companies. This £45m was part of MGN's cash resources which MGN instructed the Maxwell companies to invest in gilt-edged stocks as an alternative to holding cash. But of course the gilts were never purchased.

And all of this happened to a company which was a member of the FTSE 100 Index of the largest quoted companies – which is often assumed by many, especially foreign investors, to represent 'blue chip' companies.

But is attention to accounting any safeguard to investors against becoming involved in a company which is subject to a scandal that is the 'daddy of them all' (Ivon Fallon, *Sunday Times*, 8 December 1991)? In the original *Accounting for Growth* publication, Maxwell Communications Corporation was one of the only three companies to receive seven 'blobs' for the use of creative accounting techniques in the Major Companies Accounting Health Check:

Perhaps it should have been called a Wealth Check!

ACCOUNTING TECHNIQUES

In Parts II and III, I highlight some of the most commonly used techniques of creative accounting in the 1980s. In each case there is an example of one or more companies' use of the technique. Their inclusion is not meant to imply that their use is in some sense 'wrong'. Indeed, to my knowledge, all the techniques described accorded with UK Generally Accepted Accounting Practice (UK 'GAAP') and received a clean audit report at the time of use. Whether or not the use of the accounts received sufficiently clear information to reach an informed judgement on the companies concerned is entirely another question.

Part II looks at the accounting techniques used for acquisitions and disposals.

Part II

Accounting Techniques: Acquisition and Disposal

3

THE 1980S – DECADE OF THE DEAL

LIBERALISATION AND LAISSEZ FAIRE

Economic growth combined with a raging bull market and an easy supply of credit is a recipe for a booming market in takeovers and this is what the 1980s saw, particularly in the United States and the United Kingdom. In the UK, the takeover fires were stoked by a number of other factors. Together, these created a situation by which the 1980s has come to be known as 'the decade of the deal'.

First amongst these factors was a government committed to the freedom of the markets and to financial liberalisation. This saw the end of exchange controls, which helped to fuel cross-border investment and takeover activity, and the imposition (for that is effectively what it was) of 'Big Bang' on the cosy cartel which constituted the London Stock Exchange. This in turn led to the disappearance of most traditional stockbroking firms into integrated securities houses complete with expensive corporate finance departments keen to justify their existence. This is an important point because there is little doubt that many of the deals which grabbed the headlines in the 1980s, particularly towards the end of the decade, were hatched as much in the City's corporate finance departments as in the boardrooms of Great Britain plc. Some of the spectacular disasters involved the new generation of integrated houses rather than the more traditional merger and acquisition players such as Schroders or Warburgs. Thus it was that Barclays de Zoete Wedd were advisers to the ill-fated British & Commonwealth and Midland Montagu found themselves fighting a claim for damages in relation to the same group, as well as being advisers on the flotation of Robert Maxwell's Mirror Group Newspapers, whose 'ring fence' against the late Mr Maxwell proved to be completely ineffective.

Hand in hand with the government's liberalisation of the financial markets was a *laissez-faire* attitude to the resulting upsurge in takeover activity, particularly from the mid-1980s. Virtually no-one was safe from the rigours of the market. Thus household names such as Rowntrees were gobbled up by the Swiss, Jaguar was driven into American hands and what was left of the British computer industry (ICL and Apricot) was consumed by the Japanese.

Through all this the Bank of England was relaxed, but stood relatively firm, protecting the Clearing Banks from anyone who was not 'fit and proper' – polite language for anyone who was 1) foreign or 2) might inject any commercial reality into those most unloved of British institutions. But even the Bank of England could not resist the takeover tide completely and there were plenty of sacrificial lambs amongst the merchant banks as Hill Samuel was swallowed by TSB, Guinness Mahon by the New Zealand-based Equiticorp and Morgan Grenfell by Deutsche Bank. The fact that Equiticorp quickly went bust and was engaged in a share support operation suggests that it was neither fit nor proper, but a ready solution was soon found when Bank of Yokohama came to the rescue. No xenophobia here, one might think, except that Guinness Mahon itself then ran up huge losses and has had to be recapitalised. Perhaps the officials who allowed the Japanese to buy a member of the Accepting Houses Committee – unthinkable ten years ago – knew a thing or two after all. Here, in fact, is the clue, for all three merchant banks that were taken over had run into problems, two as a result of Big Bang. Aside from this, National Australia Bank was allowed to buy Clydesdale and Northern Banks from Midland in a £400m deal, but again this was a forced sale. The £977m takeover of Yorkshire Bank by the same Australian bank from a consortium of the Clearers contained no such element of panic, but then the sellers were more than happy to cash in their chips at what turned out to be the top of the cycle.

Apart from the Bank of England, there was little to stop the takeover tide in the 1980s. Even Britain's defence interests could not stop the demise of Plessey and the net result was a staggering flow of bids and deals which finally foundered when Hoylake failed in its record-breaking £13.4bn bid for BAT in the summer of 1989. The statistics are:

Table 3.1   Mergers and acquisitions – The 1980s (£bn)

	1980	1981	1982	1983	1984	1985	1986	1987	1988	1989	1990
UK* M&A value £bn	1.5	1.1	2.2	2.3	5.5	7.1	14.9	15.3	22.1	26.1	7.9
UK equities: total return %	35.0	13.5	28.9	28.8	31.6	20.6	27.5	8.0	11.6	36.0	–9.7
YOY RPI %	15.1	12.0	5.4	5.3	4.6	5.7	3.7	3.7	6.8	7.7	9.3
Net gearing† %	26	23	25	17	21	21	18	17	18	37	
Average Base Rate %	16.3	13.3	11.9	9.8	9.7	12.3	10.9	9.7	10.1	13.8	14.8
Real interest rate %	1.2	1.3	6.5	4.5	5.1	6.6	7.2	6.0	3.3	6.1	5.5

* *Source*: DTI. Public companies only.

† Combined balance sheets of large UK companies. Source: UBS Phillips & Drew.

The DTI series is not the most comprehensive currently available, but it does go back 20 years and it is the most useful from the point of view of long-term trends.

Table 3.2   Mergers and acquisitions – The 1970s (£bn)

1970	1971	1972	1973	1974	1975	1976	1977	1978	1979
1.1	0.9	2.5	1.3	0.5	0.3	0.4	0.8	1.1	1.7

The previous peak of M&A activity at £2.5bn in 1972 pales into insignificance compared with £26bn in 1989.

Statistics compiled by the magazine *Acquisitions Monthly*, which includes private companies, tell the same story of a merger and acquisition boom in the late 1980s. According to them, the 1988 figure for all M&A activity in the UK was £32bn, rising to £52bn in 1989.

FLAVOURS OF THE MONTH

As the table shows, economic growth, the bull market and undemanding interest rates underpinned the huge rise in takeover activity. In addition, there were a number of fashionable themes which, even without the benefit of hindsight, were founded on some highly dubious assumptions and were executed more in the heat of the moment than on any prudent assessment of the financial implications involved.

'One-stop' financial shopping

Aside from Big Bang, the liberalisation of financial markets gave rise to the concept of the 'financial supermarket' where the public could purchase everything from mortgages and pensions to home contents insurance and unit trusts. It was this concept that was a major factor in the expansion of British & Commonwealth (B&C) and the rush by insurance companies and building societies to buy estate agents. The concept was fine on paper, but it ignored one simple and very obvious fact: the clearing banks had been in a position to offer a basket of financial services for years; and had largely failed. The new generation of 'financial supermarkets' fared little better and, apart from B&C, the Prudential was forced to do an embarrassing volte-face and sell its estate agency chain, virtually giving away some of the branches for an overall loss of £350m.

1992-itis

The preparation for the single European market in 1992 was another reason to hype the takeover game, although this appeared to afflict those investing in corporate UK rather than the other way around. Indeed, corporate UK, still hamstrung by an inability to speak a foreign language, was besotted more by the United States than by the opportunities in its own backyard. This is shown by the following table:

Table 3.3 Spending on corporate acquisitions into and out of the UK

	1990		1989	
	No.	*Value £m*	*No.*	*Value £m*
UK domestic	1228	14062	1825	29572
UK into EC (excl UK)	279	4522	380	3655
UK into Europe (excl EC)	19	177	30	69
UK into US	167	4998	262	10198
UK into others	69	1326	92	1168
EC (excl UK) into UK	167	5668	122	5165
Europe (excl UK) into UK	31	436	42	1299
US into UK	47	1171	51	9171
Others into UK	51	6341	38	2025

Source: Acquisitions Monthly.

With 1992 upon us, it must be assumed that the majority of companies wishing to make a strategic move have already done so. Nevertheless, those investors who suffered the torture of Morgan Grenfell's brief quoted existence will have been grateful for the bid in 1989 from Deutsche Bank at 2.3 times book value. However, they will not be as grateful as former investors in Equity & Law or Pearl Assurance. The former was taken over by Compagnie du Midi on 54 times earnings, and the latter by AMP (Australian Mutual Provident) on 29 times earnings. Even allowing for the embedded value of the long-term life business, both exit multiples were very generous and now look even more so given the recent slow-down in life assurance and pension sales.

Unbundling

Like many of the phrases coined in the 1980s takeover boom, 'unbundling' is an ugly word which sits appropriately alongside other inventions such as the 'junk bond' and 'greenmail'. The phrase can be attributed to Sir James Goldsmith, whose Hoylake consortium planned to unbundle BAT. In the end, BAT unbundled itself, but the practice was perfected by Lord Hanson as early as 1986 with one of the UK's original mega bids, the takeover of Imperial Group. Unbundling proved to be easily exportable across the Atlantic where it was akin to taking coals to Newcastle. Indeed, Hanson was as much adept at unbundling over there as over here, SCM being perhaps the pinnacle of his US achievements. Then, of course, ICI appeared to offer the greatest prize to date.

But herein lies the catch. For growth through continued asset stripping (sorry, unbundling) is like a drug. The more successful each deal is, the bigger the next deal has to be to continue the pattern of growth and herein lies the seed of some of the creative accounting practices which came to bedevil corporate UK in the late 1980s. The takeover vehicles not only found that bigger and bigger takeovers were necessary to maintain profits growth, but also found a series of techniques associated with acquisitions and disposals which could be used to boost profits.

MBOs and LBOs

With the exception of the £2bn Isosceles deal for which Warburgs earned in the region of £20m in the summer of 1989, mega bids involving buyouts or buyins by a company's management or others have not been a major feature of the UK corporate scene to the same extent that they have been in the US. Apart from Isosceles, the three major deals involving household names were Magnet, Lowndes Queensway, and Woolworths. Unfortunately, the timing of the first two, at the top of the consumer boom, was to be catastrophic. Both deals were dashed on the rocks of rising interest rates from mid-1988 which led to crippling costs of debt servicing on the one hand and falling demand for their products on the other. In the end the clearing banks, especially The Royal Bank of Scotland, were left holding the babies. The decade was not without some success in the MBO market with the Premier Brands buyout from Cadbury Schweppes standing out in the somewhat safer area of food processing, and the Woolworths buyout (originally called Paternoster Stores) succeeded where the other retail MBOs failed – partly because it happened in an earlier stage of the retail cycle. Timing in this area of M&A activity, as much as anywhere else, is crucial.

Even a brief résumé of the LBO/MBO market in the 1980s would not be complete without mentioning the relatively small management buyout of the commercial service activities of British & Commonwealth by Bricom in June 1988 for £359m. Although B&C retained a 22.5 per cent interest this was effectively the beginning of the end for the group because it removed most of the tangible assets from the balance sheet, leaving only a highly dubious pile of goodwill relating to the newly acquired financial companies. These proved to be of little support when the Atlantic Computers takeover finally brought the house down. The Bricom buyout was done on an exit P/E of 19.6, but there was much hidden value in the various commercial service companies reflecting very conservative accounting policies over the years.

The new owners were quickly able to unlock this value. Over half the acquisition loan was repaid within 18 months, the 1990 medium–term debt instalment was paid a year early, and in March 1990 the forced sale by B&C of most of its 22.5 per cent stake to other investors was done at a price twice as high as the management buyout. Within a few months the crazy accounting at Atlantic Computers had brought B&C crashing to earth in one of the most dramatic UK corporate failures ever. And, as if to add insult to injury, the debt-free Bricom was sold to a Swedish buyer for £338m. Effectively, Bricom was the B&C of the Cayzers. Old money and prudent accounting had survived and prospered despite an initial mountain of debt; the brash, financial services conglomerate built with highly-rated paper and supported by what proved to be invisible earnings, was strangled almost at birth. How suitable an epitaph for the Decade of the Deal?

AND NOW THE HANGOVER

Now the party's over, who is paying the bill? First of all there are the successful companies who in the light of the current recession possibly feel they paid too much in the boom days. This was a factor in the stream of rights issues in 1991. Many companies which used debt for acquisition purposes may yet join the growing band of companies to call on their shareholders.

For many of course, the game is over, and shareholders have paid the ultimate price, often with a total loss of the value of their investment. In the financial services sector, B&C was joined by Dominion International, UTC, LIT and Burns Anderson. All of these in investment terms were total or near total write-offs. The collapse of a whole raft of property development/trading companies is very much part of the same syndrome. Polly Peck, the virtual collapse of Brent Walker, Coloroll and the failed MBOs referred to above make a forbidding list. And, of course, Maxwell whose highly geared acquisition of Macmillan and Official Airlines Guide in the United States, combined with perhaps great accounting opacity, has pushed the company into administration.

There is also the human factor. As well as bleeding balance sheets, soaring bad debts devastating bank profits and penniless shareholders, the scene is littered with tarnished reputations and broken careers. The companies run by the whizz-kids of the 1980s, the Gunns, Goldies, Ashcrofts, Nadirs and Maxwells are no more and will probably never rise again. There is also a seedier side to it all. Just as in the US, the high stakes involved led to rules being bent and then finally broken. In the US the arch corporate raider Ivan Boesky ended up by literally sweeping the floor, and court-room tears could not save the junk bond king, Michael Milken, from jail.

In the UK, HM Prison Service has also had to be employed. Looking at the sad, deteriorating figure of Ernest Saunders, the former Guinness chief, it was hard to envisage him at the centre of one of the most desperately fought takeovers in UK corporate history, the bid for Distillers. But that was the 1980s.

4

THE PRE-ACQUISITION WRITE DOWN

'Write down' – to reduce the *book value* of an asset
Chambers Dictionary

BASIC PRINCIPLES

The basic principle in accounting for acquisitions is that the assets of the subsidiary acquired should be brought into the acquiring group's accounts at their 'fair value' rather than the book value at which they stood in the subsidiary company's accounts prior to acquisition.

The purpose of the fair value adjustment is to obtain a good basis for the new subsidiary's assets and liabilities to be consolidated within the group. The book values at which they stand in the new subsidiary's accounts are of no use for this purpose because: 1) they are not necessarily based upon the acquiring company's accounting practices, and 2) they are based upon the original book cost of the assets not their market value from the acquiror's viewpoint. Consequently, assets are revalued for the purpose of the fair value adjustment prior to their inclusion in the enlarged group's accounts.

These fair value adjustments are explained in Statement of Standard Accounting Practice (SSAP) 22 (revised) issued in July 1989 and Exposure Draft (ED) 53 issued in July 1990 by the Institute of Chartered Accountants.

Once the fair value of the net assets acquired has been determined, any shortfall between their value and the purchase price represents goodwill which must be accounted for. The method of accounting for goodwill is in itself a minor epic of the accounting profession's confusion. Briefly, in 1980 the Accounting Standards Committee issued a discussion paper in which it proposed that goodwill should be taken on to the balance sheet like any other asset, and amortised or depreciated via an annual change to the profit and loss account. However, this was followed in 1982 by ED30, and then by SSAP 22 in 1984 which permitted a choice between amortisation through the profit and loss account or a direct write–off of goodwill to reserves at the outset, although the write–off became the preferred treatment.

In ED47 Accounting for Goodwill the ASC came back to the proposal that goodwill should be treated as a fixed asset and amortised through the profit and loss account. The latest development is that the new Accounting Standards Board Urgent Issues Task Force (UITF) has issued an Abstract on the Treatment of Goodwill on Disposal of a Business. Under existing rules, if a subsidiary is purchased for £500m and has tangible assets of only £150m, then £350m will have been written off as goodwill direct to reserves without passing through the profit and loss account. If the subsidiary was subsequently sold on for £400m then a profit of £250m would be recorded against the written down book value of £150m. Under the new UITF Abstract a loss of £100m (£500m − £400m) would be recorded in the profit and loss account.

The wider issues of goodwill accounting are to be dealt with in an ASB Financial Reporting Standard (FRS), but looking at the recent history of the subject, it is easy to see why this was not one of their first tasks.

PROVISIONS

ED53 accepts that there are occasions when provisions may be made against *possible* reductions in asset values or reorganisation costs as part of fair value adjustments upon acquisition. This is probably the area of acquisition accounting which has provided the greatest opportunity for abuse. The choice of assets to write down or raise provisions against divides most simply into current assets such as stock and debtors, and fixed assets, and the impact on the profit and loss account of these write downs is quite different:

STOCK AND DEBTOR WRITE DOWNS

Coloroll's acquisition of John Crowther in 1988 provides a good example of fair value accounting leading to a massive goodwill write-off and the uses and abuses of provisions.

Coloroll was involved in the manufacture and marketing of wallpaper, co-ordinated home furnishing fabrics and tableware. The photographs in its 1989 Annual Report seem to exemplify the designer 1980s. In June 1988, Coloroll acquired the textile company John Crowther, whose principal business was the manufacture of carpets, in a bitterly fought takeover in which one stockbroking analyst (David Buck of Barclays de Zoete Wedd) incurred the ire of Coloroll management by describing their approach to business as 'whizz-kiddery'. How he was to be vindicated by events.

Crowther was acquired for £213m in shares and cash. But Coloroll's Accounts for the year to March 1989 show goodwill written off of £247m (Exhibit 4.1), and Exhibit 4.2 shows that £224m related to Crowther. Coloroll wrote off £11m more than the total cost of Crowther!

Exhibit 4.1 **Coloroll Group Accounts for the year ended 31 March 1989**

18. Reserves

	Share premium account £000	Revalu- ation reserve £000	Other reserves £000	Profit and loss account £000	Total £000
(a) Group					
At 1 April, 1988	24,929	–	15,733	25,119	65,781
Premium on shares issued for cash	22,623	–	–	–	22,623
Premium on shares issued on acquisition of subsidiaries	–	–	183,681	–	183,681
Purchase of Coloroll Finance Limited stock (note 17)	–	–	158	–	158
*Goodwill written off	–	–	(247,257)	–	(247,257)
Retained profit for the year	–	0	0	26,879	26,879
Exchange differences	–	–	–	166	166
Property revaluation	–	8,711	–	–	8,711
At 31 March, 1989	47,552	8,711	(47,685)	52,164	60,742

Immediately before the acquisition, Crowther had net assets of £70m and therefore, subject to fair value adjustments, should have given rise to goodwill of:

$$£215m - £70m = £145m$$

i.e. Purchase price − Net asset acquired = Goodwill

The total cost of the acquisition had been raised by £75m through write-offs of stock and debtors, redundancy, relocation and incidental costs. Crowther's net assets had been written down by £4m to £66m, all of which explains how the goodwill adjustment came to be more than the acquisition cost:

Table 4.1 Coloroll – Crowther write-downs

	£m
Original goodwill	145
(excess of price over Crowther's net assets)	
Various write-offs	75
Reduction in Crowther's Net Asset Value	4
	224

* Bold or italic type indicates author's emphasis on all exhibits throughout the book

The write-offs broke down as follows:

	£m
Incidental costs	11
Stock write down	6
Debtor write down	5
Redundancy costs and temporary staff	7
Relocation costs	13
Other	33
	75

Exhibit 4.2   Coloroll Accounts for the year ended 31 March 1989

19. Acquisitions and disposals of subsidiaries

	1989 £000	1988 £000
Net assets acquired less sold:		
Tangible fixed assets	46,639	2,329
Stocks, debtors less creditors	28,279	5,183
Net borrowings	(96,061)	(28,149)
Provisions for liabilities and charges	(46,732)	(17,672)
Goodwill	(247,257)	766,667
	179,382	38,358
Less: Book values of investments (note 11)		(6,357)
		(2,711)
Interests of Coloroll Finance Limited stockholders	(20,470)	–
	152,555	35,647
Net consideration:		
Acquisitions:		
Cash paid	39,218	270
Dividends charged to cost of acquisition (note 8)	4,503	–
Shares issued	194,297	91,095
Disposals:		
Cash received and debt transferred	(90,059)	(59,595)
Fixed asset investments received (note 11)	(9,309)	–
	138,650	31,770
Add: Profit on disposals	13,905	3,877
	152,555	35,647

Goodwill includes £223,920,000 and £19,910,000 arising on the acquisition of John Crowther Group plc and William Barrett Limited in June, 1988 and September, 1988 respectively.
Proceeds of disposals relate to the sale during the year of various former subsidiaries of John Crowther Group PLC.

The significance of these pre-acquisition write-downs is that they absorb costs or *potential future* costs, at the expense of the balance sheet (to which the write-offs are applied), and thereby boost future profits. To the extent that in future trading periods the stock or debtors would have realised less than they were shown in Crowther's accounts, this loss of revenue is brought forward and dealt with through the balance sheet write-downs, as are future costs of reorganising the new subsidiary. Moreover, to the extent that stock or debtors (or any other assets) are later sold for more than their written-down value, profits will be enhanced. In practice, many provisions represent the expectation of future losses from the company acquired. ED53 regards this as no more correct than setting up an asset on the balance sheet for expected future profits of a subsidiary acquired.

As it acquired Crowther, Coloroll also used part of the fair value adjustment/goodwill to create provisions (Note 16) of £56.5m 'arising on acquisitions' as part of the additional £75m goodwill adjustment. Even

---

Exhibit 4.3   Coloroll Accounts for the year ended 31 March 1989

16. Provisions for liabilities and charges

	Deferred taxation £000	Other £000	Total £000
At 1 April, 1988	67	10,454	10,521
Arising on acquisitions	(9,781)	56,513	46,732
Charged to profit and loss account	9,553	–	9,553
Utilised during the year	–	**(51,986)**	**(51,986)**
Advance corporation tax	161	–	161
Exchange differences	–	376	376
At 31 March, 1989	–	15,357	15,357

No deferred taxation has been provided at 31 March, 1989 due to available tax losses carried forward.

The potential amount of deferred taxation comprises:

	1989 £000	1988 £000
Capital allowances	10,250	6,450
Other timing differences	(3,350)	(1,474)
	6,900	4,976
Recoverable advance corporation tax	(1,320)	(866)
	5,580	4,110

Other provisions comprise costs of reorganisation of subsidiaries acquired and business segment closures.

though £52m were utilised in 1989, provisions are more insidious than actual write downs – they are a guess at the cost of reorganising a company or writing down the value of assets. When they are utilised against costs the effect is to reduce costs which would otherwise have gone into the profit and loss account: Coloroll's provisions of £52m utilised in 1989 compared with pre-tax profits of only £55.5m! These profits would have been all but wiped out if these costs had been taken through the profit and loss account rather than debited against provisions in the balance sheet.

FIXED ASSETS

Another candidate for the pre-acquisition write-down is the acquired company's fixed assets. These can also be written down to 'fair value' in accordance with SSAP 22 (revised) and ED53.

As with write-downs in stock and debtors and provisions for reorganisation costs, such as we saw with Coloroll, these write-downs increase the goodwill incurred in an acquisition, which again hits the balance sheet by diminishing tangible net worth. The effect on the profit and loss account from a write-down of fixed assets is longer-lived than a stock or debtor write-down or reorganisation costs, which cease to be of significance once the stock is sold or the business reorganised.

The benefit of a fixed asset write-down feeds through to the profit and loss account by a reduction in the depreciation charge over the life of the asset acquired.

Tiphook – fixed asset write down

During the year to April 1990 Tiphook acquired Sea Containers' dry container and tank fleet assets. It valued these assets for the purposes of a fair value adjustment in accordance with SSAP 22 as if these containers had been acquired piecemeal, and as if it had already owned them and written them down in accordance with its own depreciation policy of writing these assets off by equal statements over 15 years down to a residual value of 15 per cent of cost.

The result was a goodwill write-off of £139m out of an acquisition cost of £350m. The average age of the assets acquired was six years, so that there was also a depreciation gain from the £139m knocked off the assets' values spread over the remaining depreciation life of nine years (15 years normal depreciation life – six):

$$£139m \div 9 = £15m \text{ p.a.}$$

This is the saving of depreciation and therefore effective boost to profits which results, compared with Tiphook's pre-tax profits of £33m for 1990.

In addition, should Tiphook dispose of any of these containers, the profits on disposal will be increased or any loss on disposal reduced since the balance sheet value of the containers has been reduced by about one third by the goodwill write-off. Tiphook credits these disposal profits to pre-tax profits (there was £2.8m of profit on sale of fixed assets in 1990), so that once again, the profit and loss account is boosted at the expense of the balance sheet.

SUBSEQUENT AMENDMENT TO FAIR VALUE (OR 'A SECOND BITE AT THE CHERRY')

Although provisions are normally set up at the time of an acquisition, there have been examples where companies have made further provisions in subsequent years.

Obviously a company making an acquisition cannot always be expected to have available all the information needed to compute a fair value adjustment immediately upon completion of the takeover, especially in the case of a hostile bid where the acquiror has only had access to published information about the target company.

But how much hindsight should be allowed? ED53 states that if accounts for the acquiring company are approved within six months of the acquisition, and there is insufficient time to complete the assessment of fair value, then a provisional adjustment to goodwill may be made and amended if necessary in the next set of accounts.

TI Group's additional goodwill adjustments

TI (formerly Tube Investments) has been transformed from a collection of low margin, commodity businesses into a specialist engineer with high market shares through a programme of acquisitions and disposals.

In 1987, TI acquired Houdaille Industries Inc in order to obtain control of John Crane USA, the sister company of Crane Packing in the UK in the mechanical seals business, and the 49 per cent of Crane Packing which it did not already own.

In 1988 TI acquired Bundy Corporation in the USA, a manufacturer of small diameter tubes for the automotive and refrigeration industries, and Thermal Scientific plc, a vacuum equipment and processing business.

In TI's 1988 Accounts the amount of goodwill written off in respect of these acquisitions is shown as £268.8m, including £88.5m during that year, relating to Bundy and Thermal Scientific (Exhibit 4.4).

The 1989 Accounts went further and provided a further £59.3m in respect of goodwill on these acquisitions including £4.2m in respect of John Crane, which had been acquired in August 1987 – two and a half years earlier! (Exhibit 4.5.)

TI's 1989 Financial Review stated that these additional goodwill adjustments arose from: 'the identification of additional investment opportunities to improve international competitiveness through major rationalisation of manufacturing facilities, systems and organisation structures'.

Exhibit 4.4 **TI Group 1988 Accounts**

28. Reserves

	Share premium account £m	Capital reserve £m	Goodwill written off £m	Profit and loss account £m
At 31 December	84.5	–	–	45.9
Reclassification of goodwill written off in 1987	–	58.5	(180.3)	121.8
At 31 December restated	84.5	58.5	(180.3)	167.7
Arising on issue of shares	0.5	–	–	–
Reduction of Share Premium account	(84.6)	84.6	–	–
Goodwill written off on acquisitions	–	–	(88.5)	–
Foreign currency translation differences	–	–	–	(7.4)
Balance for the year to 31 December 1988	–	–	–	123.2
At 31 December 1988	0.4	143.1	**(268.8)**	283.5

The goodwill arising in 1987 has been reclassified to the Goodwill written off reserve. **The total goodwill written off above arises from the acquisitions made in 1987 and 1988, principally Crane US, Bundy and Thermal Scientific.**

The cancellation of the Share Premium account and the transfer of the balance to a Capital Reserve was approved at the Extraordinary General Meeting held on 28 April 1988 and confirmed by the High Court on 23 May 1988.

The earnings retained in overseas subsidiary and related companies would be subject to further tax on distribution. The foreign currency translation differences shown above include an adverse translation movement of £6.5m in respect of foreign currency borrowings and foreign exchange instruments hedging overseas investments.

	Share premium account £m	Capital reserve £m	The company profit and loss account £m
At 31 December 1987	84.5	–	82.2
Reclassification of goodwill written off in 1987	–	58.5	36.4
At 31 December 1987 restated	84.5	58.5	118.6
Arising on issue of shares	0.5	–	–
Reduction of Share Premium account	(84.6)	84.6	–
Balance for the year to 31 December 1988	–	–	99.2
At 31 December 1988	**0.4**	**143.1**	217.8

In prior years investments in subsidiaries were held by the Company at a valuation representing the net tangible assets of the subsidiaries at the date of acquisition, less provision for any diminution in value.

Exhibit 4.5 TI Group 1989 Accounts

27. Reserves

	Share premium account £m	Capital reserve £m	Goodwill written off £m	Retained earnings £m
At 31 December 1988	0.4	143.1	(268.8)	283.5
Arising on issue of shares	38.4	–	–	–
Goodwill written off				
– current year acquisitions	–	–	(32.4)	–
– prior year acquisitions	–	–	**(59.3)**	–
Foreign currency translation differences	–	–	–	(0.2)
Retained profit for the year to 31 December 1989	–	–	–	59.8
At 31 December 1989	38.8	143.1	(360.5)	343.1

The earnings retained in overseas subsidiary and related companies would be subject to further tax on distribution. The foreign currency translation differences shown above includes an adverse translation movement of £26.7m in respect of foreign currency borrowings and foreign exchange instruments hedging overseas investments. This was offset by a favourable movement on translation of overseas assets.

Prior year acquisitions	Consideration £m	Provisional fair value of net assets £m	Provisional goodwill at 31 Dec 1988 £m	1989 Adjustments to fair values £m	Goodwill £m
John Crane	314.7	130.3	184.4	4.2	188.6
Bundy	148.5	115.2	33.3	39.0	72.3
Thermal Scientific	76.4	25.3	51.1	16.1	67.2
	539.4	270.8	268.8	**59.3**	328.1

The movements in provisions in respect of acquisitions in prior years are:

Balance at 31 December 1988	56.1
Exchange rate adjustments	3.8
Utilised	(57.7)
Released to Profit and Loss Account	nil
Additional provisions charged to goodwill	59.3
Balance at 31 December 1989	61.5

No amounts have been released to the profit and loss account. Additional provisions charged to goodwill to include major rationalisation of manufacturing facilities, systems and organisation structures.

Exhibit 4.6 **TI Group 1989 Financial Review**

Note 27 on pages 43 to 45 gives additional information on the treatment of goodwill as required by the revised accounting standard SSAP 22. Again no policy change is involved. The Standard relates only to disclosure requirements. Since 1986, when the strategy for the reconstruction of TI was initiated, a total of £580m had been invested in acquisitions. Goodwill written off on acquisitions made in 1989 was £32.4m. Also written off are goodwill adjustments to earlier years amounting to £59.3m arising from the identification of additional investment opportunities to improve international competitiveness through major rationalisation of manufacturing facilities, systems and organisation structures. Goodwill relating to acquisitions made prior to 1989 is now finally determined. Adjustments relating to acquisitions made during 1989 are not expected to be material. No provisions have been released through the Profit and Loss Account during the whole period of reconstruction.

Two points are at issue here: 1) the size of the ultimate fair value adjustment and 2) making provisions for reorganisation etc, and adjustment to the value of assets acquired over the previous two years and so writing them off to the balance sheet, rather than taking them through the profit and loss account.

TI's fair value adjustment certainly looks high in comparison with other acquisitions by engineering companies, relating the adjustment to the book value of the assets acquired, or to the price paid. The main exception is Siebe's acquisition of Foxboro. (See Table 4.2.)

The subsequent £59.3m adjustments represent 22 per cent of the original (provisional) fair values i.e. the assets were estimated to be worth over 20 per cent less than originally estimated under TI's accounting policies.

TI's subsequent 'bite of the cherry' in going back to make adjustments was certainly consistent with the then current GAAP in the form of SSAP 22, although it is worth bearing in mind that it would only have been consistent with current practice embodied in SSAP 22 (revised) issued in July 1989: 'Where the fair value of assets and liabilities, or the consideration, can only be determined on a provisional basis at the end of the accounting period in which the acquisition took place, this should be stated and the reasons given'. And ED53 issued in July 1990 goes further and states that 'fair value should be based on the circumstances at the date of the acquisition'.

That is, under current practice, TI would have had to state that its fair value adjustments and resulting goodwill write-offs were a guess which might have coloured analysts' judgement on the acquisition rather differently.

Table 4.2   Comparison of fair value adjustments

TI: Crane, Bundy, Thermal Scientific	£m
Book value assets acquired★	270.8
Fair value provisions	59.3
Fair value provisions/book value assets (%)	21.9%
Fair value provisions/consideration (%)	**11.0%**
Turner & Newall: JPI	
Book value assets acquired	159.5
Fair value provisions	14.1
Fair value provisions/book value assets (%)	8.8%
Fair value provisions/consideration (%)	**7.0%**
Vickers: Cosworth	
Book value assets acquired	27.1
Fair value provisions	2.8
Fair value provisions/book value assets (%)	10.3%
Fair value provisions/consideration (%)	**1.7%**
Siebe: Foxboro	
Book value assets acquired	112.5
Fair value provisions	48.1
Fair value provisions/book value assets (%)	42.7%
Fair value provisions/consideration (%)	**13.0%**

★Book value of assets acquired on consolidation are not available. These figures will already have been struck after fair value adjustments.

Source: UBS Phillips & Drew

For reasons explained at the beginning of this chapter, all companies must follow fair value accounting when incorporating acquisitions into their consolidated accounts. The question is whether, if subsequent adjustments to fair value are needed, these constitute a reduction in the value of the businesses bought or a cost of the ongoing business.

In none of the above cases did TI make a hostile acquisition without access to the books of the company such as the likes of Hanson seem to accomplish without subsequent goodwill adjustments.

TI's provisions account was first revealed in 1989 (Exhibit 4.7).

The 1989 and 1990 accounts state that no provisions have been released to the profit and loss account, a particularly cunning practice, when followed, in which profits are bolstered by the release of provisions – but 1) there is an obvious temptation to over-provide on an acquisition so depleting the

Exhibit 4.7 **TI Group 1989 Accounts**		
27. Reserves	*1989 £m*	*1990 £m*
Start year	56.1	67.8
Exchange rates	3.8	−7.7
Utilised – prior year	−57.7	−28.0
– current year	−0.8	−2.3
Goodwill	66.4	6.3
End year	67.8	36.1
Source: TI Group Report & Accounts		

balance sheet, and release the unwanted provisions through the profit and loss account, so bolstering profits, and 2) provisions are a non-cash item – they merely represent a transfer between shareholders' funds and another liability account called provisions, or vice versa – so that the portion of any profit generated by releasing or utilising provisions does not constitute cash generated. And where provisions are simply utilised to cover costs, this does not stop these costs representing a cash outflow, so that profits may overstate cash generated in this manner.

TI has not followed the practice of writing back provisions, but it is fair to say that without these provisions to utilise, 1989 profits would have been £58.5m lower and 1990 profits £30.3m lower. It is clear that the accounts saw significant benefits from this reorganisation expenditure viz. the Thermal Scientific companies 'underwent substantial restructuring during the year. The companies generally produced good results, and the benefits of the restructuring came through' etc., etc., so the benefits were in the profit and loss account but the costs were borne by the balance sheet in the form of utilised provisions.

Moreover, the use of provisions can become a treadmill. Unless further provisions can be created and utilised over the coming years, or organic growth in the business accelerates, the profit growth of a business will begin to slow. But then TI Group is back on the acquisition trail with its bid for the aerospace company Dowty.

WHAT HARM DOES IT DO?

The example of Coloroll at least raises the suspicion that creative use of acquisition accounting techniques could be damaging to your wealth as an investor – Coloroll was one of the most prominent corporate failures at the end of the 1980s (see Appendix I). But acquisition accounting per se was not the immediate cause of death in Coloroll – more specific problems are discussed in Chapter 8 (Off Balance Sheet Finance) and Chapter 9

Exhibit 4.8 **Charterhall Accounts for the year to 30 June 1989**

13. Acquisition and Disposal of Businesses

The net effect of the acquisition and disposal of businesses each of which have been accounted for using acquisition accounting is as follows:

	Acquisitions £000	Disposals £000	Net £000
Brand name	5,050	–	5,050
Goodwill	**49,120**	–	49,120
Tangible fixed assets	13,505	(1,078)	12,427
Current assets less liabilities	(16,119)	(274)	(16,393)
Provisions	(11,420)	–	(11,420)
Profit on disposals	–	(4,339)	(4,339)
Consideration (net)	40,136	(5,691)	34,445

Business	Consideration (incl cost of acquisition)	Effective date
Acquisitions:		
Lennards footwear retailing business	£11,326,000 cash (see note 24)	15 Aug 1988
Corah plc	£28,245,000 cash and £280,000 unsecured loan stock	18 Jan 1989
Westec Petroleum, Inc and Wasfrac, Inc	£285,000 cash	23 Mar 1989
Disposals:		
Charterhall Oil Canada Ltd	9,236,655 shares in Red Cliff Energy Inc (valued at £1,585,000)	5 Aug 1988
Charterhall Petroleum Ltd	£3,356,000 cash and 524,475 shares in De Facto 121 Limited (valued at £750,000)	30 Jun 1989

The contribution of Corah plc to the Group's operating profit for the year ended 30 June 1989 is set out in note 1. In view of the merging of the activities of certain acquisitions with existing acquisitions with existing Group companies, the Directors do not consider it feasible to identify the contributions to operating profit of the other businesses acquired during the year.

(Contingent Liabilities). So does creative accounting for acquisitions cause any real danger?

A better example is Charterhall, the former oil exploration company, which became an 'acquisition vehicle' for Australian entrepreneur Russell Gowod and in 1988–89 purchased the footwear business of Lennards from

Great Universal Stores and Marks & Spencer textile supplier Corah plc for a combined consideration of £40m. As Note 13 of the Charterhall Accounts shows (Exhibit 4.8), £40m included goodwill of £49m – the assets required had a tangible value of minus £9m. And this was after raising the inevitable provision of £16.1m.

The effect on Charterhall's balance sheet was devastating: shareholders' funds of £77.6m were more than outweighed by intangible assets (including the goodwill on these acquisitions) of £34.5m, and by borrowings of £84.2m.

Exhibit 4.9 Charterhall Accounts for the year to 30 June 1989

19. Borrowings

	Group		Company	
	1989	1988	1989	1988
	£000	£000	£000	£000
Borrowings are repayable as follows:				
Wholly repayable, other than instalments,				
Within one year	9,886	18,265	303	10,418
One to two years	22,515	12,056	22,515	–
Two to five years	–	4,910	–	–
More than five years	–	–	–	–
Repayable by instalments:				
Within one year	14,875	1,409	–	–
One to two years	15,158	1,262	4	–
Two to five years	21,505	100	5	–
More than five years	219	–	219	–
	84,158	38,002	23,046	10,418

All the borrowings are subject to commercial rates of interest.
The bank loans and overdrafts are secured by fixed and floating charges over certain assets of the Group.

These bank lenders must have become unnerved by the payment of their cash in return for businesses with no tangible assets, and the general lack of asset backing. Once profits disappeared in the first half of the year to 1990, and the Australian company which owned half Charterhall's shares and guaranteed its debts, Westmen, went into liquidation the end was inevitable and Charterhall went into administrative receivership on 21 December 1990.

5

DISPOSALS

Man proposes but God disposes
Thomas à Kempis

Just as acquisitions provide major opportunities to enhance future profits through provisioning, so too do disposals. It is quite common for companies to take the profits on the disposal of fixed assets through the profit and loss account, and indeed in some industries where it is a recurrent feature of operation this is a legitimate, if rather low quality, source of earnings.

However, an investor should be aware of the size of these items, and the extent to which they are one-off or recurrent in order to assess a company's true profitability. But this is not assisted by the differences in treatment that arise even within the same industry:

DISPOSAL OF FIXED ASSETS

Ladbroke Group is part of the FT-A Hotels and Leisure sector and P&O (The Peninsular & Oriental Steam Navigation Company) is part of the FT-A Shipping and Transport sector, but both engage in property development and investment. Ladbroke Group is best known for its betting shops, but as well as owning Hilton International Hotels and Texas DIY stores, Ladbroke engages in property investment and development in the UK and USA. P&O has Bovis, the housebuilder, Ashby & Horner in contracting, and a number of other property development and investment subsidiaries including Pall Mall, the former Laing Properties, which was formerly a joint venture with Chelsfield.

Exhibit 5.1 **Ladbroke Group – 1990 Annual Report**

12. Investment Properties

	Total	Freehold cost or valuation	Long leasehold cost or valuation	Short leasehold valuation
Held for development, third party renting and capital appreciation	£m	£m	£m	£m
At 31st December 1989	757.7	695.8	61.6	0.3
Exchange rate movements	(58.0)	(56.2)	(1.8)	–
Net additions (c)	118.7	93.9	25.0	(0.2)
Revaluation surplus	(105.9)	(97.8)	(8.1)	–
At 31st December 1990	**712.5**	**635.7**	**76.7**	**0.1**
Representing assets stated at:				
Valuation (a)	646.3	575.4	70.8	0.1
Cost (b)	66.2	60.3	5.9	–
At 31st December 1990	**712.5**	**635.7**	**76.7**	**0.1**

(a) Valued by property division directors or a professional executive of the company, following consultation with external professional advisers, or by independent external valuers, on an open market basis. The property division directors were J Anderson, AP Grant, H Harris or PG Martin FRICS and the executive was JD Broughton ARICS.

(b) At cost in the course of development, the current value being estimated by the directors to be not less than the book amount.

(c) Net additions comprise additions of £205.1m including a transfer of £67.9m from dealing properties, freehold disposals of £86.2m and short leasehold disposals of £0.2m.

(d) The amount of investment properties determined according to the historical cost accounting rules, as at 31st December 1990, is £670.7m (1989 £566.2m) which includes capitalised interest of £113.6m (1989 £88.4m).

(e) Investment properties are accounted for in accordance with SSAP19. Where the requirements of SSAP19 conflict with those of the Companies Act 1985, SSAP19 has been followed as the directors believe this is necessary in order to present a true and fair view.

In 1990, Ladbroke sold investment properties for £86.2m, as shown above in Note 12 of the Accounts. But none of this was included in the extraordinary items, proving that the income from disposals was taken 'above the line'.

Exhibit 5.2 **Ladbroke Group – 1990 Annual Report and Accounts**

Note 6 Extraordinary Items

	1990 £m	1989 £m
Extraordinary (loss) profit after taxation relief of £7.2m (1989 nil)	(13.5)	4.9

The extraordinary loss for the year arises mainly from the decision to terminate the contract under which betting services are provided in The Netherlands. The extraordinary profit in 1989 arose from the disposal of peripheral businesses.

Exhibit 5.3 **Ladbroke Group – 1990 Annual Report and Accounts**

Consolidated profit and loss account

	1990 £m	1989 £m
Turnover	3,800.5	3,659.5
Cost of sales	3,382.1	3,250.9
Gross profit	418.4	408.6
Administrative expenses	59.4	60.3
Income from associated companies	6.9	5.2
Operating profit	365.9	353.5
Interest	60.3	51.3
Profit on ordinary activities before taxation	305.6	302.2
Tax on profit on ordinary activities	76.2	88.4
Profit on ordinary activities after taxation	229.4	213.8
Minority interests	0.4	6.7
Profit for the financial year attributable to shareholders before extraordinary items	229.0	207.1
Extraordinary items	(13.5)	4.9
Profit attributable to shareholders	215.5	212.0
Dividends	91.5	83.8
Retained profit for the year	124.0	128.2
Earnings per share		
Actual	26.69	24.26
Fully diluted	25.78	23.76

In contrast, P&O's accounting policies note states that: 'Properties (excluding development and dealing properties) . . . Capital profits on the sale of these properties . . . are recognised in extraordinary items.'

Exhibit 5.4 P&O Accounting Policies

Properties (excluding development and dealing properties) are included in the accounts at their latest valuations plus subsequent additions at cost, and surpluses and deficits are included in the revaluation reserve. A substantial proportion by value, including the largest properties, is valued annually by the group chief surveyor and triennially by external valuers. The remaining small value properties are valued triennially, a third each year, by the group chief surveyor. Capital profits on sale of these properties, including realised valuation surpluses, are recognised in extraordinary items. In certain subsidiaries such realised capital profits are not available for distribution and accordingly an amount equivalent to the appropriate net sum is transferred to other reserves. Properties held for development are not revalued during development or refurbishment. Interest and other outgoings less income receivable are charged in the profit and loss account during development, except in respect of certain overseas properties where the development period is extensive and in respect of certain United Kingdom properties which will be retained by the Group after development. In these cases such amounts are capitalised. Realised profits on development properties are recognised in arriving at the operating profit.

Dealing land and properties are stated at the lower of cost and net realisable value.

No charge for amortisation is made in respect of freehold or long leasehold properties. The book value of leasehold properties with less than 21 years to the termination of the lease is written off over the remainder of the period on a straight line basis.

Exhibit 5.5 P&O 1989 Accounts

Note 4. Extraordinary items

	1989 £m	1988 £m
Capital profits on sale of properties (including £10.8m (1988 £30.4m) realised revaluation surplus)	25.5	68.7
Other	(0.1)	(0.4)
Taxation (note 3)	(5.3)	(19.4)
	20.1	48.9

The taxation charge in respect of capital profits on the sale of properties has been reduced by the utilisation of capital losses.

This is one of the reasons why P&O's profits for the past three years would have been significantly higher under the new ASB Exposure Draft which allows almost no extraordinary items – P&O has been including substantial gains in extraordinary items (and therefore not in Earnings per Share) – £48.9m in 1988, £25.5m in 1989 and £25.0m in 1990.

Property disposals are probably the commonest area for differences in the treatment of disposal profits. Nowhere is this more evident than in the retail sector where the simple fact of operating a branch network means that most retailers are constantly engaged in the activity of buying and selling property. But for such a common item, treatments differ enormously.

The 1989 accounts for WH Smith and 1990 accounts for Asda show diametrically opposed treatment of property profits. In the case of WH Smith the property profits are taken, and disclosed above the line:

Exhibit 5.6 Profit and loss account – W H Smith Group plc		
	53 weeks to 3 June 1989 £m	52 weeks to 28 May 1988 £m
Turnover note 2	1,940.5	1,662.0
Cost of sales	(1,357.3)	(1,158.1)
Gross profit	583.2	503.9
Other net expenses note 3	(487.1)	(427.5)
Trading profit	96.1	76.4
Share of profits in related companies	1.5	2.1
Trading profit including related companies note 2	97.6	78.5
Exceptional item note 4	(2.5)	–
Net interest note 5	(11.0)	(8.7)
Profit on ordinary activities before profits and taxation	84.1	69.8
Property profits	**5.6**	**0.6**
Profit on ordinary activities before taxation note 6	89.7	70.4
Tax of profit on ordinary activities note 7	(32.3)	(24.7)
Profit on ordinary activities after taxation	57.4	45.7
Minority interests	1.1	0.1
Profit before extraordinary items	58.5	45.8
Extraordinary profit after taxation note 8	39.2	–
Profit for the financial period note 9	97.7	45.8
Dividends note 10	(20.5)	(17.5)
Transfer to reserves note 19	77.2	28.3

Whereas Asda shows property disposals (admittedly used to finance the Gateway acquisition) as an extraordinary item:

Exhibit 5.7 Asda Group PLC

Note 7 Extraordinary items

	1990 £m	1989 £m
Profits on disposals of property to refinance the Gateway acquisition, principally to The Burwood House Group	88.8	–
Provision for costs of disposal of businesses of subsidiary companies	(2.1)	–
	86.7	–

No taxation charge has arisen on the extraordinary item due principally to the utilisation of rollover relief on capital gains.

Nor does the variation in disclosure of property profits merely vary between exceptional and extraordinary items. In a study of 34 retail company accounts in 1989–90 KPMG Peat Marwick McLintock found the following variation in treatment of property profits:

Table 5.1 Treatment of 'profit' on property sales

	Number of companies	
	1990	1987
Describing profit on sale of properties as an exceptional item	5	1
Treating 'profit' as part of 'other operating income'	4	2
Including profit on sale of properties as an 'other item' or other income	4	3
Specifying 'surplus on sale of properties' separately on the face of the profit and loss account or in a note to the accounts analysing trading profit	3	10
Including profit on sale of properties as an extraordinary item	3	4
Including 'profit' or 'loss' on property sales as part of ordinary activities or operating charges in the notes to the accounts	4	2
No mention made	11	11
Total	34	33

Source: KPMG Peat Marwick McLintock, *The Retail Industry*

Some would maintain that an efficient stock market will see through such obvious nuances of accounting in valuing shares. But there is precious little evidence that it does: analysts are too often mesmerised by Earnings per Share (EPS) and oblivious to what goes on 'below the line' in the profit and loss account at which EPS is calculated, let alone what goes on in the balance sheet. But possibly all this will change with the implementation of the ASB's proposals.

COMPANY DISPOSALS

If the disposal of fixed assets causes some confusion this is even greater when complete operations incorporated as subsidiaries are being sold. The basic principles enshrined in SSAP 14 and ED50 would appear to be quite straightforward: the results of the company being sold should be included as part of the group's profit and loss account until the effective date of disposal, and the gain or loss on disposal should be determined by comparing the value of the subsidiary's net assets with the sale proceeds. Certainly the justification for including proceeds from the sale of a subsidiary as part of a group's trading profit or even as an exceptional item would seem to be much less than, say, is the case for sales of fixed assets.

Tootal – use of company disposal to boost profits

Tootal agreed a phased sale of its 49.8 per cent stake in the Da Gama Textile Company in January 1989 for a total of approximately £25m payable in five equal tranches. Da Gama contributed the lion's share of Tootal's £8.5m related company income and therefore an outright sale for £25m would have caused a serious shortfall in continuing profits since the annual interest income on £25m is a lot less than £8.5m. Alternatively, booking approximately £17m disposal gain to the P&L in the year that disposal terms were agreed would have caused a discontinuity in the profit trend, particularly as Tootal would probably have credited the profit as a trading item rather than treating it as an extraordinary or exceptional item.

The solution was elegant in accounting terms. In 1988/89, the first tranche of the disposal profit, £3.4m, was payable on completion and this was booked to pre-tax profits. As this deal was completed at the year end, Tootal also enjoyed a full year's related company contribution on its 49.8 per cent stake in 1988/89. Between them these two contributions accounted for around 25 per cent of Tootal's reported pre-tax profits in 1988/89 despite the company entering into a contract to dispose of its complete interest in Da Gama. In subsequent years the disposal profit would be likely to be lower, reflecting the fact that the retained earnings of Da Gama will increase its book cost. In addition, the related company income was also likely to decline as the effective percentage owned falls.

Exhibit 5.8 Tootal 1989/90 Accounts

Profit on Ordinary Activities Before Tax

	1989/90 £000	1988/89 £000
Is arrived at after crediting		
Sales	529,844	491,551
Income from investments (note 4)	158	538
Profits on disposals (see below)	**6,524**	3,411
Other operating income	7,324	9,606
Share of profit of related companies (note 5)	**5,901**	8,487
	549,751	513,593
And after charging		
Raw materials and consumables	262,210	231,984
Change in stocks of finished goods and work in progress	(12,842)	(5,462)
Other external charges	105,768	100,920
Staff costs (note 7)	132,040	121,887
Depreciation of tangible fixed assets	11,270	9,590
Operating lease charges	3,687	4,028
Directors' emoluments	874	748
Auditors' remuneration	725	649
Interest (note 6)	10,300	6,958
	514,032	471,302
Profit on ordinary activities before tax	35,719	42,291

Profits on disposals

During the year the Group disposed of the second tranche, within the terms of the agreement it entered into during the year ended 31 January 1989, for the progressive disposal of its interest in Da Gama Textile Company Limited. The profit arising from the sale of the second tranche, amounting to £3,028,000 (1988/89 £3,411,000) is included in the profits analysis under the heading of Group in Note 2. Also included is the profit on the disposal of Sandhurst Marketing PLC, details of which are referred to in Note 24.

A more prudent approach in accounting terms to this transaction might have been to take all the profit on disposal as an extraordinary item. There is also some justification for regarding the entire disposal as taking place on agreement of the sale and treating the deferred proceeds as a long–term debtor.

Clearly the profits on the disposal of a subsidiary has very little to do with the on-going trading performance of Tootal and should therefore be ignored by the stock market as far as assessing an appropriate Price/Earnings ratio for the shares.

DECONSOLIDATION ON DISPOSAL

Another option used by some companies which is provided by some conflict between SSAP 14/ED50 and SSAP6 (Extraordinary items) is to deconsolidate the results of a subsidiary from the group accounts at the time a disposal is announced rather than later when the sale is completed. The trading profits (or losses) for the subsidiary between the announcement and completion are included in the extraordinary capital profit or loss on disposal. But for some reason this technique is most commonly used when the subsidiary is loss-making!

TSB/Target Deconsolidation

TSB took the decision to dispose of its interest in the life assurance and fund management group Target, early in its 1989/90 financial year. When it published its results for the half year to April 90, it did not consolidate the Target Group results and included its £55m investment in Target as 'other accounts receivable' in the TSB balance sheet.

Target reported a pre-tax loss of £17m for the first half of 1989/90 against a profit of £3m in the comparable period. Had this result been consolidated in TSB's interim figures, the pre-tax profits would have shown a decline of five per cent rather than the seven per cent growth reported (see Table 5.2). A useful contribution at a time when TSB was under pressure because of its poor performance post flotation. TSB still had not sold Target at its year end (October 1990).

Table 5.2 TSB 1990 interim results – Deconsolidation of Target

	1990 £m	1989 £m	% change
Reported Pre-tax Profits	175	164	+7
Target Group *	(17)	3	
Restated TSB Results	158	167	−5

* Not consolidated because decision taken to dispose of Target

Exhibit 5.9   **TSB Interims announcement to 30 April 1990**

Target Group
The results for Target Group for the half year to 30 April 1990 have not been
consolidated as the decision to dispose of the business was taken early in the
period. The results of Target Group in the relevant periods were:

	Half year to *30 April 1990*	*Half year to* *30 April 1989*	*Year to* *31 October 1989*
Pre-tax (loss)/profit	(17)	3	3

The results for the period include a reduction in the embedded value of the life
and pensions business in force of some £15m due mainly to changes in
taxation and more conservative assumptions on lapse rates. They also include
provision for likely ex gratia payments to clients of Garston Amhurst together
with associated costs.

In the full year results, the loss for the period to date will be included in the
extraordinary profit or loss on disposal.

The Group's investment in Target Group is included in 'other accounts
receivable' in the amount of £55m.

Midland/EAB – taking deconsolidation a stage further

Midland's disastrous foray into Californian banking in the 1980s through
Crocker National Bank is now infamous. But prior to this direct entry into
international banking, Midland's overseas representation was via a number
of so–called consortium banks – banks which have a group of other banks as
their shareholders. In New York, Midland had a 15 per cent shareholding in
a consortium bank called European American Bancorp (EAB).

Midland was required to reduce its shareholding in EAB when it bought
Crocker because of the then US laws restricting inter–state banking. So the
approval for the Crocker acquisition given by the Federal Reserve Board in
1981 required Midland to reduce its stake in EAB to five per cent or less.
But this became urgent in 1983–84 for other reasons: in 1983 Crocker lost
£17m before tax and in 1984 this soared to £222m, reducing Midland Group
pre–tax profit from £251m in 1982 to just £135m in 1984. The attributable
profit of £45m after tax, minorities and extraordinary items in 1984 left the
dividend of £58m uncovered. But when things go wrong, they rarely go
wrong in just one place, especially in banking. In 1984 EAB made a loss net
of tax of £133m, of which Midland's share was some £20m.

From the time of the Federal Reserve approval in 1981, Midland
continued to treat its holding in EAB as an associate company, even though
the holding was below the 20 per cent level which is normally required for
an associate treatment by the definition contained in SSAP1, since
Midland's EAB holding qualified as an associate on another part of the
SSAP1 definition, that of 'significant' influence since Midland had a

Exhibit 5.10 **Midland 1984 Accounts**

27. Trade investments

At cost less provisions	Book amount	Valuation 1984	Book amount	Valuation 1983
Group				
Listed elsewhere than in Great Britain	1	1	2	2
Unlisted	59	72	23	36
	60	73	25	38
Midland Bank plc				
Unlisted	47	58	13	26

Listed investments are valued at middle market prices and unlisted investments at Directors' valuation.

The principal trade investments at 31 December 1984, all of which were held directly by Midland Bank plc, were as follows

	Country of incorporation	Interest of Midland Bank plc
The Agricultural Mortgage Corporation Limited		
Issued share capital £8.5m	Great Britain	13%
The Bankers' Clearing House Limited		
Issued share capital £1.5m	Great Britain	17%
European American Bancorp		
Issued share capital US$70m	USA	20%
European Banking Company Limited		
Issued share capital £12.2m	Great Britain	14%
European Banking Company SA		
Issued share capital BFrs 3,500m	Belgium	14%
Euro-Pacific Finance Corporation Limited		
Issued share capital A$ 12.5m	Australia	15%

Under the terms of approval given by the Board of Governors of the Federal Reserve Board dated 25 August 1981 to the Midland Bank plc application to acquire a majority interest in Crocker National Corporation it was necessary for the interest in European American Bancorp (EAB) to be reduced to not more than 5% by October 1984, now extended to 15 October 1985. Midland Bank plc has reduced its representation on the Board of EAB and has treated its holding in EAB as a trade investment rather than an associated company from 1 January 1984. As a trade investment, EAB is stated in the accounts at £35m, after an extraordinary write-down of £6m. The share capital and reserves of EAB at 31 December 1984 amounted for 1984 to US$ 133m.

Exhibit 5.11 **Midland – Consolidated Profit and Loss Account**			
	Notes	1984	1983
Year ended 31 December 1984		£m	£m
Profit before taxation			
Group excluding Crocker National Corporation		357	242
Crocker National Corporation	11	(222)	(17)
		135	225
Taxation	12	160	100
(Loss) profit after taxation		(25)	125
Minority interests		87	(7)
Profit before extraordinary items		62	118
Extraordinary items	13	(17)	(4)
Profit attributable to members of Midland Bank PLC		45	114
Dividends	14	58	58
(Deficit) retained profit		(13)	56
Reserves at 1 January		1,396	1,269
Effect of Finance Act 1984 tax changes	12	(230)	–
Other movements in reserves	22	25	71
Reserves at 31 December		1,178	1,396
Earnings per share	15	27.1p	60.6p

The results for Crocker National Corporation, which are after charging £456m (1983 £120m) for bad and doubtful debts, include a profit arising from the disposal of the freehold of its headquarters buildings amounting to £134m (1983 Nil).

representative on EAB's Board. As a result, Midland took into its profit and loss account its share of EAB's profits.

Suddenly, in 1984, Midland reduced its representation on EAB's Board and redefined the holding from an associate company to a trade investment in the 1984 Accounts. What did this rather obscure change of nomenclature achieve? If EAB had remained as an associate, Midland would have been forced to show a £20m loss in its own profit and loss account to reflect EAB's performance. But for the trade investments only any dividend paid is taken to the profit and loss account. EAB's loss was reflected in Midland's accounts as a fall in the value of its trade investment taken to reserves – i.e. it appeared in the balance sheet, not the profit and loss account.

Once again, the profit and loss account escaped unscathed, and the balance sheet suffered.

Once more it is necessary to ask – it may be lamentable that companies appear to play fast and loose with their accounts when it comes to disposals, but does anyone lose as a result of this?

Two that failed – Charterhall and Leading Leisure

The example of the acquisition vehicle Charterhall has already been cited. Charterhall had been an oil exploration company, and its 1989 pre-tax profit of £13.1m included disposal profits of £8.5m covering properties and petroleum interests in the UK and North America (Exhibit 5.12).

Exhibit 5.12 Charterhall Accounts for the year to 30 June 1989			
	Year ended 30 June 1989 £000	Year ended 30 June 1988 £000	18 months ended 30 June 1988 £000
2. OTHER INCOME			
Profit on sale of:			
Properties	2,650	418	532
UK petroleum interests	4,246	2,158	3,058
North American petroleum interests	1,624	–	–
Investments	–	4,324	7,120
	8,520	6,900	10,710

Removing this disposal profit reduced the apparent interest cover of 3.1 times to 1.7 times in a company where goodwill on acquisition had eaten into the tangible asset base. This treatment was certainly unhelpful for anyone trying to establish the cover which regular trading profits provided for interest payable. But the banks of course were not confused. The end result was Charterhall's administrative receivership.

In 1989, Leading Leisure showed a profit before tax of £6.7m.

This was struck after a number of items for which the Accounts will feature again and again under various headings of accounting creativity: capitalising costs, reclassification of properties, but of most interest in this context is the £10m from the sale of properties to Duchy Parklands Limited and other joint ventures involving ... Leading Leisure included in Operating Profit of £12m (see Exhibit 5.13).

Exhibit 5.13 Leading Leisure Accounts for December 1989

1. TURNOVER AND OPERATING PROFIT

	Turnover £'000	14 months 31 December 1989 Operating profit £000	Turnover £'000	12 months 31 October 1988 Operating profit £000
Leisure	38,931	4,348	41,060	2,719
Construction, property development and dealing	54,360	9,796	32,955	7,734
Other activities	3,752	(292)	4,490	(1,550)
Central administration	378	(1,869)	–	(1,590)
	97,421	11,983	78,505	7,313

Trading profit generated by the disposal of properties to Duchy Parklands Limited and other joint ventures with Wykeham Group PLC included in the operating profit for the 14 months to 31 December amounted to £10,000,000.

Leading Leisure held 50 per cent of Duchy Parklands Limited (Exhibit 5.14) and all ten million of its five per cent preference shares:

Exhibit 5.14 Leading Leisure 1989 Accounts

Note 13

On 15 May 1990, following the completion of the acquisition of certain properties from both Leading Leisure and Wykeham Group, Duchy Parklands Group Limited allotted 1,153,998 £1 ordinary shares and 10,000,000 cumulative redeemable 5% preference shares. 576,998 of the ordinary shares and all the preference shares were allotted to Leading Leisure.

Leading Leisure had booked a profit on disposal of an asset to a company of which it controlled 50% and supplied more than half the finance. Meanwhile, net interest payable before interest capitalised, was £11.3m (£4.9m + £6.4m)

Leading Leisure Plc 1989 Accounts

4. NET INTEREST PAYABLE

	14 months 31 December 1989 £000	12 months 31 October 1988 £000
On bank loans and overdrafts repayable wholly within five years	4,347	525
On bank loans and overdrafts repayable partly after five years	6,995	3,462
On other loans	588	340
Interest capitalised	**(6,412)**	(1,903)
Interest receivable	(643)	(17)
	4,875	2,407

Given that the Operating Profit of £11.9m barely covered net interest payable of £11.3m and £6.7m of the Profit was from a sale to a company which Leading Leisure had financed, it is hardly surprising that on 9 November 1990, Leading Leisure went into administrative receivership. The comparison of reported interest cover with the reality shows why:

Table 5.3 Leading Leisure 1989 – interest cover

	£000s	
	As reported	Adjusted*
Operating profit	11983	5283
Interest payable	4875	11287
Cover (times)	2.5	0.5

* Operating profit less property sale to Duchy Parklands
Interest payable ignoring capitalised interest

6

DEFERRED CONSIDERATION

Delays have dangerous ends
Henry VI, Part I (III.ii.33)

Finally, on the subject of creative accountancy in the area of buying and selling things, or to give the practice its corporate name, acquisitions and disposals, there is the practice of deferred consideration.

As with a number of the other acquisition related techniques discussed, the application of accounting to deferred consideration is governed by ED53 – Fair value in the context of acquisition accounting.

Deferred consideration is a payment, the value of which is contingent upon the future performance of the business acquired. More commonly known as 'earn-outs' (from the point of view of the vendors of the business acquired) this technique became popular in structuring acquisitions in the 1980s, particularly for companies within the FT-Actuaries Agencies Sector comprising mainly advertising agencies (this sector ceased to exist from the end of 1990 which gives some indication of the impact of the technique).

Typically in an earn-out the acquiring company would make an up-front payment with further payments in either cash or shares based on a multiple of future profits of the acquired company. This method of acquisition has a number of advantages.

1. Limited downside risk – if the acquisition performs badly, the future deferred consideration payments could be adjusted downwards accordingly.
2. In the 'people' businesses of the Agencies sector, in particular, tying-in the vendors of a business is important as the success of the business often depends heavily upon their creative talents and most companies have few tangible assets.
3. There was often an immediate enhancement to earnings as the profits of the acquired company were consolidated at once, but the additional consideration was only paid some time later.

But problems can arise. These relate to the ability of the acquiror to finance the future deferred consideration payments, if they are in cash, to the dilutive effect of the shares to be issued and to the resulting cost of maintaining the dividend payment.

It is usual to disclose these potential liabilities rather than providing for them, as the amount is uncertain. An example is Saatchi & Saatchi's 1989 accounts which show contingent liabilities for deferred consideration payments of a maximum of £119.5m (Exhibit 6.1).

The Group balance sheet at the end of 1989 already showed negative net worth of £264.2m after deducting £434.6m goodwill, and this would have

---

Exhibit 6.1   Saatchi & Saatchi 1989 Accounts

18. COMMITMENTS AND AUTHORISATIONS NOT PROVIDED

Additional capital payments may be made to the vendors of acquired companies in the years to 1995. Such payments are contingent on the future levels of profits achieved by these companies. The Directors estimate that, at the rates of exchange ruling at 30 September 1989, the maximum payments that may be made are as follows:

	£m
Within one year	26.0
From two to five years	92.2
After five years	1.3
	119.5

At 30 September 1989, the Group had the following other commitments in respect of capital expenditure and non-cancellable operating leases for the following year:

	1989 £m	1988 £m
CAPITAL EXPENDITURE		
Committed but not provided for	1.3	3.1
Authorised but not contracted for	5.1	4.9
	6.4	8.0

	Land and buildings £m	Other £m	Total £m
OPERATING LEASES which expire:			
Within one year	5.4	1.6	7.0
From two to five years	14.4	3.0	17.4
Over five years	20.8	0.4	21.2
	40.6	5.0	45.6

been increased significantly by the payment of the deferred consideration, as well as increasing its gearing, with bank loans and overdraft already standing at £121.5m (Exhibit 6.2)

Neither are all these problems overcome if the deferred consideration is payable in shares. If the share price of the acquiring group is depressed at the time of payment, the result is often the need to issue a greater number of shares in order to fulfil the deferred consideration obligations, which has a highly dilutive effect on Earnings per Share and increases the cost of the total dividend often to a level where the dividend per share must be cut or passed in its entirety, as it has been by WPP:

WPP – Deferred consideration commitments

WPP made over 30 small acquisitions by earn-outs, and in 1990 had a total maximum of further payments of around £130m. The payment schedule looks like this (WPP estimates assuming 15 per cent post-tax profits growth):

Table 6.1   WPP – Deferred consideration commitments

	1991	1992	1993	1994	1995	Total
Shares £m	12	6	17	12	2	**49**
Cash £m	19	10	33	17	3	82

Source: WPP

WPP's share price has fallen dramatically due to trading difficulties, caused by the downturn in advertising spend during the recession and the cost of acquisition, most notably Ogilvy and Mather. With the share price at about 48p in early 1992, against 700p at the beginning of 1990, there was a substantial impact on the future number of shares to be issued:

£49m shares at 700p =   7.0 million shares
£49m shares at 48p = 102.0 million shares

The company had 43 million shares in issue at the beginning of 1992 – so assuming that these earn-out targets are met, when the share price was 48p, the number of shares in issue would have to be increased nearly 2½ times to meet these commitments, and by over 100 per cent even at the price at the time of writing (92p) which is showing some recovery. The result is potentially devastating dilution of earnings per share and the impossibility of paying a maintained dividend on the enlarged share capital.

Exhibit 6.2 **Saatchi & Saatchi 1989 Accounts**

13. Creditors

| | GROUP | | | | COMPANY | | | |
| | 1989 | | 1988 | | 1989 | | 1988 | |
	Due within one yr £m	Due after one yr £m	Due within one yr £m	Due after one yr £m	Due within one yr £m	Due after one yr £m	Due within one yr £m	Due after one yr £m
Loan stock	–	6.2	–	6.3	–	6.2	–	6.3
Bank loans and overdrafts	107.1	121.5	7.4	109.4	93.1	60.0	45.0	–
Trade creditors	499.5	–	461.1	–	–	–	–	–
Subsidiaries	–	–	–	–	281.5	–	276.9	–
Related companies	8.5	0.7	9.2	–	–	–	–	–
Deferred purchase consideration	0.6	1.4	9.4	–	–	–	2.8	–
Finance leases	1.9	2.8	1.6	2.4	–	–	–	–
Taxation and social security	51.2	48.0	49.4	34.2	4.8	–	8.9	–
Other creditors	227.2	32.5	180.4	11.9	3.9	–	2.2	–
Proposed dividends	8.1	–	19	–	5.6	–	16.6	–
	904.1	213.1	737.7	164.2	388.9	66.2	352.4	6.3

The loan stock is convertible and unsecured. It bears interest at 6% and is repayable in 2015 unless previously converted into Ordinary shares. Conversion into Ordinary shares may take place at the option of the Loan stockholders during a specified period in the years to 2015 at £2.465 nominal of Ordinary shares for every £100 nominal of Loan stock. An amount of £6.3 million (1988 – £4.6 million) included in bank loans and overdrafts is secured by mortgages on property.

| | GROUP | | COMPANY | |
Analysis of bank loans and overdrafts by years of repayment	1989 £m	1988 £m	1989 £m	1988 £m
From one to two years	2.6	0.6	–	–
From two to five years	118.7	107.4	60.0	–
Over five years	0.2	1.4	–	–
	121.5	109.4	60.0	–

Gross obligations under finance leases due after more than one year	1989 £m	1988 £m
From two to five years	3.4	3.0
Less future finance charges	0.6	0.6
	2.8	2.4

Exhibit 6.3 **WPP 1990 Accounts**

21b. Contingent Liabilities – Acquisitions

Acquisitions made in 1990 together with earlier acquisitions (excluding JWT Group, Inc and the Ogilvy Group, Inc) may give rise to further consideration resulting in goodwill, in addition to the initial payments referred to above. Any further payments will be payable in cash and Ordinary shares of the Company dependent upon the level of profitability of these acquired entities over various periods up to 31 December 1995. It is not practicable to estimate with any reasonable degree of certainty the total additional consideration to be paid. However, the directors estimate that the maximum additional payments which may be payable in respect of all subsidiary undertakings, including amounts accrued in the balance sheet at 31 December 1990, would be:

	Shares £000	Payable in Cash £000	Total £000
Within one year from 31 December 1990	12,951	26,307	39,258
Within two to five years	35,978	35,278	71,256
	48,929	61,585	110,514

The above analysis assumes that the vendors choose cash rather than shares where the option exists. The analysis also assumes that the Company issues shares where the option exists, although in many cases it has the right to settle with cash if it so wishes. Consideration received as shares must generally be retained by the vendors for a minimum period of three years.

WPP's performance has obviously been affected by a number of factors other than its deferred consideration commitments: the recession, Gulf War, the Ogilvy & Mather acquisition and attendant property write-offs. The ordinary dividend was passed in 1990, and the convertible preference dividend in 1991.

Whilst the Saatchi & Saatchi Accounts show the details of the cash deferred consideration commitment in the Note to the Accounts which is usually designed to cover capital expenditure authorised and/or contracted, Cray Electronics Holdings shows under Note 20 – 'Share Capital' – the maximum deferred consideration commitments for ten acquisitions requiring a maximum of £17.1m which at 67p per share (the price in early 1992) would require an issue of 25.5m shares at Cray's option against 87.4m already in issue.

Figure 6.1 WPP share price chart 1985-92

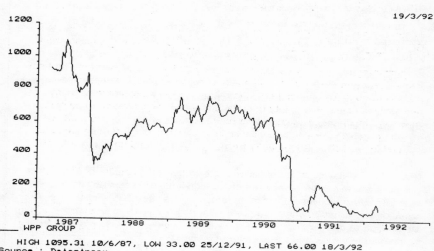

Source : Datastream

Cray Electronics

Cray's origins, like those of many other electronics related companies, are in the defence industry. It had operated as a subcontractor for many years, with equipment and subsystems going mainly to the Royal Navy. Some diversification away from the defence area was made in the 1970s largely to utilise fully the manufacture of microfiche readers, engineering consultancy services and telecoms equipment.

Results, however, continued ever upward. Acquisitions came thick and fast, all for shares and virtually all on a deferred consideration basis. The grand plan did actually have some merit – to build a diverse, leading edge technology concern, able to make money from new processes and products, such as the development of composite materials.

So why didn't the warning bell ring louder? The main reason was that this was the mid 1980s when attention to financial detail was infinitely more relaxed than it is now. The sector was doing well, acquisitions were the order of the day and as long as the results were OK, it seemed best to give the group the benefit of the doubt. Trading in the shares had been freed up with the withdrawal of Capital for Industry who disposed of all their holding and the appetite for the shares from institutions was strong.

In July 1989, Cray announced its full year figures. The cracks started to show in the figures with such items as capitalised R&D, merger accounting and property profits, together with an increasing outflow of shares as deferred considerations became payable. Also, the true costs associated with the composite materials venture were difficult to unravel since a Swiss nominated holding company and a complicated marketing agreement with the Spanish steel giant, Inespal were involved.

Exhibit 6.4 **Cray Electronics 1989 Accounts**

d) Research and development

In previous years up to 30 April 1988, the policy has been as follows:

'Research and development expenditure is written off as incurred, except that development expenditure incurred on an individual project is carried forward when its future recoverability can be foreseen with reasonable assurance. Any expenditure carried forward is amortised during the years following completion of the development in line with the sales from the related projects. The period of write-off is a maximum of 3 years.'

This policy has been changed with effect from 1 May, 1988 to:

'Expenditure on research and development is charged against income in the period in which it is incurred except to the extent that such expenditure is recoverable on contracts with third parties.'

The result of this change in accounting policy which has been applied retrospectively has been to reduce the retained profit at 30 April, 1987 and the profit for the financial period 1987/88 by £2,476,000 and £1,537,000 respectively.

Additionally this change in accounting policy has impacted the results for the year to 29 April 1989 to the extent that profits have been reduced on ordinary activities before taxation by £4,196,000 inclusive of costs in work-in-progress compared with the results that would have been stated had this policy not been changed.

After a short period of time the Chairman and Chief Executive resigned. A new management team was announced – that from UEI, which had recently been taken over by Carlton. 1989 figures were finally restated at a pre-tax profit of just £1.33m versus £17.03m originally reported (see Exhibit 6.4).

Both Saatchi & Saatchi and WPP are now operating in reduced circumstances partly as a result of their deferred consideration commitments. But marketing services group FKB Group was pushed into administration by these commitments. Note 25 of the 1989 accounts shows a maximum liability for deferred consideration of £58.8m in comparison with shareholders' funds of just £4.7m, after deduction of goodwill on previous acquisitions of £40.1m.

Exhibit 6.5 **FKB Accounts to 31 March 1989**

25. FINANCIAL COMMITMENTS

Additional payments may be made to the vendors of certain acquired companies in the years to 1993. These payments are contingent on the future profits of the respective companies. It is not practicable to estimate with any reasonable degree of certainty the total additional consideration to be paid. However, the Directors estimate that the maximum payments that may be made, using the rates of exchange ruling at 31 March 1989, are as follows:

	£000
Within one year	3,400
Between two and five years	55,400
	58,800

Part III

Other Accounting Techniques

7

EXTRAORDINARY AND EXCEPTIONAL ITEMS

'The single most important figure affecting the analysts' and hence the market's view – is forecast earnings per share'
Ian Hay Davidson

ABOVE OR BELOW THE LINE?

SSAP6 covers items over which some of the most frequent debates in accounting rage: extraordinary and exceptional items. Never more than in this area does a conversation between accountants and financial analysts sound more like a debate on linguistic philosophy. So why all the heat and lack of light created by these items?

The answer lies in Earnings per Share ('EPS'). EPS is usually taken as the single biggest determinant of a share's value, through the ubiquitous Price/Earnings Ratio ('PER').

> 'At 8.15 each weekday morning the security salesmen and analysts at my firm meet to consider the ideas that will be put to our 300 or so institutional customers during the day. Analysts give their recommendations for specific shares: buy, hold or sell. It is these recommendations together with similar conclusions reached at twenty or so other security houses, that collectively drive the share prices in the market. The single most important figure affecting the analysts' and hence the market's view – is forecast earnings per share' (Ian Hay Davidson, then Chairman of Alexanders Laing & Cruickshank).

And since EPS is normally calculated by taking earnings *before* extraordinary items there is a keen interest in deciding whether an item is an exceptional item taken 'above the line' and therefore included in the EPS calculation ('the line' being the line in the profit and loss account at which EPS is calculated) or an extraordinary item taken 'below the line'. This interest increases exponentially if the item is a debit item. Incidentally, for those interested in records, the phrase 'above the line (below the line)' is probably one of the most frequently used/least understood in financial analysis (although 'dilution' runs a close second).

All this seems surprising given that SSAP 6 (revised) gives some apparently clear definitions:

Extraordinary items: are material items which derive from events or transactions that fall outside the ordinary activities of the company and which are therefore expected not to recur frequently or regularly.

Exceptional items: are material items which derive from events or transactions which fall within the ordinary activities of the company, and which need to be disclosed separately by virtue of their size or incidence if the financial statements are to give a true and fair view.

Table 7.1 Examples of exceptional and extraordinary items SSAP6 (revised paras 2 and 4)

	Exceptional	*Extraordinary*
Rationalisation, reorganisation and redundancy costs	costs relating to continuing business segments	costs arising from the discontinuance of a business segment, either through termination or disposal
Fixed assets	profits/losses on disposals arising from an exceptional event	profits/losses on disposals arising from an extraordinary event
	previously capitalised expenditure on intangible fixed assets written off other than as part of a process of amortisation	provisions for a permanent diminution in value of fixed assets (including investments), because of an extraordinary event
		profits/losses arising from expropriation of assets
		profits/losses arising from the sale of an investment not held for resale, such as investments in subsidiaries and associates

	Exceptional	*Extraordinary*
Employee share schemes	amounts transferred to employee share schemes	
Bad debts	abnormal bad debt charges	
Stocks and long-term contracts	abnormal write–offs of stocks or provisions for losses on long–term contracts	
Insurance claims	surpluses arising on the settlement of insurance claims; amounts received in settlement of insurance claims for consequential loss of profits	
Taxation		effect of a change in the basis of taxation or a significant change in Government fiscal policy

Clear enough? But if this is clear, how could the following differences arise:

Exhibit 7.1   **Reckitt & Colman Accounts for 1988**

7. EXTRAORDINARY ITEMS	1988 £m	1987 £m
Extraordinary income:		
Surplus on disposal of businesses and major sites	15.84	19.45
Extraordinary charges:		
Reorganisation and integration costs of newly acquired businesses	(11.86)	(9.51)
	3.98	9.94
Tax relief	3.76	6.19
	7.74	16.13

Reckitt & Colman's 1988 Accounts show an extraordinary gain which includes profits from disposal of businesses and major sites (Exhibit 7.1), whereas British Aerospace's 1989 Accounts show an exceptional items profit on the share of the shares in Daf NV and Istel Holdings Ltd (Exhibit 7.2).

Exhibit 7.2 **British Aerospace 1990 Accounts**		
EXCEPTIONAL ITEMS	*1990*	*1989*
	£m	*£m*
Costs associated with industrial action	(28)	(28)
Profit on sale of investments	4	68
	(24)	40
There is no tax charge arising on the profit on sale of investments		

How extensive is the use of exceptional and extraordinary items?

Table 7.2   Exceptional costs as a percentage of profits

	Year	Pre-tax profit £m	Extraordinary costs as % pre-tax profits %
Costain Group	1990	5.5	245.5
Saatchi & Saatchi	1990	35.6	216.0
Storehouse	1991	6.2	180.7
Unigate	1991	75.5	125.8
Greenhall Whitley	1990	62.2	91.6
Tootal Group	1990	23.2	67.4
Burton Group	1990	133.1	63.0
Amstrad	1990	43.8	55.3

In all these cases, extraordinary costs represented more than half reported pre–tax profits, up to a maximum 2½ times pre–tax profits. In all the cases in Table 7.3, exceptional profits represent more than one third of reported profits. One name manages to make an entry in both tables – Storehouse. Obviously, a part of the problem here is that Storehouse's profits were so depressed that they were dwarfed by other items.

Exhibit 7.3 Storehouse 1991 Accounts

4. EXCEPTIONAL ITEMS	1991 £m	1990 £m
Store closure and related costs	(5.5)	(17.9)
Rationalisation and redundancy costs	(12.9)	(9.0)
Discontinued operations	–	(4.4)
	(18.4)	(31.3)
Profits arising from the sale of property	3.6	11.5
	(14.8)	(19.8)

Note 4 of the Storehouse Accounts for 1991, however, shows that the exceptional profits on sale of properties of £3.6m was also in fact overshadowed by exceptional losses of £18.4m on closures, rationalisation costs and redundancies. The extraordinary costs is made up of a series of gains and losses on disposals.

Table 7.3 Exceptional profits as a percentage of profits

Company	Year	Pre-tax profit £m	Exceptional profits as % pre-tax profits %
Stakis	90	30.6	60.4
Storehouse	91	6.2	58.1
George Wimpey	90	43.3	44.1
Daily Mail & General Trust	90	44.2	40.5
Sears	91	146.9	37.0

Source: UBS Phillips & Drew

Stakis, which exceeds Storehouse in its reliance on exceptional profits, actually does not include gains on sale of trading units and properties of £17.6m (57.5 per cent of pre-tax profit) as an exceptional item, but rather shows it as 'Other Operating Income' (Exhibit 7.4). Although as a property developer, development gains would legitimately be taken into operating profits in the year of disposal, only £9.6m of the gains related to 'trading units' and the balance is not identified as development projects.

Exhibit 7.4 **Stakis 1990 Accounts**		
2. OTHER OPERATING INCOME	*1990* *£000*	*1989* *£000*
Gains on sale of trading units	9,605	2,986
Gains on sale of other properties	463	421
Gains on sale of freehold interests in properties	8,420	673
Non-recurring development costs	(917)	–
Other items	45	112
	17,616	4,192

Nor is the size of extraordinary items relative to profits the only problem. Some companies seem to report extraordinary items with anything other than extraordinary frequency. The table below shows the use of extraordinary items to cover closure costs for RHM (Ranks Hovis McDougall) over the past eight years:

Table 7.4 RHM – Extraordinary Closure Costs

£m	1984	1985	1986	1987	1988	1989	1990	1991
Extraordinary								
Closure Costs	14	15	12	20	21	14	24	11
Post–tax profits	45	44	59	74	105	125	93	105
Ratio %	31	34	20	27	20	11	26	10

As can be seen, extraordinary closure costs have averaged over 22 per cent of reported net profits over this period. A common–sense approach would suggest that this use of the word 'extraordinary' strains the English language, if not SSAP 6.

Probably one of the most famous changes in treatment of an item between extraordinary and exceptional in recent times concerns Midland Bank's treatment of its provisions for bad debts on lending to Third World countries in 1987. Lending to certain heavily indebted Less Developed Countries (LDCs) had been a problem for the UK clearing banks since Mexico defaulted on its debt servicing in 1982. The reality that these loans were at least doubtful, if not probably lost, was conveniently swept under the carpet for several years by so–called rescheduling (or lengthening the repayment period) and practices such as lending the countries the money with which to pay the interest due. The reason for this sudden burst of creativity was that without playing for time, some of the banks, such as Midland and Lloyds (where at peak, LDC loans were over twice shareholders' funds – i.e. the bank's shareholders' funds were wiped out twice over if the loans were written off) would have gone bust. By gaining some breathing space, the banks were able to milk the strong profitability of UK banking in the 1980s (much to the recent disgust of consumers and small businesses) and have a string of rights issues with which to repair their balance sheets:

Table 7.5   Bank Rights Issues in the 1980s

		Amounts raised £m
1983	Standard Chartered	98
	Midland	155
1984	Bank of Scotland	42
	NatWest	236
1985	Royal Bank	115
	Barclays	507
	Bank of Scotland	81
1986	NatWest	714
1987	Midland	700
1988	Barclays	921
	Standard Chartered	304
		3873

Source: UBS Phillips & Drew

By 1987 this process had been taken far enough, and the position of the LDCs had deteriorated enough, for the banks to admit that some of their LDC loans would probably never be repaid. Led by Citibank of the United States in May 1987, the banks raised provisions against these loans to 25–30 per cent of the LDC exposure outstanding.

These provisions were raised at the time of the UK clearers' interim profit announcements in the main, and Midland Bank broke rank with the other banks by placing its LDC loan provisions of £653m below the line as an extraordinary item. This seemed rather odd. To allege that making a provision against bad and doubtful loans was outside the ordinary activities of a bank and therefore not expected to recur per SSAP6 seemed to fly in the face of reality. Bad debts are of course a normal part of banking, and had been an even more regular feature of Midland's performance. Midland had been the bank which acquired Crocker National Bank in 1981 which had produced substantial bad debts in California real estate. Indeed, the Crocker deal was the genesis of Midland's LDC exposure – Crocker's management had used the capital supplied by its new parent, Midland, to expand its loan book including loans to Latin America, which was a pretty easy market to penetrate!

Exhibit 7.5 Midland Bank 1987 Interim Report

4. Extraordinary items

As announced on 7 July 1987, Midland Bank is taking a series of actions which will strengthen its capital position. As part of this series of actions, it has created additional specific provisions of £916m following a fundamental review of loans to borrowers in 30 countries identified as having actual or potential payments difficulties. After anticipated tax relief of £263m these additional specific provisions give rise to an **extraordinary charge** amounting to £653m.

Midland's treatment of its LDC provisions seemed to owe less to the letter of SSAP6 than to the fact that it was a very large negative item. If the LDC provision had been taken above the line, Midland's dividend would have been uncovered and yield support was one of the few attractions of Midland's shares in the 1980s. Midland also probably felt vulnerable to predators if its earnings were seen to collapse and the dividend was cut, as indeed it was: Hanson bought a stake in 1987, as did Hongkong Bank, and even Saatchi & Saatchi made a bid approach.

This treatment of LDC provisions was even more curious given that Midland and Nat West shared the same auditors (Ernst & Whinney). Of course, interim results are not audited, but it seems incredible that the auditor of these two banks would not have been consulted on the treatment of such a major item. Nat West was then a stronger bank, with good capital ratios, and domestic and US profits, and could afford a more stringent treatment. But no doubt it was not amused that a competitor bank audited by its own auditors intended to 'get away with' an extraordinary debit in this instance.

The net result was that by the time Midland's final results and Accounts for 1987 were published, the extraordinary item had to be changed to an exceptional item and Midland disclosed a loss before tax of £505m, and a loss per share of 125.3p. Midland had bitten the bullet, but reinforced with the capital injected by Hongkong Bank, it was by then able to hold the dividend per share at 20.1p, despite the loss.

Exhibit 7.6 **Midland Bank 1987 Accounts**

7. Exceptional item

	1987 £m	1986 £m
Exceptional provisions against loans to borrowers in countries identified as having actual or potential payment difficulties	1,016	–

But possibly the award for extraordinary use of an extraordinary item should go to Pennant Properties, a company which went into administrative receivership on 24 October 1990. In 1989, Pennant tried unsuccessfully to sell its US subsidiary, Bay Financial Corporation, and when it could not sell it wrote down the value of its subsidiary as an extraordinary item, *which included the cost of financing the investment*:

Exhibit 7.7 **Pennant Properties 1989 Accounts**

9. EXTRAORDINARY ITEMS

	1989 £000	1988 £000
Extraordinary items comprise the following:		
a) Bay financial corporation:		
Write down of investment	(31,386)	(8,615)
Costs of financing investment	(2,857)	(4,144)
Realised currency gains on related debt, now retired	5,080	–
b) Profit on sale of UK and Caribbean retail operations	241	–
c) Advice to the Company in respect of prospective offers for its share capital during 1987	–	(615)
d) Profit on sale of shares in Jermyn Investment Co. Plc	–	311
	(28,922)	(13,063)

Bay Financial Corporation
A provision has been made to write down the investment in Bay Financial Corporation ('Bay'), a subsidiary quoted on the New York Stock Exchange. It is the Director's intention to dispose of the investment in Bay in the year to 30 June, 1990 and the write down and associated interest costs are treated as extraordinary as this will represent the sale of an investment not originally acquired with the intention of resale.

If all of this seems, as we earlier remarked, like an interesting subject for debate before the Oxford Union rather than a live issue which affects companies' welfare or even survival and that of investors, it is worth looking at the coincidence of the creative use of exceptional and extraordinary items with company failures in recent years:

Table 7.6 Company failures and extraordinary items

Company	Year	Pre-tax Amount £m	profit £m	Reason
Arley	1989	(0.970)	0.632	Included cost of reorganising an existing site (note 25)
Bestwood	1988	(5.341)	2.613	Reorganisation expenses £1m, losses on investment £2.8m
A Goldberg & Sons	1988	(0.756)	3.232	Cost of conversion to specialist retailing on non-apparel i.e. stopping selling items other than clothing
Reliant	1989	(0.537)	1.938	Reorganisation costs

Source: UBS Phillips & Drew

In every case, the extraordinary debits taken below the line (often offset against extraordinary credits for disposals) were substantial in relation to trading profits, and in two cases were actually larger. The outcome for all four companies was the same:

Company	Date of administrative receivership
Arley	27.11.90
Bestwood	24.4.90
Goldberg	8.6.90
Reliant	2.11.90

The problems of distinguishing exceptional and extraordinary items live on. In the 1991 interim results from BTR, disposal profits from the sale of its investment in Pretty Polly were taken above the line, causing some criticism.

Exhibit 7.8 Arley Holdings 1989 Accounts

25. EXTRAORDINARY ITEMS

	1989 £000	1988 £000
Profit on sale of land & buildings at Eastbourne (transferred from revaluation reserve)	610	–
Loss on sale of land & buildings at Leighton Buzzard	(90)	–
Expenditure relating to closure of factories at Eastbourne, Leighton Buzzard and Potters Bar and in setting up a new factory at Tipton and reorganising existing site at Borehamwood	(970)	–
Less taxation credit	311	–
	£(139)	–

Bestwood 1988 Accounts

6. EXTRAORDINARY ITEMS

	1988 £000	1987 £000
Extraordinary items comprise:		
Reorganisation expenses	1,024	–
Losses on investments	2,769	–
Loss on sale and discontinuation of businesses	2,605	295
Abortive acquisition costs	30	68
	6,428	363
Less: tax relief	1,087	165
	5,341	198

A Goldberg & Sons 1989 Accounts

6. EXTRAORDINARY ITEMS

Extraordinary Income for the year ended 26 March 1988 amounted to £4,930,000 before deduction of corporation tax of £1,728,000 and comprised the surplus on revaluation of the investment in Style Financial Services Limited of £5,836,000 less costs of conversion to specialist retailing and discontinuance of non-apparel of £756,000 and the costs of improvements to the group pension scheme and changes to employee conditions of £150,000.

Reliant 1989 Accounts

9. EXTRAORDINARY ITEMS

	Group	
	1989 £000	1988 £000
Profit on sale and leaseback of Two Gates South site	–	(463)
Reorganisation costs associated with the relocation from part of the Two Gates site	–	221
Reorganisation costs, including closure of the engineering division	537	–
	537	(242)
Taxation thereon – current	(92)	130
– deferred	(96)	–
	349	(112)

The Accounting Standards Board has now decided to address this problem, and in an Exposure Draft published in April 1991 maintained that extraordinary items should be restricted to:
a) the expropriation of assets i.e. their confiscation or nationalisation by government
b) a fundamental change in the basis of taxation.
The result, if this Exposure Draft is applied, will be to make extraordinary items very rare indeed. Items which have been included as extraordinary items such as redundancy, reorganisation costs, disposal profits/losses, write downs, provisions, legal and insurance claims should be included above the line, albeit as exceptional items, and will affect earnings per share, which will therefore swing around a lot more and not always follow the neat upward progression so beloved of managements and some analysts.

The ASB has already gone further and in an emergency ruling has barred the classification of redundancy and reorganisation costs as extraordinary items. The intention now is that the new Financial Reporting Standard which will replace SSAP 6 will ban the use of all extraordinary items including even the two limited exceptions proposed in the April 1991 Exposure Draft.

This emergency ruling may have come in response to two examples of companies using the existing accounting standard, believed to be ICI which made a £300m extraordinary charge to cover the expected costs of 'reshaping' the ICI business portfolio, and Unilever, which in February 1991 made an extraordinary charge of £195m after tax (£305m before tax) to cover the costs of restructuring its manufacturing operations as a result of the legislation leading to the single European market.

Taking the UK shipping and transport sector as an example, the implementation of this Exposure Draft could have a powerful effect in many cases:

Table 7.7 Shipping and transport Sector – Extraordinary item analysis

| | Last three years total | | | Historic PER | |
Company	Pre-tax £m	Extraordinaries £m	Ratio %	Reported	Adjusted
AB Ports	164	−43	−26	11.1	24.3
Ocean	133	−33	−25	11.7	12.1
LEP	74	−11	−15	9.1	12.8
NFC	255	−6	−2	11.9	12.3
Powell Duffryn	101	−1	−1	9.5	7.7
P&O	955	85	9	13.8	12.7
Tiphook	61	7	12	9.4	9.7
TDG	127	29	23	14.5	17.1

Source: UBS Phillips & Drew

AB Ports has had the highest level of extraordinary costs relative to its pre-tax profits among the major companies in the sector over the last three years. The extraordinary items relate to the cost of redundancies as a result of the abolition of the National Dock Labour Scheme in July 1989, and these would be treated as an exceptional cost under the new system.

In addition, ABP wrote down some of its retail developments by £25m after transferring £85.1m of development properties from the development property to the investment property category, thereby taking the write down of £25m against reserves rather than profits. It is not clear whether such a write down would be able to avoid reported profits under the new system, although we have calculated the adjusted P/E without this further factor in the table above, but it would certainly be revealed in the proposed new statement of recognised gains and losses detailed in the ASB's Exposure Draft on the Structure of Financial Statements (see Survival Techniques in the Accounting Jungle, Chapter 17).

Profits would be considerably lower in some cases and higher in others which would substantially affect the rating of the stocks through the ubiquitous Price/Earnings ratios.

8

OFF BALANCE SHEET FINANCE

'The creative accounting trick which improves companies' balance sheets'
The Guardian, 22 December 1987

OFF BALANCE SHEET

Another frequently quoted term in modern accounting and finance is 'off-balance sheet'. It has been defined as 'the funding or refinancing of a company's operations in such a way that, under legal requirements and existing accounting conventions, some or all of the finance may not be shown on its balance sheet' (ICEAW, Technical Release 603, Off balance sheet finance and window dressing). Assets as well as liabilities are removed from the balance sheet of the company concerned, and there may also be some impact on the profit and loss account. But the usual aim of off-balance sheet finance is to reduce a company's ostensible gearing.

There have been several steps towards developing an accounting standard for off-balance sheet items. ICEAW Technical Release 603 in December 1985 suggested for the first time that financial statements should be concerned with the substance rather than the legal form of transactions.

ED42 issued by the Accounting Standards Committee in March 1988 also dwelt upon the need to report the substance rather than the form of transactions in order to provide a 'true and fair view'. It introduced the concept of the 'special purpose transaction' – briefly, this was a transaction which could be accounted for differently depending upon whether its elements were taken step by step, or the transaction was viewed as a whole. Greater disclosure of the effect of such transactions was required to provide a true and fair view. ED42 also introduced the concept of the 'controlled non-subsidiary' being a company which fell outside the Companies Act definition of a subsidiary, but which is nonetheless controlled by the company which places assets and liabilities within it in order to place these items off-balance sheet. ED42 maintained that such controlled non-subsidiaries should be consolidated in the group accounts.

WHEN A SUBSIDIARY IS NOT A SUBSIDIARY

ED49, published in May 1990, went on to define what it called 'quasi subsidiaries'. Most of the forms of off-balance sheet finance involve the use of a company which a holding company controls, but which is not consolidated as a subsidiary. Rather it is usually accounted as an associate company, shown in the consolidated account as a single item representing the cost of the net investment in the associate, plus post-acquisition retained profits (or minus losses), less dividends received from the associate. For a company which has high gearing and is able to place an asset (such as property) and its attached borrowing into a quasi-subsidiary the advantage is that these items are removed from its balance sheet. If they were placed in a real subsidiary, the gross assets and liabilities of that subsidiary would be included in the group consolidated accounts, so increasing gearing. And gearing or debt/equity ratio is used by analysts in valuing the company – hence the desire to show low, or conservative gearing.

Prior to the 1989 Companies Act, the definition of a subsidiary was given by the Companies Act 1985 as:

'A company is deemed to be a subsidiary of another if:

a) that other either:

    (i) is a member of it and controls the composition of its board of directors, or

    (ii) holds more than half in nominal value of its equity share capital, or

b) the first mentioned company is a subsidiary of any company which is that other's subsidiary.'

There are loopholes in this definition of a subsidiary. Firstly, it concentrates on equity holding rather than control through voting rights. Thus, a company could hold all of another company's *ordinary* shares, yet the company was not a subsidiary because a third party held more than 50 per cent of the company's *total* equity capital. Even if the company holding the ordinary shares had superior voting rights and was entitled to virtually all the profits of the quasi-subsidiary, it would not qualify as a subsidiary under the Companies Act 1985. The problem revolves around the definition of equity, which made it possible to structure a class of equity with limited voting and dividend rights, which nonetheless allowed a company to escape from the definition of a subsidiary if this class of shares representing 50 per cent or more of the equity was held by a third party.

The second area of difficulty relates to the control of the Board of

Directors. Control of the composition of the Board, which is the Companies Act 1985 definition of a subsidiary, is not the same as controlling the decisions of the Board, especially if the directors were given differential voting powers.

EXAMPLES

Sale of Assets

Most of the off-balance sheet finance also involves the sale of assets (and the associated liabilities) by a company to its quasi-subsidiary. This could reduce the gearing shown in the balance sheet and produce a profit (or loss) in the same way as the sale of any other asset. However, it is debatable whether these profits have been realised in any sense that would be understood by the average investor.

LEP – Sale of St Paul's Vista – Off Balance Sheet

In 1988, LEP sold a development property, St Paul's Vista, for £120m to an associate company called St Paul's Vista Limited. St Paul's Vista Limited had a complex share structure in which LEP had an effective interest of approximately 90 per cent although under the UK companies' legislation, it was regarded as an associate and therefore consolidated as a net investment, without the debt appearing on LEP's balance sheet. At that time the St Paul's Vista property had a net book value of £111.3m which meant that a profit of £8.7m was realised on the transaction. This profit was credited to group pre-tax profits as an exceptional gain. However, because the Inland Revenue regarded it as an intra-group transaction, the profit was not subject to tax and therefore £8.7m flowed through directly to earnings. This accounting treatment more than doubled LEP's reported earnings per share in 1988. The transaction also enabled LEP to transfer £2.86m from its revaluation reserve into the profit and loss reserves i.e. it became distributable in the form of a dividend even though by most common sense approaches no profit had been realised by the sale to an entity controlled by LEP.

The amount of cash actually received by LEP as a result of the deal was substantially less than the £120m disposal consideration. The associate's borrowings were secured on the property without recourse to the group. In fact group borrowings, net of cash, rose by £5m net of acquisition effects during the year of the transaction. However, in the following year, LEP reduced its loans to St Pauls's Vista by £42.5m, thereby benefiting the published net gearing ratio of LEP. In addition to St Paul's Vista, LEP had joint property venture net assets of £18.7m at December 1989. Financing for these ventures was supported by irrevocable letters of credit issued by LEP (Contingent Liabilities, see Chapter 9) for a total of £59.5m at that date.

The benefits from LEP's point of view of this complex restructuring were summarised as:

- Removed debt from the published balance sheet

- Substantially improved EPS in the year of the transaction

- Enabled capital reserves to be transferred to distributable reserves.

But the ultimate outcome for LEP has been disastrous. The St. Paul's Vista transaction was eventually reversed, bringing the property (now known as Swiss Bank House) back on balance sheet.

The effect is shown by comparing the borrowings in Lep Group's 1989 Accounts with the restated figures in the 1990 Accounts:

Exhibit 8.1   LEP Group 1989 Accounts

19. BORROWINGS

	Group		Holding Company	
	1989	1988	1989	1988
	£000	£000	£000	£000
Bank loans, overdrafts and other loans:				
Not wholly repayable within five years	98,187	31,276	–	–
Wholly repayable within five years	98,303	150,798	96,636	97,787
Included in creditors due after one year	196,490	182,074	96,636	97,787
Included in creditors due within one year	34,989	19,094	2,718	3
Gross borrowings	231,479	201,168	99,354	97,790
Cash balances	(16,822)	(12,046)	(13)	(238)
Borrowings net of cash at bank	**214,657**	189,122	99,341	97,341

LEP Group 1990 Accounts

20. BORROWINGS

	1990	1989	1990	1989
	£000	£000	£000	£000
Bank loans, overdrafts and other loans				
Included in creditors due after one year:				
– Not wholly repayable within five years	97,320	98,187	–	–
– Wholly repayable within five years	226,121	173,303	97,550	96,636
	323,441	271,490	97,550	96,636
Included in creditors due within one year	93,120	83,346	50,723	2,718
Gross borrowings	416,561	354,836	148,273	99,354
Cash and short-term deposits	(17,099)	(21,110)	(3)	(13)
Borrowings net of cash and short-term deposits	399,462	**333,726**	148,270	99,341

The result is an increase in stated net borrowings from £214.7m for 1989 to a restated £333.7m. As the Chairman's statement said, 'The economic relationship between St Paul's Vista Ltd and LEP has not changed as a result'! Quite – and the obverse applied – having St Paul's Vista off balance sheet had not reduced LEP's actual gearing.

The net result for LEP was even worse than this restatement of 1989 net debt. LEP finished 1990 with gearing of 189 per cent.

Obviously general recessionary conditions in the transport business were partly to blame, but LEP's results for the six months to June 1991 were catastrophic:

	Six months to 30 June 1991 £m	31st Dec 1990 £m	Year ended 1990 £m
Operating profit	20.1	23.3	55.7
Share of related companies and property joint ventures	(1.1)	(0.4)	(0.1)
Profit before Interest and Tax	19.0	22.9	55.6
Net interest payable	(17.1)	(12.5)	(26.2)
Pre-tax profit	**1.9**	**10.4**	**29.4**

Exhibit 8.2 **LEP Group 1990 Accounts**

Profits collapsed by over 80 per cent and the dividend was passed, with the soaring interest bill being the main cause. Gearing was over 200 per cent with the Swiss Bank House back on balance sheet, and in October 1991 LEP was forced into a refinancing agreement with its bankers owing £470m of debt. Once again it had declared 'profits' of £29m. In 1990 LEP's net interest charge was just £26m on net debt of over £400m – an intriguing position brought about by borrowing in currencies with low interest rates (notably US dollars) to finance sterling assets – a mismatch which came home to roost in 1991 (see Chapter 15, Currency Mismatching).

By the end of 1991, LEP's shares were down to 7½p from 187p in March and the Chairman and Chief Executive, John Reed, had resigned.

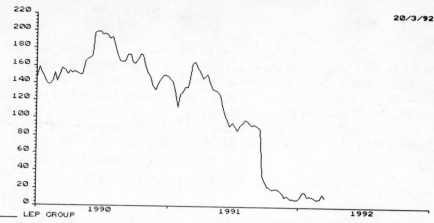

Figure 8.1   LEP Share price chart 1990-92

20/3/92

LEP GROUP

1990   1991   1992

HIGH 199.00 18/6/90, LOW 9.00 23/12/91, LAST 11.50 16/3/92
Source : Datastream

The effect on LEP's share price is equally well illustrated by its position in *The Sunday Times'* 1991 table of stock market winners and losers:

Table 8.1   The Winners and Losers of 1991

BIGGEST SHARE-PRICE RISES   BIGGEST SHARE-PRICE FALLS

Rank	Company	% change	Rank	Company	% change
1	Airtours	432	1	**LEP Group**	−94
2	ML Laboratories	310	2	NSM	−90
3	Next	239	3	YJ Lovell	−89
4	Hi-Tec sports	239	4	Rosehaugh	−89
5	Betterware Con Prods	191	5	Richmond Oil & Gas	−87
6	Domestic & Gen	177	6	Mountleigh	−85
7	Misys	174	7	Cannon Street Inv	−84
8	Medeva	172	8	First Nat Finance	−83
9	Yule Catto	149	9	Ratners	−82
10	Etam	140	10	Thomas Robinson	−77
11	Domino Printing	133	11	Buckingham International	−76
12	Kalon Group	133	12	Cairn Energy	−72
13	Kwik-Fit	128	13	Greycoat	−70
14	Silentnight	123	14	Asda	−69
15	Wellcome	122	15	Stanhope Properties	−68
16	Owners Abroad	119	16	Costain	−67
17	Scottish TV	119	17	Marina Dev	−65
18	Spring Ram	114	18	Union discount	−65
19	Sherwood Group	114	19	Enterprise Comp	−65
20	Pentland	108	20	Hodgson Kenyon	−65

Source: Sunday Times 29.12.91

The scope for this type of off-balance sheet finance is likely to be limited in the future by the adoption of ED49, which was issued in May 1990. This will bring many off-balance sheet structures back on to the group balance sheet unless new share structures can be developed to avoid this measure.

The sale of assets to a quasi-subsidiary does not mean that the vendor company cannot use or regain full control/bring the assets back on to its balance sheet. Use can be achieved by the quasi-subsidiary granting an

---

Exhibit 8.3 **Burton Group 1986 Accounts – sale to Hall & Sons Ltd**

25. Related Companies
The principal related companies are:

	Country of Operation	Country of Registration	Activity	Equity Shareholding
BG Holdings Ltd	UK	England	Financial Services	42%
Burton Group Personal Account Ltd	UK	England	Financial Services	46%
Welbeck Finance plc	UK	England	Financial Services	10%
Hall & Sons Ltd	UK	England	Property Investment	50%

Income from related companies comprises the Group's share of the profits of BG Holdings Ltd and Welbeck Finance plc. Consistent with prior years, income from management services provided to Burton Group Personal Account Ltd and investment income attributable to the Group's interest in this company is included in the Group's turnover.

BG Holdings Ltd: The net assets attributable to the Group's investment are £7.0 million represented mainly by debtors and other assets £27.2 million less bank loans and other creditors £20.2 million.

Burton Group Personal Accounts Ltd: The net assets attributable to the Group's investment are £26.1 million, represented mainly by debtors £162.5 million less bank loans and other ceditors £136.4 million.

Welbeck Finance plc: A subsidiary owns the whole of the ordinary share capital of Welbeck Finance plc (which represents 10% of the equity share capital) and the whole of the restricted share capital. The remainder of the equity share capital is represented by deferred shares, none of which is held by the Group. The net assets attributed to the Group's investment are £52.7 million, represented mainly by debtors and other assets, £324.1 million less bank loans, and other creditors £271.4 million.

Exhibit 8.4 **Burton Group 1986 Accounts**

CONSOLIDATED BALANCE SHEET

At 30 August 1986 (£m)	1986	1985
Fixed assets		
Tangible assets	593.9	660.5
Investments	120.0	83.6
	713.9	744.1
Current assets		
Stocks	178.3	171.0
Debtors	94.6	79.9
Properties held for sale	14.9	44.5
Investments	0.4	14.4
Bank balances and cash	66.2	9.1
	354.4	318.9
Creditors (due within one year)	429.9	498.0
Net current liabilities	75.5	179.1
Total assets less current liabilities	638.4	565.0
Creditors (due after one year)	144.1	114.2
Provisions for liabilities and charges	39.1	66.5
Minority interests	14.7	15.0
	440.5	369.3
Capital and reserves		
Called up share capital	274.4	135.1
Share premium account	0.9	1.9
Revaluation reserve	30.1	102.4
Other reserves	0.2	0.2
Retained earnings	134.9	129.7
	440.5	369.3

operating lease on the asset (building, plant or whatever) to the vendor/ parent company. Under the terms of SSAP 21, operating lease commitments do not need to be capitalised so the vendor/lessee can still lease the asset but keep it on his balance sheet. This method of ensuring that the asset can be bought back on balance sheet is called a sale and leaseback.

The Burton Group 1986 Accounts show the sale and leaseback of £100m of properties together with £70m borrowings to a quasi-subsidiary, Hall & Sons Ltd, in which its equity interest was only 50 per cent. No profit was booked on this transaction as the book and market value of the properties, as defined by the sale, were equal, but the borrowings were taken off balance sheet, which made nonsense of the implied gearing of 50 per cent suggested by the Consolidated balance sheet.

More information on Hall & Sons Ltd (now called High Street Property Investments Ltd) was revealed in the 1988 Accounts, from which it can be seen that the Burton Group's 50 per cent equity shareholding related to all of one class of ordinary shares (the 'B' shares). In addition it also held all of the far more numerous £1 Preference Shares:

Exhibit 8.5 **Burton Group 1988 accounts**

Note 25 Related companies

The principal related companies are:

	Country of Operation	Country of Registration	Shares in Issue	Group's shareholding
Burton Group Financial Services (Hgs) Limited	UK	England	150 £1 'A' Ordinary	100%
			150 £1 'B' Ordinary	–
			2,000 £1 Preference	100%
High Street Property Investments Limited	UK	England	52 £1 'A' Ordinary	–
			52 £1 'B' Ordinary	100%
			19,948 £1 Preference	100%

Burton Group Financial Services (Holdings) Limited (BGFSH)
BGFSH holds the whole of the issued share capital of BG Holdings Limited, Burton Group Personal Accounts Limited and Welbeck Finance plc, the principal companies who provide financial services for the Group.

High Street Property Investments Limited (HSPI)
In August 1986 the Group entered into sale and leaseback arrangements with HSPI (formerly Hall and Sons Ltd), in respect of properties with a book and market value of £100.1 million. HSPI has granted ten-year options to certain Group companies to repurchase the individual properties at market value and pre-emptive rights over the properties or in respect of the repayment of loans made to HSPI by its lending banks. The Group is entitled to, and accounts for, the retained profits of HSPI under the equity method of accounting, including any profits which may arise on the sale of properties to third parties.

But perhaps more revealing is the admission in Burton's 1989 Accounts: 'The recently enacted Companies Act 1989 is likely to require consolidation of the Group's financial services activities. . . . Consideration is also being given to the implications of the Act for the Group's other related company, High Street Property Investment Limited. . . . The new Companies Act will have no effect on the commercial operations, profitability, cash flow or existing banking arrangements of the Group'. Quite so, and neither therefore did the off balance sheet structure using quasi–subsidiaries which the Act forced companies to disclose!

And finally, in the 1991 Accounts, Burton's new Finance Director moved to consolidate the assets and liabilities of High Street Property Investments Limited as a subsidiary rather than an associate:

Exhibit 8.6 **1991 Burton Accounts**

1. ACCOUNTING POLICIES

B. Changes in accounting bases and the presentation of financial information

In the light of the introduction of the Companies Act 1989 and likely developments in accounting practice, a comprehensive review of accounting policies and the presentation of financial information has been undertaken. As a result, certain changes have been made to the bases of accounting for fixed assets and the presentation of financial information adopted in previous years as follows:

(i) The results and liabilities of High Street Property Investments Limited (HSPI) have been consolidated. HSPI was formerly treated as an associated undertaking;

(ii) Certain properties disposed of in 1988 under the terms of sale and leaseback transactions with a capital value of £75 million have been reflected in the Group's fixed assets and the related lease obligation included in creditors. These transactions were previously treated as operating leases in accordance with provisions of Statement of Standard Accounting Practice No. 21;

(iii) The redeemable preference shares owned by banks in Debenhams (Aruba) NV, one of the Group's subsidiary undertakings, have been treated as a component of borrowings rather than as a minority interest;

(iv) Certain items of income and expenditure and certain balance sheet figures have been reclassified; and

(v) Certain changes have been made to the economic lives applied to and basis of providing depreciation on certain of the Group's fixed assets as described below.

The comparative figures for 1990, shown in these accounts, have been restated to reflect items (i) to (iv) above. The profit for the financial year ended 1 September 1990 previously reported, of £12.4 million, is unchanged and the net assets at that date previously reported, of £737.5 million, have been restated at £741.3m.

Together with other changes described in the changes in Burton's accounting policies note, such as bringing sale and leaseback properties back on balance sheet (see next section) and counting redeemable preference shares issued by subsidiaries which carried a dividend equivalent to a commercial rate of interest as debt not as a minority interest, this completely changed the picture presented by Burton's balance sheet. Gearing before these changes of 24.3 per cent was increased to 43.1 per cent (although in itself this was a big reduction from the previous year's actual position). But it is obvious that these devices had virtually halved Burton's apparent gearing. The difference is apparent from a comparison of the creditors due over one year of £183.4m shown in the 1990 Group Accounts with the restated figure of £331.5m for 1990 shown in the 1991 Accounts:

Exhibit 8.7   Burton Group 1990 Accounts

15. Creditors – due after one year

	Group 1990 £m	Group 1989 £m	Company 1990 £m	Company 1989 £m
Debenture loans (note 16)	158.2	220.5	144.4	148.2
Loans from group companies	–	–	152.1	177.6
Term loan	1.0	1.0	–	–
Lease obligations (note 21)	0.6	3.0	–	1.3
Other creditors	0.6	1.3	27.4	1.3
Loan from related company	23.0	–	166.2	–
	183.4	**225.8**	**490.2**	**328.4**

Burton Group 1991 Accounts

18. Creditors – due after one year

	Group 1991 £m	Group 1990 £m	Company 1991 £m	Company 1990 £m
Debenture loans (note 19)	42.8	158.2	34.3	144.4
Redeemable preference shares				
between one and two years	3.1	3.1	–	–
between two and five years	–	3.0	–	–
Bank loans repayable				
between one and two years	1.0	1.0	–	–
between two and five years	64.5	7.0	–	–
after five years	–	58.5	–	–
Loans from subsidiary undertakings	–	–	33.0	152.1
Term loan	–	1.0	–	–
Finance lease obligations (note 24)	–	0.6	–	–
Property lease obligations (note 24)	75.5	75.5	–	–
Other creditors	–	0.6	–	27.4
Loan from associated undertaking	–	23.0	–	166.3
	186.9	**331.5**	67.3	490.2

Redeemable preference shares carry a right to a dividend equivalent to a commercial rate on interest.

Sales and repurchase of assets

This method of off-balance sheet finance does not normally involve quasi-subsidiaries but rather the existence of an option for the vendor to repurchase an asset sold. If the repurchase price is calculated as the original sale price plus compound interest to the date of repurchase, then the purchaser is merely financing the asset for a period but also taking it off the owner's balance sheet.

In determining whether such a transaction is a form of off-balance sheet finance it is necessary to explore where the risks and rewards of ownership rest, often indicated by the price of the two transactions. If both transactions are to be at market value, then the risk and rewards of ownership are passed, and the sale and repurchase is genuine and not a form of off-balance sheet finance. But if the repurchase price is fixed, for example, to include interest it is evident this is a lending transaction conducted off-balance sheet.

The nature of the contract of repurchase has also to be examined. It can be a contract binding on both parties, or a put or call option (or both). In the case of binding commitment and the existence of *both* put and call options, only the price remains as a determinant of whether the transaction is a form of off-balance sheet finance.

A put option would tend to suggest that the vendor has retained the risks of ownership, since the put option will only be exercised by the purchaser when the strike price for the put option is above the market price of an asset, so that the vendor has secured a form of financing rather than genuinely disposing of the asset. Obviously, the existence of a call option for the vendor would suggest the reverse – it is a genuine disposal and any profit on it should be recognised, even though the vendor has held on to the rewards of ownership through the call option.

Joint ventures

Frequently used in property development, joint ventures can represent a form of off-balance sheet finance. SSAP1 deals with associate companies and equity accounting, and attempts to apply the same principles to other unincorporated forms of joint venture such as partnerships.

Rush & Tompkins' 1989 Accounts show net investment of £7.78m in property development joint ventures, which is shown in the Stocks and work-in-progress Note in the accounts, and we are told that a further £17m of working capital provided for these joint ventures is included in Note 15 (Exhibit 8.9) where amounts owed by related companies total £20.1m out of total Debtors of £42.2m. But probably the key item is the mention of £89m of non-recourse or limited recourse bank facilities provided to these joint ventures.

Exhibit 8.8   Rush & Tompkins 1989 Accounts

Note 13 Stocks and work-in-progress

	1989 £000	1988 £000
Work in progress:		
Contracting	685,220	598,197
Cash received on account	(631,766)	(553,200)
	53,454	44,997
Development land, buildings and work-in-progress	27,482	26,613
Net investment in joint venture developments (note 14)	**7,780**	16,513
	88,716	88,123
Stocks of consumables	1,164	1,091
	89,880	89,214

The net contracting work-in-progress of £53,454,000 includes £37,459,000 (1988 £27,997,000) certified and unpaid.

The total amount of interest included in development land, buildings and work-in-progress including investments at the year end was £8,220,000 (1988 £7,783,000)

The net investment in joint venture developments of £7,780,000 represents the group's share of the equity of various schemes. In addition to the equity invested, **the group had provided additional working capital amounting to £17,033,000** (see notes 15 and 16) and the joint venture companies have entered into **a number of non-recourse and limited recourse banking arrangements.** At 31 March, 1989 the value of each development considerably exceeded the total of such loans (which amounted to approximately **£89 million** (1988 £65 million) and other outstanding commitments. As a result, the directors consider the risk of any claim which would have a material effect on the group's financial position to be remote.

Whilst no further construction work remains to be carried out in the former international civil engineering business, finalisation of outstanding accounts will take some considerable time. The provision established in 1987 still appears to be adequate.

Obviously this bank finance was not shown in Rush & Tompkins' consolidated balance sheet, where bank borrowings of £25m compared with shareholders' funds of £35m. The joint venture structure had kept Rush & Tompkins' disclosed gearing down, quite correctly, since the loans were non-recourse i.e. the bank lenders had no recourse to Rush & Tompkins if they lost money lending to the joint venture developments. But (1) some of the lending was 'limited' recourse not non-recourse (2)

Exhibit 8.9 **Rush & Tompkins 1989 Accounts**

Note 15 Debtors	Group		Company	
	1989	*1988*	*1989*	*1988*
	£000	*£000*	*£000*	*£000*
Amounts falling due within one year:				
Trade debtors	14,838	6,557	–	–
Amounts owed by subsidiaries	–	–	56,854	49,152
Amounts owed by related companies	20,084	9,876	7,035	4,902
Other debtors	2,545	2,316	1,359	1,499
Prepayments and accrued income	657	548	224	81
	38,124	19,297	65,472	55,634
Amounts falling due after more than one year:				
Trade debtors	4,082	424	–	–
Total debtors	42,206	19,721	65,472	55,634

'non-recourse' was one of the terms bandied around at the height of the property bull market with little or no certainty in its definition, and (3) many property companies underestimated or misjudged the practical implications when the bank which lent directly to their company was also the non-recourse lender to one of their off-balance sheet developments. The souring of relationships which could result from the company allowing its bankers to lose money in a non-recourse loan raised practical difficulties in dealing with the same bank for its group facilities, particularly as the companies which indulged in non-recourse off-balance sheet finance tended to be highly geared anyway.

When Rush & Tompkins went into receivership in May 1990 it was reported as owing over £300m compared with the £25m shown in the 1989 Accounts!

Dissimilar activities

SSAP 14 grants exemption to exclude subsidiaries from group accounts where 'its activities are so dissimilar from those of other companies within the group that consolidated financial statements would be misleading' and information for the holding company's shareholders and other users of the statements would be better provided by presenting separate financial statements for such a subsidiary! But it should be noted that SSAP 14 is concerned with whether a subsidiary should be *consolidated*, not whether it should be excluded from the financial statements.

But it is also likely that companies will wish to exclude activities because they increase the group's gearing ratio since they involve leasing, property, credit card lending or other financial services. In these cases, the degree of dissimilarity to the group's core business may not be sufficient to warrant deconsolidation under SSAP14. Moreover, SSAP14 still requires separate financial statements for the deconsolidated subsidiaries.

A better way to disclose as little as possible about these activities has been once again to move them off-balance sheet through the device of quasi-subsidiaries.

The Burton Group 1988 Accounts reveal three quasi-subsidiaries involved in financial services: BG Holdings, Burton Group Personal Accounts and Welbeck Finance. Welbeck's shareholding structure is particularly indicative of a quasi-subsidiary: 'A subsidiary owns the whole of the ordinary share capital of Welbeck Finance plc (which represents ten per cent of the equity share capital) and the whole of the restricted share capital. The remainder of the equity share capital is represented by deferred shares, none of which is held by the Group'.

These three finance quasi-subsidiaries conducted a business which was an important part of Burton Group's operations – financing credit purchases within its stores and related companies contributed £22.2m to Burton's pre-tax profit of £148.7m in 1986. Their combined borrowings of £428m compared with Burton Group's shareholders' funds of £440.5m in 1980, and total borrowings on the consolidated balance sheet of £218.3m. The effect on apparent gearing from their deconsolidation is obvious.

ED49, ED50 and the Companies Act 1989

Chapter 4 of the Companies Act 1989 introduced a new definition of a subsidiary undertaking, which is based on *de facto* control. The definition is that a subsidiary undertaking is one in which:

(1) the parent has a majority of the voting rights, or

(2) the parent is a member and can appoint or remove a majority of the board, or

(3) the parent is a member and controls voting rights by agreement with other members, or

(4) the parent can direct the operating and fiscal policies through the Memorandum and Articles or a control contract, or

(5) the parent has a participating interest and either exercises a dominant influence or manages·both companies on a unified basis.

There are obvious differences from the Companies Act 1985, with voting rights replacing equity, which limits the scope for schemes based upon different classes of share capital. Another obvious change is a reference elsewhere in the Act to those directors who control a majority of the voting rights on the board, which prevents schemes based upon differential voting rights for board members. But the most far-reaching change is the introduction of concepts such as a 'participating interest' and 'dominant influence'. For example, a participating interest includes unexercised options and conversion rights.

ED49 requires quasi-subsidiaries to be included in consolidated accounts in the same way as other subsidiaries. ED49 defines a quasi-subsidiary as 'a company, trust or other vehicle which, although not fulfilling the Companies Act definition of a subsidiary undertaking, is directly or indirectly a source of benefits or risks for the reporting enterprise or its subsidiaries with the emphasis on benefits rather than risks since all subsidiaries confer upon their parent companies risk reduction through limited liability.

The combination of ED49 and the Companies Act 1989 clearly make it more difficult to exclude quasi-subsidiaries from consolidation as a form of off-balance sheet finance, whilst ED50 contains proposals that unincorporated joint ventures should normally be consolidated with the owners accounting for a proportional share of assets, liabilities, revenues and expenses in the consolidated balance sheet and profit and loss account.

9

CONTINGENT LIABILITIES

Contingency: accident, casualty, chance, event, fortuity, happening, incident, possibility, uncertainty
Oxford English Dictionary

Closely allied to the subject of off-balance sheet finance is that of contingent liabilities, since both involve liabilities that are literally not shown on the balance sheet. Nor is it coincidence that the term contingency has several meanings, most of which are close to common parlance for an accident. Most investors' grasp of contingent liabilities in the last few years has been accidental, and the outcome has often been disasterous.

A contingency is defined by SSAP18 as 'a condition which exists at the balance sheet date where the outcome will be confirmed only on the occurrence or non-occurrence of one or more uncertain future events'! Contingencies are not intended to cover the nominal uncertainties associated with accounting estimates, such as a valuation of assets, the lives of assets, the amount of bad debts, etc. A contingency also requires uncertainty as to the outcome of an event, for example, where a company has litigation pending against it.

Frequently the last or penultimate Note in a set of Accounts, the Contingent Liabilities often makes apparently dull reading. Certain types of contingency are disclosed almost in a litany, as a matter of course by most companies, for example:

Exhibit 9.1 **Lloyds Bank PLC 1990 Accounts**

27. Contingent Liabilities

	Group		Bank	
	1990 £m	1989 £m	1990 £m	1989 £m
Acceptances	910	1,085	589	521
Guarantees and similar obligations	4,026	4,902	4,152	6,079
	4,936	5,987	4,741	6,600

In addition, contingent liabilities exist in respect of forward contracts for the sale and purchase of foreign currencies, financial futures, option contracts and other facilities to customers which are not reflected in the balance sheets.

Banks take on substantial contingent liabilities in their normal course of business, such as the issue of guarantees and indemnities and dealing with customers in financial instruments which only become exercisable in the future, such as forward foreign exchange markets, options, futures etc. so that they nearly all have a common wording for these activities in the Contingent Liabilities note, but with little quantification:

COMMON TYPES OF CONTINGENT LIABILITIES

(a) Guarantees of subsidiary overdrafts: where a bank lends to a subsidiary within a group it will normally require the holding company's guarantee; otherwise if the subsidiary gets into difficulties the holding company could rely upon its limited liability as an equity holder in the subsidiary and walk away, leaving the bank with the loss.

(b) Performance bonds – many types of performance bond are required. For example a housebuilder will be required to supply a bond from his bank to ensure that the roads, drains etc. on an estate he constructs will be up to the standard that the local authority is willing to maintain subsequently. Since the bank will only issue such a bond if the builder counter-indemnifies it the builder will have a contingent liability to his bank if the bond is ever called.

(c) Discounted bills – where a company raises finance by selling (discounting) bills of exchange it has received or factoring debtors with recourse, the bank or finance house will have recourse to it if the bills or debts are not met at maturity. Having been on-sold, the bills do not appear on the company's balance sheet, but there should be a contingent liability shown.

Perhaps a typical example is contractor and developer Mowlem.

Exhibit 9.2 Mowlem 1990 Report and Accounts

23. Guarantees and other financial commitments

	Group		Company	
	1990 £m	1989 £m	1990 £m	1989 £m
Loan guarantees outstanding in respect of subsidiary companies	–	–	60.5	65.2
Associated companies				
Bonding support	0.4	8.3	0.4	8.3
Loan Guarantees	26.7	7.6	26.7	6.9
	27.1	15.9	27.1	15.2
Capital Expenditure				
Contracted for	–	2.1	–	0.2
Authorised but not contracted for	4.7	2.5	–	1.4
	4.7	4.6	–	1.6

Annual commitments under non-cancellable operating leases are as follows:

	Group		Company			
	Land and buildings	Plant and machinery	Land and buildings	Plant and machinery	Land and buildings	
Operating leases which expire	1990 £m	1990 £m	1989 £m	1989 £m	1990 £m	1990 £m
Within 1 year	0.6	2.6	0.3	2.1	–	–
In 2 to 5 years	2.0	10.3	0.8	10.2	–	–
Over 5 years	3.4	5.8	4.4	0.5	1.1	1.1
	6.0	18.7	5.5	12.8	1.1	1.1

The Company issued counter-indemnities to financial institutions in respect of tender, advance payment, retention and performance bonds. Terms and conditions of such bonds vary but may prescribe payment on demand. Contractual commitments have been entered into by the Company which, by agreement, have been performed by and reflected in the accounts of its subsidiaries.

This shows the normal contingent liabilities that you might expect for a building contractor – bonds, loan guarantees and capital expenditure authorised. And the Note points out that Mowlem counter-indemnifies banks for bonds issued on its behalf.

But as in the accounts for another builder and developer, Costain Group, a much more dangerous item may lurk behind the contingent liabilities Note:

Exhibit 9.3 **Costain Group 1990 Report & Accounts**

27. Contingent Liabilities

	Group		Company	
	1990	1989	1990	1989
	£m	£m	£m	£m
Under guarantee of bank overdrafts, mortgages and loans:				
To subsidiary undertakings	–	–	98.2	122.8
To associated undertakings	52.0	28.2	52.0	28.2
To long-term joint ventures	–	1.5	–	1.5
To other joint ventures	19.1	4.6	19.1	4.6

There are also contingent liabilities in respect of:

The creditors of joint ventures which are less than the book value of their assets.

Performance bonds and other undertakings entered into in the ordinary course of business.

Preference shares issued by a subsidiary undertaking (note 24).

No security has been given in respect of any guarantee given by the Group.

The Note mentions liabilities for guarantees to banks of borrowings by associates, and other contingent liabilities for joint ventures in the form of bank guarantees and creditors. But Costain is a member of the Trans-Manche Link (TML) consortium which is constructing the Channel Tunnel, and which is in dispute with Eurotunnel to the tune of £800 million at 1985 values (equivalent to some £1.1bn at 1991 values) claimed by TML from Eurotunnel. But the French members of the TML consortium have already raised provisions for losses on the contract which imply total provisions of maybe £200m for TML which have yet to be adopted by the British members, Costain, Tarmac, Taylor Woodrow, Wimpey and Balfour Beatty.

And as with other accounting practices, failing to pay due regard to contingent liabilities can prove fatal or just expensive:

The example of Coloroll has already been cited in the section in the Pre-Acquisition Write Down, and a fuller history of Coloroll's rise and fall is given in Appendix I. This reveals that in an attempt to reduce debt after its acquisition splurge, Coloroll 'sold' the cloth and clothing divisions of the recently acquired John Crowther Group. The sale was to an MBO called Response Group Limited, and as a consideration, Coloroll received £53m cash, £7.5m of redeemable preference shares in Response and £14.25m of loan notes issued by Response, plus £1m of shares in Response. At this point, Coloroll had not so much sold the Crowther interests to Response, as exchanged the Crowther interests for a share in Response. Consequently, Coloroll on-sold the loan notes and redeemable preference shares 'with recourse' i.e. the purchaser could ask for their money back from Coloroll, which they duly did when the Response MBO hit financial problems in January 1990:

Exhibit 9.4   Coloroll 1989 Report and Accounts

23. Contingent liabilities

At 31 March 1989 the group had contingent liabilities in connection with the following matters:

(a) the sale with recourse of £7,500,000 of redeemable preference shares and £14,250,000 senior and subordinated loan notes in Response Group Limited which were received as part consideration for the sale of the clothing interests of John Crowther Group plc;

(b) the guarantee of borrowings and other bank facilities of Homfray Carpets Australia Pty Limited equivalent to £13,000,000 following the sale of the group's majority interest in that company. The guarantee provides for recourse by the group to the assets of Homfray Carpets Australia Pty Limited by way of a second charge;

(c) the guarantee of borrowings of £4,580,000 of the purchaser of land for development from the group (see note 6);

(d) the guarantee of borrowings of the owners of properties occupied by a subsidiary which at 31 March, 1989 amounted to £1,150,000 (1988 £1,141,000).

By this time the liability had become £22m as the loan notes yielded 12 per cent payable as a premium upon redemption. The disclosure of this item in Coloroll's Note on contingent liabilities reveals that similar liabilities had been assumed in order to sell other assets: the guarantee of Homfray Carpets bank borrowings in order to sell a *minority* interest in the company and a guarantee of borrowings for the purchaser of land sold by the group.

The question has to be asked whether an ordinary individual would consider that he had sold his house if he guaranteed repayment of the mortgage of the purchaser. Clearly he would not be free of the liabilities which went with the asset. If Coloroll was only able to sell assets such as Response MBO's preference shares by guaranteeing to repurchase them in the event of a default by Response, it is equally evident that there was something deeply wrong with the Response Group if a 'clean' sale could not be achieved.

So contingent liabilities need to be carefully examined. But unfortunately even that is not always a guarantee of protection for investors:

Exhibit 9.5 **Allied Lyons Report and Accounts 1990**

29. CONTINGENT LIABILITIES

	1990 £m	1989 £m
Group		
Guarantees by the company and by subsidiary companies, uncalled liability in respect of partly paid shares and bills discounted by group companies	79	67
Parent company		
Guarantees of stocks, bonds and notes of subsidiary companies	163	144
Value added tax of certain subsidiary companies under group registration scheme	28	22

No security has been given in respect of any contingent liability

---

The Contingent Liabilities note for Allied Lyons seems reasonably revealing. It even shows that Allied Lyons is part of a VAT group with certain group subsidiary companies, and therefore has joint and several liability for the payment of the group VAT. What it does not reveal is the foreign currency transactions undertaken by the group treasury which cost the group £147m and lead to the resignation of the Finance Director and early retirement by the Chairman.

Why was this massive foreign exchange transaction not revealed by the Contingent Liabilities note? Because contingent liabilities by definition do not form part of the double-entry bookkeeping system which is at the heart of all accounting. Normal transactions are recorded by posting (or writing in a ledger or in this automated age typing into a computer record) equal and opposite entries – 'for every debit there is a credit' should be engraved above the bed of every junior accountant. So that when, for example, a company purchases a property using funds borrowed from a bank, the assets are increased by the cost of the property, and liabilities are increased by the amount of the bank borrowing.

Contingent liabilities by definition are liabilities which *may* become concrete in the future. Consequently, there are no equal and opposite assets, and no entry in the double-entry bookkeeping system which can be checked by the mechanism of a trial balance which auditors use: adding up all the debit items and all the credit items to see if they balance. This should reveal any unrecorded liabilities for a transaction which has taken place, since debit and credits would then fail to balance. Because of this absence of a need for double entry book-keeping for contingent liabilities, even major public companies may have their contingent liabilities recorded in a simple card index system, and the auditors are reliant upon the Directors' assurances that all contingent liabilities have been recorded and revealed.

The great grand-daddy of recent disasters substantially caused by unrecorded contingent liabilities was the collapse of British & Commonwealth:

Exhibit 9.6 **British & Commonwealth Report & Accounts 1988**

26. CONTINGENT LIABILITIES

a) The company has guaranteed bank overdrafts and other substantial trading liabilities of certain subsidiaries which have arisen in the normal course of their business and which are not expected to give any financial loss.

b) The directors are confident that there is no contingent liability arising out of counterclaims by Quadrex Holdings Inc in respect of proceedings referred to in note 11.

Few Contingent Liability Notes could appear more innocuous than B&C's in 1988, with the usual litany about guaranteeing bank overdrafts and trading liabilities of certain subsidiaries. The only specific item mentioned was legal action against Quadrex which had failed to complete a deal to buy the money broking interest of B&C's Mercantile House acquisition. No numbers were mentioned at all.

But during July 1988, B&C had taken over Atlantic Computers plc. Atlantic started life in 1975 as a computer consultancy, founded by John Foulston, moving into computer leasing and eventually controlling an estimated 70 per cent of the UK computer leasing market. Foulston remained the entrepreneurial drive behind the company until his death in a motor racing accident at the Brands Hatch circuit, which he owned, in September 1987. The company was taken over by B&C the following year.

The cornerstone of Atlantic's business was the 'Flexlease' contract. Atlantic acted as an intermediary between the banks who were willing to lease computer equipment (just another form of lending, similar to hire purchase, as far as the bank is concerned) and the lessee who uses the equipment.

Atlantic's Flexlease was a separate contract with the lessee/user. The original lease might typically be for a period of seven years. Flexlease gave the user two additional options: 1) the 'Flex' – this allowed the user to return the equipment after three years providing he leased replacement equipment of greater value, and 2) the 'Walk' which enabled the user simply to terminate the lease by handing the equipment back to Atlantic after five years, leaving Atlantic to service the original lease payments to the bank.

Atlantic could cover its liability after the 'Walk' option was exercised to meet the payments to the bank under the original lease, firstly from sale of the equipment, although the residual or second-hand value of the equipment was rarely sufficient to meet this liability. If the user was exercising the Flex option, Atlantic would of course also have the income on the lease of the new equipment although this was not available if the user had 'Walked'. Thus Atlantic's operations became virtually a form of pyramid selling with the liabilities on original leases which Atlantic had to cover because a Flex option had been exercised, covered by payments under a new lease.

As an aside, there was often customer resistance to the higher lease payment required on the new lease under the Flex option. Atlantic usually overcame this by setting lease payments in the initial years of the new lease at the same level as the old lease, with a rapid escalation in the later years of the lease. But these higher payments in later years were often never reached as the user Flexed again or Walked so that the higher payments were never received. No wonder Atlantic's Flexlease gave it such a high market share! It gave users the flexibility which they wanted during a period when upgrading of computer systems was rife due to technological change.

But the outcome for Atlantic was a burgeoning set of contingent liabilities to meet the payments due to banks on leases on which the lessees might Walk or Flex, which could only be covered by leasing ever greater amounts of new equipment.

But there was no sign of this contingent liability in the accounts of Atlantic or B&C. This apparent omission also called into question the diligence exercised when B&C acquired Atlantic in an agreed takeover i.e. one in which B&C had full access to Atlantic's books.

The dénouement rapidly followed. Immediately after Easter 1990, B&C announced that Atlantic was to go into administration less than one year after it was acquired. At the same time B&C wrote off some £550m to cover the cost of the original investment plus capital subsequently injected. It had, it claimed, 'ring-fenced' Atlantic to save the group – a polite way of saying that it was relying upon the principle of limited liability as an equity investor in its subsidiary and walking away to let the banks pick up the pieces.

But it was not as easy to erect a so-called 'ring-fence', as the advisers to Mirror Group have also now found as a result of the Maxwell debacle. As can be seen in the table in Appendix II, B&C was a heavily indebted company and the liquidation of a subsidiary of the size of Atlantic produced fears that the trustees of B&C's bonds would be forced to call an event of default (company borrowings by means of bond issues are governed by trust deeds which define events of default such as the failure to pay interest on the bonds, and less obvious events such as the liquidation of major subsidiaries, sale of assets, etc. which could endanger the bond holders' interests and also require repayment), as well as unrest amongst B&C's bankers. The final nail in the coffin came on 1 June when the Securities and Investment Board (SIB) removed British & Commonwealth Merchant Bank (BCMB) from the list of banks authorised to accept clients' money under the Financial Services Act. This threatened a classic liquidity crisis for BCMB, and the response to this and the withdrawal of a £70m standby facility for BCMB from three major banks, triggered B&C's administration on 3 June.

Not bad going for a liability which was not shown in the accounts.

10

CAPITALISATION OF COSTS

or How to make an expense become an asset

Many different expenditures may be capitalised, although by far the commonest capitalised cost is interest on property under development. Capitalisation is a process by which an item which would otherwise be seen as an expense or debit in the profit and loss account is instead classified as an asset in the balance sheet. As with all the accounting treatments described, capitalisation of costs is a legitimate technique. The Companies Act 1985 allows the inclusion in the cost of production of an asset of:

(a) a reasonable proportion of the costs incurred by the company which are only indirectly attributable to the production of that asset; and

(b) interest on capital borrowed to finance the production of that asset, to the extent that it accrues in respect of the period of production.

The Listing Agreement requires disclosure of interest capitalised by companies listed on the International Stock Exchange and USM companies. EDS1 proposes that companies should be allowed to choose whether or not to capitalise borrowing costs on projects which take time to be brought into use.

CAPITALISING INTEREST

This is a practice normally associated with property development or the construction of properties for the use in a business e.g. stores or supermarkets but there are other uses. For example, ships, aircraft and stocks of goods which take a long time to mature such as whisky:

Exhibit 10.1 **Guinness 1989 Report & Accounts**

16. STOCKS

	1989 £m	1988 £m
Raw materials and consumables	134	105
Work in progress	28	19
Stocks of maturing whisky	1,085	860
Finished goods and goods for resale	169	144
	1,416	1,128

Stocks of maturing whisky include financing costs amounting to £481m (1988 £417m). A net adjustment to stocks of £10m (1988 £12m) has been credited to the profit and loss account comprising £97m (1988 £98m) of interest incurred during the year less £87m (1988 £86m) in respect of sales during the year. Following the review of the Distillers fair value accounting (Note 11) the amount at which maturing whisky stocks are stated as at 31 December 1989 has been uplifted by £157m including £49m relating to financing costs.

But capitalisation of interest on property development remains the commonest form of capitalisation of costs:

Table 10.1 UK Major quoted Property Companies

		Net Interest		
Company	Year to	Total	Capitalised	Pre-tax Profit
British Land	Mar 91	61.4	1.3	31.0
Great Portland	Mar 91	16.1	nil	33.8
Hammerson	Dec 90	70.8	29.8	70.7
Land Securities	Mar 91	79.1	nil	215.2
MEPC	Sep 91	119.2	39.5	143.3
Slough	Dec 90	84.3	59.8	22.6

Source: UBS Phillips & Drew

Capitalisation of interest remains common practice within the sector, although it has never been adopted by the largest company Land Securities. More recently, the practice has been dropped by Great Portland and by smaller companies such as Property Security Investment Trust:

Exhibit 10.2 **Statement by the Chairman – Property Security Investment Trust**

A conservative accounting policy has always been the byword for the Company. Interest and other costs on investment properties being developed are written off against Revenue. On the other hand interest in developing dealing properties was capitalised. **That was justifiable in a buoyant market**, but the economic climate has now changed. To extend the conservative approach your Board has decided to change the Company's accounting policy so that from the commencement of the current financial year interest on all dealing properties will no longer be capitalised but charged against revenue.

The obvious problem which these companies can encounter is that the cost of the property plus capitalised interest can easily exceed the market value, which leads to write-downs of the difference by which cost exceeds market.

The arguments for capitalisation are that interest is a legitimate cost of the project and therefore it is as appropriate to capitalise as the cost of bricks and mortar. Witness the fact that no property developer ever computes the viability of a project without including the cost of interest until the project is complete and/or sold.

Where property is under construction for use in a company's activities, such as a hotel or store, it is also argued that capitalising interest gives a better match between income and expense in future since the interest cost only begins to bear on the profit and loss account once the project is complete and generating income.

Finally, it is worth noting that if companies were not permitted to capitalise interest there would be a lower asset cost but also a lower profit (because interest would be charged through the profit and loss account) for a company which built its own factory or hotel, compared with the same company if it purchased the property once completed by a developer (who would certainly seek to include his interest cost in computing the sale price).

There are counter arguments, but these are much less important than simply understanding the impact of capitalised interest in published accounts. This is perhaps best illustrated with an example:

Exhibit 10.3 **Broadwell Land 1989 Accounts**

CONSOLIDATED PROFIT & LOSS ACCOUNT 1989
for the year to 31 March, 1989

	Notes	1989 £	1988 £
Turnover	1	33,678,720	16,864,484
Operating expenses	2	(26,719,406)	(12,703,965)
Operating profit		6,959,314	4,160,519
Interest receivable	4	244,459	24,222
Interest payable	5	(148,270)	(39,585)
Profit on ordinary activities before taxation		7,055,503	4,145,156
Taxation	6	(2,510,406)	(1,447,097)
Profit for the year after taxation		4,545,097	2,698,059
Dividends	7	(1,280,582)	(65,700)
Retained profit for the year	21	3,264,515	2,632,359
Earnings per share – basic	8	19.08p	14.35p

The comparative figures for 1988 have been restated to comply with Statement of Standard Accounting Practice 9 (revised).

Broadwell Land 1989 Accounts

5. Interest payable

	1989 £	1988 £
On bank loans, overdrafts and other loans:		
Payable within five years	3,892,684	1,456,032
Less: Interest added to developments-in-progress	(2,215,024)	(979,520)
Interest included as a cost of sale of developments	(1,270,195)	(436,927)
Interest capitalised in investment properties	(152,886)	–
Interest capitalised in other tangible fixed assets	(107,309)	–
	148,270	39,585

Interest cover is an important measure of the financial health of a company. It measures the company's ability to cover the interest payments due to its bankers, and the margin of cover if profits should fall. Normally it is calculated by dividing operating profit by net interest payable. But Broadwell Land ostensibly had no problem confronting this measure in 1989: there was no net interest payable, with interest receivable of £244,459 and interest payable of £148,270 to give *net* interest receivable of £96,189 against oeprating profit of £6,959,314, as shown in the Profit and Loss Account.

But Note 5 reveals that the actual interest payable was £3,893,684, all but £148,270 of which was capitalised. Ignoring capitalised interest, i.e. bringing it back into the profit and loss account, gives a very different interest cover computation:

Interest payable of £3,893,684 minus interest receivable of £244,459 = net interest payable of £3,649,225

Operating profit £6,959,314 / £3,649,225 = 1.9 times cover

This can hardly be considered generous. Interest cover below two times would usually be regarded as a warning signal. This is even more true when profits are at a speculative peak, which was demonstrated in 1990 when property profits collapsed and Broadwell Land went into administrative receivership.

An analysis of 45 listed, USM or Third Market companies which had receivers or administrative receivers appointed in 1989 and 1990 shows the following pattern for interest cover in the final year before they were declared insolvent.

Table 10.2   Interest cover

Cover	Number of Companies
No cover	6
Under 1×	1
1× – 2×	14
2× – 3×	6
3× – 4×	5
over 4×	13

Source: UBS Phillips & Drew

60 per cent were less than three times covered in their final accounts.

There are plenty of examples of capitalised interest from property developers and others which was one of the factors which disguised the precarious nature of a company's finances. The following table shows the capitalised interest position and true interest cover ignoring capitalised interest, for companies which have all been placed in receivership or administrative receivership:

Table 10.3 True interest cover

Company	Capitalised interest as a percentage of operating profit %	Interest cover in profit or loss account x	Interest cover taking capitalised interest into paid x
Broadwell Land	53.8	–*	1.9
Citygrove	31.3	2.0	1.4
Kentish Properties	57.6	–*	1.7
Leading Leisure	53.5	2.5	1.1
Reliant	75.3	5.1	1.1
Rockfort	19.3	3.5	2.1
Rush & Tompkins	88.1	7.2	1.0

* net interest receivable in the profit and loss account.

Source: UBS Phillips & Drew

Exhibit 10.4 **Rockfort Group 1989 Report & Accounts**

8. INTERST PAYABLE AND SIMILAR CHARGES

	1989 £000	1988 £000
Interest on bank loans and overdrafts		
Repayable otherwise than by instalments within five years	2,455	748
Repayable by instalments wholly within five years	509	547
Other interest	240	152
Licence fee	1,637	222
	4,841	1,669
Less: Interest capitalised on development land and properties	1,288	702
	3,553	967

Rush & Tompkins Group 1989 Report & Accounts

4. INTEREST

	1989 £000	1988 £000
On bank loans, overdrafts and finance leases:		
Repayable within 5 years, not by instalments	11,697	5,678
Repayable within 5 years by installments	145	155
	11,842	5,833
Interest receivable	1,972	711
Net interest payable for the year	9,870	5,122
Less: interest added to developments in progress	8,521	3,885
Net interest charged in the profit and loss account	1,349	1,237
Share of related companies interest included above:		
Net interest payable	7,240	2,810
Less: interest added to developments in progress	5,737	2,037
Net interest charged in the profit and loss account	1,503	773

Exhibit 10.5 **Citygrove 1989 Report & Accounts**

3. INTEREST PAYABLE

	1989 £000	1988 £000
Loans repayable wholly or in part over five years	33	30
Bank overdraft and loans repayable wholly or in part within five years	4,829	1,877
Hire purchase and finance lease interest	82	45
Other interest	–	2
	4,944	1,954
Less: Interest capitalised	(1,448)	(258)
	3,496	1,696

Kentish Property Group 1987 Report & Accounts

3. INTEREST PAYABLE AND SIMILAR CHARGES

	1987 £000	1986 £000
On bank overdrafts and short-term borrowing	2,313	794
On directors' loans	–	14
Other loans	4	15
	2,347	823
Included as cost of sales and capitalised	(2,292)	(776)
	52	47

Leading Leisure 1989 Report & Accounts

4. NET INTEREST PAYABLE

	14 months 31 December 1989 £000	12 months 31 October 1988 £000
On bank loans and overdrafts repayable wholly within five years	4,347	525
On bank loans and overdrafts repayable partly after five years	6,995	3,462
On other loans	588	340
Interest capitalised	(6,412)	(1,903)
Interest receivable	(643)	(17)
	4,875	2,407

Reliant 1989 Report & Accounts

3. INTEREST PAYABLE

	Group	
	1989 £000	1988 £000
Bank loans and overdrafts wholly payable within five years	3,082	1,279
Other loans	37	57
Finance lease charges	31	16
	3,150	1,352
Capitalised	(2,494)	(978)
	656	374

In all cases the actual interest cover was obviously significantly lower once capitalised interest is taken into account, and dangerously low to withstand a downturn in profits.

Ignoring the use of capitalised interest, and the calculation of interest cover from the net interest payable shown in the profit and loss account can be dangerous. The bankers who lend the money and make the decision on whether companies survive during a downturn include capitalised interest in their calculations of cover. And if investors wish to understand how the decisions of the banks are likely to impact their investments it is necessary to understand their methods of analysis. The banker is not interested in whether his quarterly interest charge is capitalised as part of an asset or is expensed in the profit and loss account. His sole interest is in cash: is there enough cash coming in to cover the whole of the interest charged to the company's account? If not, there is a problem.

Obviously including (i.e. adding back) capitalised interest in the calculation of interest cover helps to get closer to the banker's viewpoint, although even then the assumption that operating profit is equal to cash inflow is far from realistic (see Chapter 17).

Capitalisation of interest is not confined to the property development sector. There are examples above of companies in other areas such as leisure and motor manufacturing. A list of capitalised interest as a proportion of pre-tax (operating) profit shows the following major companies involved in this practice:

Table 10.4   Capitalised interest

Company	Year	Capitalised interest as a percentage of pre-tax profits %
Stakis	1990	89.5
Costain	1990	87.3
ABP	1990	59.5
Ladbroke	1990	27.1
Enterprise Oil	1990	23.2
Asda	1990	21.1
Queens Moat Houses	1990	19.5
Burton	1990	19.0
BAA	1990	18.6
Lasmo	1990	13.6
Clyde Petroleum	1990	12.6
Wm Morrison Supermarket	1991	11.5
Forte	1991	10.7
Taylor Woodrow	1990	10.4
J Sainsbury	1991	10.1

Source: UBS Phillips & Drew

The list is dominated by companies from a few industries: Hotels –
Stakis, Ladbroke, Queens Moat House, Forte; Oil – Enterprise, Lasmo,
Clyde; Food Retailing – Asda, Wm Morrison; and Construction – Costain
and Taylor Woodrow. Obviously some of these industries are particularly
identified with the development of premises for the company's use and
most notably hotels and hyper-markets in food retailing which had
particularly high development expenditure in 1991 from the capital raised
by the main food retailing groups.

Capitalisation of interest also produces problems of comparability
between companies using the technique. EDS1 does not give detailed
guidance, and it is possible to have wide variations between when a
company may begin to capitalise interest on a project and to end it:

Start of capitalisation	*End of Capitalisation*
Exchange of contracts on a development site	When the property is completed
Completion of a purchase of a site	When the property is fully let
When planning consent is obtained	When trading commences
Upon entering into a building contract	When the property is x% let
Commencement of work	When rental income equates to x% of that anticipated
	When rental income exceeds interest

Nor is interest only capitalised on property. Corton Beach took this concept
a stage further as its Accounting Policy Notes indicate:

Exhibit 10.6   Corton Beach 1990 Report and Accounts

(b) Basis of consolidation

The Group financial statements consolidate the financial statements of the
Company and all its subsidiaries made up to 31 January 1990.

The results of the subsidiaries acquired or disposed of are included in the
Group profit and loss account from the date of acquisition or up to the date of
disposal. At the acquisition date the fair values of the net assets, excluding
goodwill, are determined and these values are incorporated in the Group
financial statements. The excess of the purchase consideration (including costs
of acquisition and due provision for reorganisation costs) over the fair value of
assets acquired (after due provision is made for all potential liabilities, asset
write downs and asset revaluations) represents goodwill (for further
explanations see 1(f) below).

**Interest relating to acquisitions is capitalised, as part of the acquisition cost,
from the effective date of acquisition until the acquired company is
substantially integrated within the Group, or for one year, whichever is
sooner. The amount of such capitalised interest for the year ending
31 January 1990 was £757,000 (1989 nil).**

No profit and loss account is presented for the Company as provided by S228(7)
of the Companies Act 1985. Of the Group profit for the financial year £1,021,000
(1989 £187,000) has been dealt with in the accounts of the Company.

This is a novel concept: that where a subsidiary is acquired for debt, the interest on the debt should be capitalised until the acquisition is fully integrated into the group (whatever that means). This seems to be taking to extremes the concept that capitalisation of interest is designed to protect the profit and loss account from distortion whilst an asset generates rent or trading income. Corton Beach presumably had some income from its acquisition prior to 'full integration'. Corton Beach is now in administrative receivership.

CAPITALISING OTHER COSTS

Interest is not the only cost which companies can capitalise. SSAP13 permits the capitalisation of research and development expenditure which may affect drugs companies, electronics, biotechnology, engineering etc.

Exhibit 10.7 **Siebe Annual Report and Accounts 1990**

Research and development expenditure

Expenditure on research and development is written off when incurred. Prototype expenditure on defined commercial projects is included within intangible assets and amortised over a period of between three and ten years.

Nonetheless not all companies with substantial R&D expenditure take advantage of the possibility of capitalising it:

Exhibit 10.8 **SmithKline Beecham Annual Report 1989**

Research and development expenditure

Laboratory buildings and equipment used for research and development are included as fixed assets and written off in accordance with the Group's depreciation policy. Other research and development expenditure is written off in the year in which it is incurred.

SmithKline Beecham shows research and development expenditure of £390m as an expense in the profit and loss account, capitalising only the laboratory buildings and equipment used for research work.

Contrast this with the treatment adopted by Rockwood, another company which has gone into administrative receivership. Rockwood was a holding company engaged in freight forwarding, distribution, warehousing and security – hardly high-tech companies. It, nonetheless, capitalised patents and development expenditure to the tune of £957,000:

Exhibit 10.9 Rockwood 1988 Accounts

10. Intangibles

	Development cost £000	Other £000	Total £000
Group			
Cost at 1 January 1988	159	190	349
Additions	586	22	608
At 31 December 1988	745	212	957

Other intangible fixed assets consist of patents held by the Hilton Gun Company. The development expenditure is principally incurred by the Defence Systems group and relates to initial set-up costs in new areas of activity.

Note c) DEPRECIATION AND AMORTISATION

Depreciation is provided by equal annual instalments to write off the purchase costs over the expected useful life of assets. The useful life assumed for freehold buildings is 50 years for leasehold property over 50 years. For fixtures and fittings it is 10 years and for motor vehicles it is between 4 and 7 years. Freehold land is not depreciated.

Intangible assets comprise patents and development costs, which are written off to profit and loss account over the appropriate period between 3 and 10 years.

What harm does it do? MTM the speciality chemicals group announced in March 1992 that its results for 1991 would be substantially below expectations, and that the announcement of these results would be delayed. The reason given was that the auditors wished to change certain accounting policies, particularly relating to MTM's capitalisation of product registration and development costs. It can only be assumed that the auditors now wish to see these costs charged in the Profit and Loss Account:

Exhibit 10.10   MTM Report and Accounts 1990

Note c) Intangible fixed assets

Intangible fixed assets comprise product registration costs and development expenditure incurred by the Group. Amortisation of product and process development costs commences with commercial production by reference to the lesser of life of the product or process, or ten years. Upon commencement of commercial production the costs are transferred to tangible fixed assets.

Note 13. Intangible fixed assets

	Product & Process Development £000	Market Development £000	Total £000
Group			
Cost			
1 January 1990	2,217	140	2,357
Exchange adjustment	(10)	–	(10)
Additions	1,252	–	1,252
Acquisition of subsidiaries	24	–	24
Transfer to tangible fixed assets	(362)	–	(362)
31 December 1990	3,121	140	3,261
Depreciation			
1 January 1990	428	36	464
Charge for year	185	14	199
31 December 1990	613	50	663
Net book amount			
31 December 1990	2,508	90	2,598
31 December 1989	1,789	104	1,893
Company			
Cost			
1 January 1990 and 31 December 1990	27	–	27
Depreciation			
1 January 1990	11	–	11
Charge for year	2	–	2
31 December 1990	13	–	13
Net book amount			
31 December 1990	14	–	14
31 December 1989	16	–	16

The immediate impact on MTM's share price from this announcement is obvious:

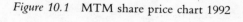

Figure 10.1   MTM share price chart 1992

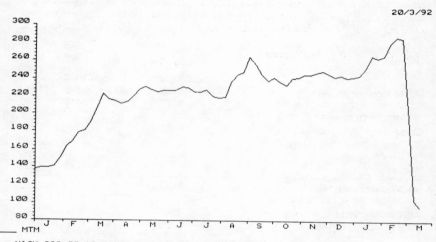

HIGH 288.00 18/2/92, LOW 97.00 17/3/92, LAST 97.00 17/3/92
Source : Datastream

The long-term impact was a loss of £20.5m before tax for 1991 and a restatement of the 1990 results to show a reduced profit of £7.9m as a result of writing off development expenditure and product registration costs against the profit and loss account rather than capitalising them.

There is obviously some debate about whether R&D expenditure meets the normal definition of an asset. Clearly it only does it if it leads to the creation of a saleable product. But R&D is not the most unusual example of capitalising items, as the following examples, all of which are taken from companies in receivership or administrative receivership, seem to illustrate:

Exhibit 10.11 **Musterlin 1989 Report & Accounts**

Note 11 TANGIBLE FIXED ASSETS
(a) The Group

	Archive £000	Book Properties £000	Leasehold Improve- ments £000	Other Assets £000	Total £000
COST OR VALUATION					
At 31 December 1988	877	6,557	260	1,159	8,853
On acquisition of subsidiary	–	–	–	66	66
Additions	32	2,296	24	489	2,841
Disposals	–	–	–	(166)	(166)
At 31 December 1989	909	8,853	284	1,548	11,594
DEPRECIATION					
At 31 December 1988	14	1,350	–	450	1,814
On acquisition of subsidiary	–	–	–	60	60
Charge for year	17	697	30	210	954
Disposals	–	–	–	(136)	(136)
At 31 December 1989	31	2,047	30	584	2,692
NET BOOK VALUE					
At 31 December 1989	878	6,806	254	964	8,902
At 31 December 1988	863	5,207	260	709	7,039

(i) Included in additions to book properties is an amount of £250,000 (1988 £155,000) in respect of interest capitalised. Cumulative interest capitalised is £641,000.

(ii) Cost of book properties includes work in progress with a value of £1,285,000 (1988 £669,000). This is not depreciated.

(iii) The archive includes £515,000 (1988 £515,000) arising from a 1981 revaluation. This is not depreciated. The historic cost of the archive at 31 December 1989 was £339,000 (1988 £362,000).

(iv) Other assets include vehicles and equipment held under finance leases with a cost of £628,000 (1988 £375,000) and depreciation of £269,000 (1988 £197,000). Depreciation charges in the year were £109,000 (1988 £47,000).

Musterlin, a publisher, included Book Properties (i.e. books which it had bought publication rights to) as tangible fixed assets with a value of £6.8m out of total tangible fixed assets of £11.6m, and Capital and Reserves of £11m.

Sharp & Law, a shopfitting company, capitalised computer software products which were *to be* sold externally i.e. that had not already been sold.

Exhibit 10.12 **Sharp & Law Accounts Annual Report 1988**

Intangible assets

Development costs in respect of computer software products to be sold
externally are amortised over the estimated life of the product, at an annual
rate of not less than 25 per cent.

Arguably another unusual example of capitalisation of costs by a major
company is Cable & Wireless, which capitalises some employee costs:

Exhibit 10.13 **Cable & Wireless – Report and Accounts 1990**

Note 5. Employees

(a) The average weekly number of persons employed by the Group during the
year was:

	1990 Number	1989 Number restated
Asia and Pacific	18,856	18,051
Middle East, Indian Ocean and Africa	1,445	1,292
Western Hemisphere	8,255	3,946
United Kingdom and Europe	9,018	6,031
Associated companies	107	96
	37,681	29,416

(b) The aggregate remuneration and associated costs of Group employees
including amounts capitalised were:

	1990 £m	1989 £m
Salaries and wages	420.1	276.7
Social security costs	18.3	9.9
Pension costs	9.7	13.2
	448.1	299.8

11

BRAND ACCOUNTING

Another chance for the UK accountancy profession to indicate to the world that it has utterly failed to get its act together!
Neil French, Finance director of APV, formerly with Touche Ross, describing Brand Accounting in *Financial Weekly*, 12 April 1990

OF BIDS AND DEALS

Brand Accounting has its genesis in takeovers, mainly within the food manufacturing and processing, and drinks industries. On the one hand, placing a valuation on brands was seen as a defence against a takeover 'on the cheap'. On the other, predators who had acquired companies with brand names but few tangible assets found in brand valuation a way to make their balance sheet look better, and to overcome some technical problems caused by the intangible nature of brands. The result is a total lack of consistency in comparing companies which possess consumer brands.

Brand accounting really is a recent phenomenon. Its history is to be found in deals such as the 1978 bid by Allied Breweries for J. Lyons at a price which was considered too high by conventional yardsticks, but gave Allied control of J. Lyons' brands. Hanson's battle with United Biscuits for control of Imperial Group in 1986 gave Hanson the ability to sell off brand name food operations such as Golden Wonder and Ross to leave the tobacco interests at a net cost of only some £197m for a business (Imperial Tobacco) which produced operating profits of £240m in 1991:

Table 11.1 Hanson–Imperial break-up

			£m
1986	Acquisition	Imperial	2,500
	Sale	Hotels etc	−186
	Sale	Beer	−1400
	Sale	Crisps	−87
1987	Sale	Finlay	−19
	Sale	Bonds	−4
	Sale	Corners	−3
1988	Sale	Food	−335
	Sale	Food	−199
	Sale	Distribution	−9
1989	Sale	Food	−25
	Sale	Hardy	−9
	Sale	Food	−7
	Sale	Food	−20
	Residual cost		197

Ignoring: capital tax
　　　　 acquired debt
　　　　 retained profits

Source: UBS Phillips & Drew

Conventional wisdom had required break up bids for poorly run companies to come out at below asset value in order to achieve a profit for the predator. These bids suggested that the stock market was not valuing brand assets correctly.

Much of brand accounting's origins lie in the rival bids launched in 1988 by Nestlé and Jacobs Suchard, the Swiss confectionery groups, for Rowntree. Rowntree possessed valuable brands such as Kit-Kat, Quality Street, Polo, After Eight and Yorkie. Its shares were trading at 477p before the bid, compared with the final winning bid from Nestlé of 1075p per share.

During the knock-down, drag-out fight which a contested bid becomes, many defences were used against the Nestlé/Suchard bids, including the fact that Nestlé and many other Swiss companies were protected from foreign takeover by their shareholding structure. Another was that the bid seriously undervalued Rowntree's brand names.

Merger and acquisition activity has continued as a potent driving force behind the development of brand accounting. In the first instance, as for Rowntree, this is because a potential victim wishes to establish the value of its brand to prevent a predator getting them 'on the cheap' since they were not reflected in the company's balance sheet net asset value. A good example is Cadbury Schweppes, with brands in confectionery and soft drinks, which faced stake building by the US company General Cinema at the time of the Rowntree bid. Cadbury Schweppes 1989 Accounts introduced the value of brands acquired since 1985 including Trebor and Bassett at cost, thereby doubling shareholders' funds with over £300m of intangible assets. By doing so Cadbury also reduced its stated gearing.

Secondly, the intangible nature of brands has presented problems for acquisitive companies in the food and drinks industry which purchase companies whose main assets are their brands. In particular, if a company has significant brands it is likely to be taken over at a premium to net asset value which will leave the acquiror with substantial goodwill financed by borrowed funds.

Grand Metropolitan brand accounting

Grand Metropolitan has adopted an accounting policy whereby significant brands, acquired since 1985, the value of which is not expected to diminish in the foreseeable future, are recorded in the balance sheet as fixed intangible assets. No amortisation is provided on these assets but the value is reviewed annually by the directors and the cost written down as an *exceptional item* where permanent diminution in value has occurred.

As at 30 September 1990, Grand Met's brands were included in the balance sheet at £2317m. This compares with shareholders' funds of £3,427m and net borrowings of £2,888m. Therefore balance sheet gearing on a published basis amounts to 84 per cent and this rises to 260 per cent if the intangible brand name were written off. There were no exceptional items in the year to September 1990 to reflect any change of view in the directors' brand name valuation.

In fairness it is worth stressing that the brand names do have value, albeit somewhat difficult to determine. Grand Met had interest cover of 4.8 times despite the high level of capital gearing, ex tangibles, in that year. We calculate that its return on capital was around 17 per cent in the last reported year so it appears to be making an adequate return on its intangible assets.

Brand valuation is a common problem in food and drink industry takeovers:

Table 11.2 Food and drink industry takeovers

Acquiror	Target	Goodwill as a percentage of price paid %
Nestlé	Rowntree	83
Grand Met	Pillsbury	86
Cadbury Schweppes	Trebor	75
United Biscuits	Verkade	66

Source: UBS Phillips & Drew

It also produces problems with the Stock Exchange Listing Agreement (or 'Yellow Book') which measures the permissions which a company must obtain for an acquisition in part by reference to the acquiror's shareholders' funds, which may be quite small in relation to its market capitalisation (and that of its target), and requires a Class 1 circular and an EGM for quite small acquisitions.

Exhibit 11.1 Cadbury Schweppes 1989 Financial Review

Historically we have written off goodwill arising on an acquisition consequently reducing shareholders' funds. Intangibles – goodwill and brand values – have not been recognised in the Balance Sheet. In 1989 the International Stock Exchange introduced new rules for assessing the value of the Company's assets in relation to acquisitions and disposals which eliminated the discretionary right of the Stock Exchange to recognise the value of intangible assets unless they are shown in the accounts. This affects their assessment of the level at which circulars to shareholders, and possibly extraordinary general meetings, are required.

Consequently, we have included in our Balance Sheet the values of major brands acquired since 1985 at cost. We have decided that no amortisation is necessary as our accounts reflect significant expenditure in support of these brands, principally by advertising and sales promotion. The values will be reviewed annually and reduced if a permanent diminution arises. Our auditors have reviewed the basis and calculations of the brand values included in the balance sheet and endorse this approach.

ACCOUNTING FOR INTANGIBLES

There is no separate accounting standard for brand accounting – the initiative having originated in industry rather than the accounting profession. But brand accounting is currently governed by ED52 – 'Accounting for intangible fixed assets'. ED52 maintains that an intangible fixed asset should only be recognised in the balance sheet if:

(1)   the historical costs associated with the asset are known or ascertainable,

(2)   the characteristics of the asset can be clearly distinguished from goodwill and other assets, and

(3)   its cost can be measured independently of goodwill and other assets.

It is evident from this that ED52 does not envisage the capitalisation of brand or other intangible assets 'created' from scratch within a business rather than acquired, when it may be possible to identify separate characteristics (1) – (3) above. Nonetheless one company stands out as having adopted brand accounting for brands created rather than acquired – Ranks Hovis McDougall:

Exhibit 11.2   **Ranks Hovis McDougall Annual Report and Accounts 1989**

Intangible Assets

The accounting treatment for additions to goodwill is considered on an individual basis and elimination against reserves has been selected as appropriate for the current year.
Brands, both acquired and created within the Group, are included at their 'current cost'. Such cost, which is reviewed annually, is not subject to amortisation.

Note 13. INTANGIBLE ASSETS

	The Group 1989 £m	The Company 1989 £m
Brands		
At 3 September 1988	678.0	–
Additions	27.1	–
Disposals	(1.1)	–
Revaluation	36.0	–
At 2 September 1989	740.0	–

The Group has valued its brands at their 'current use value to the Group' in conjunction with Interbrand Group plc, branding consultants.

The basis of valuation ignores any possible alternative use of a brand, any possible extension to the range of products currently marketed under a brand, any element of hope value and any possible increase of value of a brand due to either a special investment or a financial transaction (e.g. licensing) which would leave the Group with a different interest from the one being valued.

The criteria in ED52 are clearly restrictive showing that they view the inclusion of brands in the balance sheet as undesirable. It rejects the idea of homegrown brands being in the balance sheet as historical costs associated are unknown (RHM). It also rejects the policy of turning all potential goodwill from an acquisition into an intangible asset (Grand Metropolitan, Guinness, Cadbury).

Interbrand's approach to brand valuation

The ASC did not approve of assigning values to brands based on the capitalisation of earnings which they contribute. However, market leader Interbrand Group assists companies to calculate the earnings directly attributable to the brand and multiplies this by an earnings multiple which is determined by the assessed strength of the brand based on its stability.

$$\text{Brand Valuation} = \star \text{ Brand Earnings}$$
$$(\text{where } \star = \text{the multiple applied})$$

Brand earnings are calculated from the profit before tax figure minus profits from own label manufacture. This figure is then manipulated in two ways: firstly figures for the last x years are used and restated at present values, and then a weighted factor is applied to reflect the importance of each year's profits. Often they use the last three years with a weighting of ½ to the present year, ⅓ to last year and ⅙ to the year before that. Note also that future profits are not taken into account, so a declining brand name will be overestimated in value and a growing brand name understated.

The resultant figure could over-estimate the asset value, as much of the value should be attributable to the other assets employed such as tangible fixed assets and management as well as the brands, and therefore could result in double counting on the balance sheet.

The multiple applied is derived indirectly from a mark given out of 100. The mark is based on the brand's strength in seven areas, where strength is defined by reliability; each area is weighted in order of importance. These are:

- *Leadership*
  Marks are given for its perceived influence on its market, its ability to resist competitive 'attacks' and its market share.

- *Market*
  Value of a brand is highly correlated with the market it operates in so consumer brands will score better than production brands. Areas prone to fashion changes will also receive a low rating.

- *Internationality*
  International brands are less affected by competitive attack in a particular country and by changes in its economic climate. Also a brand that is capable of crossing cultures and overcoming competition from foreign domestic firms is going to be more stable and therefore valuable.

- *Trend*
  The long-term earnings trend gives the view of the brand's future stability and prospects.

- *Investment*
  A brand which has received high advertising spending which is of high quality generally is a better quality brand.

- *Protection*
  Marks are also given for trade marks and patents dependent on their width and length, for example a patent for a drug such as aspirin with a wide range of pain-killing applications would be more valuable than a patent for a drug specifically to alleviate toothache.

These calculations seem somewhat arbitrary and subjective. The brands are valued at current cost although it is continually stressed that the valuation is not meant to be the estimated cost of the brand to develop or the total of the future discounted cashflows.

But even where brand accounting is adopted within the framework of ED52 i.e. for acquired brands, there are still problems. Probably the greatest is that where a company after an acquisition assigns a value to intangible assets such as brands rather than goodwill, it avoids having to apply either of the treatments required for goodwill, namely writing it off against reserves or amortising it over a period by a depreciation charge to the profit and loss account. Consequently, the brands are shown in the balance sheet without the profit and loss account bearing any charge for maintaining their value, unlike any other fixed asset (except freehold land). As companies usually claim, the substitute for this is advertising and marketing expenditure to maintain the value of the brand:

Exhibit 11.3 **Cadbury Schweppes 1989 Accounts**

n) Intangibles

Intangibles represent significant owned brands acquired since 1985 valued at historical cost. No amortisation is charged as the annual results reflects significant expenditure in support of these brands but the values are reviewed annually with a view to write down if a permanent diminution arises.

Note 13. INTANGIBLES

	Group 1989 £m
Cost at beginning of year – as restated	104.3
Exchange rate adjustments	17.5
Additions	185.6
Cost at end of year	307.4

The restatement arises as a result of the change in accounting policy on intangibles.

But this is not a substitute for a stated depreciation policy in attempting to achieve consistency between companies in their treatment of fixed assets.

Other problems are hinted at by Guinness's explanation of its policy on brands:

Exhibit 11.4 **Guinness Report and Accounts 1989**

BRANDS

The fair value of businesses acquired and of interests taken in related companies includes brands, which are recognised where the brand has a value which is substantial and long term. Acquired brands are only recognised where title is clear, brand earnings are separately identifiable, the brand could be sold separately from the rest of the business and where the brand achieves earnings in excess of those achieved by unbranded products.

No amortisation will be provided except where the end of the useful economic life of the acquired brand can be foreseen. The useful economic lives of brands and their carrying value are subject to annual review and any amortisation or provision for permanent impairment would be charged against the profit for the period in which they arose.

Guinness's policy is therefore to recognise brands where:

1. The title is clear – this would exclude a lease on a brand such as Whitbread's on Heineken,

2. Brand earnings are separately identifiable – so that sales, costs and overheads must be known for each individual brand,

3. The brand could be sold separately from the rest of the business – implying a value purely on its own merits, and

4. The brand achieves earnings in excess of unbranded products – a brand of baked beans such as Heinz would have no value if it could not command greater earnings than supermarkets' own label products.

It is rare for an asset to be able to satisfy all of these criteria including separately identifiable earnings and the ability to be sold separately from the rest of the business. How many of the brands in the following table are truly separable from the business acquired with them?

Table 11.3 Brand accounting

Company	Main brands	Value £m	Date adopted
Cadbury Schweppes	Sunkist, Bassett, Gini, Oasis, Canada Dry, Trebor	308	1.3.90
Grand Metropolitan	Burger King, Pillsbury, Smirnoff	2464	30.9.89
Guinness	Johnnie Walker, Gordons, Bells	1375	31.12.86
Ladbroke	Hilton	277	Sept 1988
	Vernons	100	Dec 1989
RHM	Mothers Pride, Bisto, Mr Kipling, Hovis, McDougall, Robertson's	608	Nov 1988
Reckitt & Colman	Colmans, Weslite, Dettol Airwick, Lemsip, Mr Sheen	573	26.3.91
United Biscuits	Ross Young's, Callard & Bowser, Verkade	155	Mar 1990
Lonrho	Newspaper titles	117	Sept 1989
WPP	J Walter Thompson, Hill & Knowlton, Ogilvy & Mather	350	1988

Source: UBS Phillips & Drew

There is also a wider concern about comparability. One must suspect that Marks & Spencer and St Michael are two of the strongest consumer brand names in the UK, and although they were not acquired and therefore should not be capitalised as brands under the terms of ED52, it is also likely that Marks & Spencer would not feel the need to do so even if it were permissible. The complete absence of brand valuations from some consumer companies' balance sheets does raise an even bigger problem of comparability than the lack of amortisation on brand value. Unilever does not capitalise brands, unlike the other food manufacturers shown in Table 11.3 on Brand Accounting. Ladbroke includes the value of the Hilton name in the Accounts whereas Forte does not include the value of its name. None of the brewers has followed Guinness's example.

But perhaps the final word on brand accounting should be left to two sources: WPP and Michael Renshall, Chairman of the ASC:

Exhibit 11.5 WPP Group Annual Report and Accounts 1989

Note 3. Intangible Fixed Assets

Intangible fixed assets comprise certain acquired separable corporate brand names. These are shown at a valuation of the incremental earnings expected to arise from the ownership of brands. The valuations have been based on the present value of notional royalty savings arising from the ownership of those brands and on estimates of profits attributable to brand loyalty.

The valuations are subject to annual review. No depreciation is provided since, in the opinion of the directors, the brands do not have a finite useful economic life.

Note that no depreciation was provided as, in the opinion of the directors, brands do not have a finite economic life. Mr Renshall in contrast drew an analogy with the Blackpool football team which would have appeared very attractive to anyone wanting to buy the club back in 1953 when Blackpool won the FA Cup. 'There would have been a lot of goodwill in the price someone would have paid then' he said 'But it is obvious now that the goodwill did not have an indefinite life' (Blackpool is now in Division Three and has not won the FA Cup since).

12

CHANGES IN DEPRECIATION POLICY

Q. **What would aviators have thought about BAA's policy of depreciating runways over 100 years a century ago in 1892?**

A. **Not a lot. There were no aeroplanes in 1892.**

Changes in depreciation methods, periods and policies have long been a favourite source of manipulation of published profits. But why must companies charge depreciation in the first place?

SSAP 12

Depreciation is defined in SSAP 12, published in 1977, as 'the measure of the wearing out, consumption or other reduction in the useful life of a fixed asset whether arising from use, effluxion of time or obsolescence through technological or market changes'. It is worth noting that it is intended as a measure of consumption, not a measure of change in value. SSAP 12 requires depreciation of all fixed assets except investment properties, goodwill, development costs and investments.

The most commonly used method of depreciation is the straight line method, followed by the reducing balance method (in various guises), the annuity method and the unit of production method. A great deal of discretion is left to the management in the choice of depreciation method, as SSAP12 states: 'There is a range of acceptable depreciation methods. Management should select the method regarded as most appropriate to the type of asset and its use in the business so as to allocate depreciation as fairly as possible to the periods expected to benefit from the assets' use.'

A change in the method of depreciation is only allowed if the new method will better represent the company's results and financial position. But a change of method is not a change of accounting policy, and profits can be adjusted without even adopting a change of method, simply by altering the life of an asset over which a method is applied.

CHANGE OF USEFUL ECONOMIC LIFE

The useful economic life is the period over which the owner expects to benefit from the asset, and once it, a residual value and a depreciation method have been arrived at, a depreciation charge can be calculated.

BAA (British Airports Authority) has made two significant changes in depreciation lives in recent years:

Table 12.1   BAA – useful economic life of certain assets

Year to 31 March	*1988*	*1989*	*1990*
Terminal lives (years)	16	30	50
Runway lives (years)	23.5	40	100

Exhibit 12.1   **BAA 1989 Report and Accounts**

Depreciation

No depreciation is provided in these Group financial statements in respect of freehold or long leasehold (leaseholds with an unexpired term of over 50 years) investment properties or land.

Short leashold properties are depreciated over the period of the lease.

In the case of other assets, depreciation is calculated to write down the cost of these assets to their residual values on a straight line basis. The following table sets out the Group's standard term for each asset category:

Terminals	30 years
Runways, taxiways and aprons	40 years
Airport plant and equipment including runway lighting	15-25 years
Motor vehicles and office equipment	Over useful life which in most cases is 4-8 years
Furniture and fittings	5 years

A review carried out during the year of the useful lives of various airport assets has resulted in a revision in the case of terminals (previously depreciated over 16 years), runways (previously 23.5 years) and furniture and fittings (previously charged to the profit and loss account on a replacement basis). In addition, aircraft pavement maintenance expenditure previously capitalised is now charged to the profit and loss account as incurred.

The effect of the reassessment of useful lives of fixed assets and maintenance expenditure incurred during the year has not had a material effect on profit before tax but expenditure of £16.2m capitalised in prior years has also been charged in this year's financial statements.

Exhibit 12.2 **BAA 1990 Report and Accounts**

(d) Depreciation

No depreciation is provided in these Group financial statements in respect of freehold or long leasehold (leasehold with an unexpired term of over 50 years) investment properties or land. Short leasehold properties are depreciated over the period of the lease.

In respect of other assets, depreciation is calculated to write down the cost of these assets to their residual values on a straight line basis.

It is the Group's policy to maintain certain properties occupied by Group members in a state of good repair so the residual values exceed the costs of these properties in the Group's accounts. As a consequence, no depreciation is provided on these properties.

The following table sets out the Group's standard term for other asset categories:

Terminals	50 years (but see below)
Runways, taxiways and aprons	100 years
Airport plant and equipment including runway lighting	15-25 years
Motor vehicles and office equipment	Over useful life which in most cases is 4-8 years
Furniture and fittings	5 years

As part of a continuing review carried out in respect of the useful economic lives of its airport assets, the Group has reassessed the lives of terminal buildings (previously depreciated over 30 years) and runways, taxiways and aprons (previously 40 years) in the light of recent technological advances and an increasing volume of relevant historical data.

In respect of terminals, certain components have a life shorter than the life of the main structure. These components which were previously written off over the life of the terminals are now depreciated over a period of 10-20 years.

In the case of runways, taxiways and aprons, major periodic maintenance expenditure continued to be charged to the profit and loss account as incurred.

What is the significance of these changes? During this period, 1989–91, BAA undertook the following projects:

1. Terminal 3 Heathrow development – cost £110m

2. Heathrow runway resurfacing – £11.5m

3. Gatwick runway resurfacing – £6.5m

4. Gatwick refurbishment of South Terminal baggage and check-in systems – £22m

5. Stansted – new terminal – £395m

6. Glasgow Airport terminal refurbishment – £47m

No depreciation was, of course, provided on the assets under construction during this period:

Exhibit 12.3 BAA 1991 Report and Accounts

Notes on the financial statements

11 Tangible fixed assets

(a) Airport assets

The movements in the year in airport assets were as follows:	Terminal complexes £m	Other freehold properties £m	Airfields £m	Sundry plant and equipment £m	Assets in the course of construction £m	Total £m
Cost						
Balance 1 April 1990	940.9	69.8	209.8	133.2	344.8	1,698.5
Reclassification	(14.9)	10.7	(11.5)	(3.6)	1.1	(18.2)
Transfers from non-airport investment properties (note 11b)	–	4.9	–	–	11.6	16.5
Additions at cost	356.9	14.1	49.9	59.0	(149.8)	330.1
Amounts capitalised	–	–	–	–	54.5	54.5
Disposals at cost	(9.2)	(0.3)	(0.3)	(2.4)	–	(12.2)
Balance 31 March 1991	1,273.7	99.2	247.9	186.2	262.2	2,069.2
Depreciation						
Balance 1 April 1990	290.6	0.2	74.6	77.2	–	442.6
Reclassification	(9.9)	–	(8.2)	(0.1)	–	(18.2)
Charge for the year	34.7	0.3	4.1	14.6	–	53.7
Disposals	(6.9)	–	(0.2)	(2.0)	–	(9.1)
Balance 31 March 1991	308.5	0.5	70.3	89.7	–	469.0
Net book cost 31 March 1991	965.2	98.7	177.6	96.5	262.2	1,600.2
Revaluation surplus	–	699.7	–	–	–	699.7
Total airport assets	965.2	798.4	177.6	96.5	262.2	2,299.9
Net book cost 31 March 1990	650.3	69.6	135.2	56.0	344.8	1,255.9
Revaluation surplus	–	767.0	–	–	–	767.0
Total airport assets	650.3	836.6	135.2	56.0	344.8	2,022.9

Once they emerged from construction, the assets were depreciated in accordance with the longer economic lives – the largest capital expenditure, Stansted's new terminal building, was completed in March 1991. It is not possible to give an accurate picture of the effect on BAA's profits, even though all the assets are depreciated on the straight line method, because the estimated residual values are still unknown. But clearly a move from 16 to 50 years economic life for terminals over two years with £574m of terminal work authorised or under construction makes a substantial difference. The 1990 Report and Accounts estimated that the effect on *current year* profits of those depreciation changes was a reduction of £8.6m if the changes had *not* been introduced. This amounted to just 3.4 per cent of 1990 pre-tax profits. But the impact on future profits should grow in line with expenditure on the assets.

The sums involved are smaller for runway resurfacing, but it is worth bearing in mind with a shift in estimated economic life from 23.5 to 100 years that 100 years ago man had not achieved powered flight. So will BAA be deriving economic benefit from aircraft using its runways in 2091?

CHANGES OF LIFE AND METHOD

Exhibit 12.4 **Cable & Wireless Report and Accounts 1990**

(d) TANGIBLE FIXED ASSETS AND DEPRECIATION

Depreciation of tangible fixed assets is set aside on the basis of providing in equal annual instalments for the cost or valuation over the estimated useful lives of these assets, namely:

Telephone cables and repeaters	up to 25 years
Landlines	20 to 40 years
Freehold buildings	40 years
Leasehold land and buildings	up to 50 years or term of lease if less
Plant	2 to 33 years
Cableships	up to 30 years

Depreciation provided on capital projects relating to major network development is calculated by reference to network usage as a proportion of expected usage when the network is complete.

The provision of depreciation on the basis of usage means that part of Mercury's depreciation charge has become a variable cost growing in line with usage in later years of the project. Cable & Wireless is far from being the only company to use the unit of production or usage method of depreciation. It is most frequently used in the mineral extraction and oil and gas industries when depreciation is linked to estimated depletion of the assets:

Exhibit 12.5 **BP Annual Report and Accounts 1989**

Depreciation

Oil, coal and mineral production assets are depreciated using a unit-of-production method based upon estimated proved reserves. Other tangible and intangible assets are depreciated on the straight line method over their estimated useful lives.

In 1988, depreciation of Cable & Wireless's major network developments was changed to a unit of usage basis. Annual depreciation is calculated by comparing the network usage to the estimated total usage over the estimated life of the network. This method prevents a high depreciation charge in the early years of the network's life when usage may not have built up and losses may therefore be declared after depreciation, or at least, profits depressed. The main potential problem is of course estimating usage over the full economic life of the network. If this is overestimated then the unit of usage charge in the early years will be too low, thereby storing up trouble for later years when the network will be overvalued in the balance sheet and will need to be written down.

Cable & Wireless's other main move, in common with BAA, has been to extend the lives of digital exchanges from ten to 15 years:

This change was not evident for the Cable & Wireless Report and Accounts:

Exhibit 12.6 **Cable & Wireless Report and Accounts 1987**

D) TANGIBLE FIXED ASSETS AND DEPRECIATION

Depreciation of tangible fixed assets is set aside on the basis of providing in equal annual instalments for the cost or valuation over the estimated useful lives of these assets, namely:

Telephone cables and repeaters	up to 25 years
Land lines	20 to 40 years
Freehold buildings	40 years
Leasehold land and buildings	up to 50 years or term of lease if less
Plant	**2 to 33 years**
Cable ships	up to 25 years

During initial development of major capital projects depreciation is charged to accounting periods having regard to the utilisation of those assets.

Freehold land, where the cost is distinguishable from the cost of the building thereon, is not depreciated.

Certain land and buildings are included at open market value for existing use.

Surpluses and deficits on disposals of tangible fixed assets are determined by reference to sale proceeds and revalued net book amounts.

Cable & Wireless Report and Accounts 1990

(d) TANGIBLE FIXED ASSETS AND DEPRECIATION

Depreciation of tangible fixed assets is set aside on the basis of providing in equal annual instalments for the cost or valuation over the estimated useful lives of these assets, namely:

Telephone cables and repeaters	up to 25 years
Landlines	20 to 40 years
Freehold buildings	40 years
Leasehold land and buildings	up to 50 years or term of lease if less
Plant	**2 to 33 years**
Cableships	up to 30 years

Depreciation provided on capital projects relating to major network development is calculated by reference to network usage as a proportion of expected usage when the network is complete.

Freehold land, where the cost is distinguishable from the cost of the building thereon, is not depreciated. Certain land and buildings are included at open market value for existing use.

In previous years furniture, fittings and motor vehicles were written off in the year of acquisition. It is considered that this treatment is no longer appropriate and these items are now capitalised as plant. The previous year's amounts have been restated. The adoption of this policy in previous years would not have had a significant effect on profits for these years. Surpluses and deficits on disposals of tangible fixed assets are determined by reference to sale proceeds and revalued net book amounts.

Digital exchanges evidently fall within the category of 'Plant' where depreciation lives vary from two to 33 years.

Referring to the accounts of the subsidiary concerned, Mercury, produces more detail, but still not sufficient to identify the change in depreciation lives:

Exhibit 12.7 **Mercury Communications Limited Report and Accounts 1987**

(c) Tangible fixed Assets and Depreciation

Depreciation of tangible fixed assets is set aside on the basis of providing for their cost over their estimated useful lives. During initial development, depreciation of assets forming part of the communications network is charged to accounting periods having regard to the utilisation of those assets. Depreciation of other assets is provided in equal annual instalments.

The estimated useful lives of the assets are:

Communications Network
Fibre optic cable, ducting and plant	10 to 40 years
Microwave plant	8 to 20 years
Earth station plant and equipment	10 to 20 years
Terminal equipment	**5 to 15 years**
Other plant and equipment	3 to 10 years
Short leasehold property	Over the terms of the lease
Rights of use	Over the term of the agreement

Mercury Communications Limited Report and Accounts 1991

Tangible fixed assets and depreciation

Depreciation of tangible fixed assets is set aside on the basis of providing for their cost over their estimated useful lives. During initial development, depreciation of assets forming part of the communications network is charged to accounting periods having regard to the utilisation of those assets. Depreciation of other assets is provided in equal annual instalments.

The estimated useful lives of the assets are:

Communications Network
Fibre optic cable, ducting and plant	10 to 40 years
Microwave plant	8 to 20 years
Earth station plant and equipment	10 to 20 years
Terminal equipment	5 to 15 years
Other plant and equipment	3 to 10 years
Digital switches	**15 years**
Short leasehold property	40 years or over the term of the lease if less
Rights of use	Over the term of the agreement

The 1987 accounts for Mercury show Terminal equipment lives estimated at five to 15 years. But by 1991 a separate category for Digital Switches with estimated lives of 15 years had been identified. It would be difficult to determine the change in depreciation lives from this information.

The effect of the change has been to reduce the rate of growth in the depreciation charge at a time of heavy capital expenditure on digitalisation by Hong Kong Telecom and Mercury. Also in March 1990, the life of cable ships was extended from 25 to 30 years. The move on digital exchanges, for example, from ten to 15 years cut the depreciation charge on these items by a third. But, as ever, it is necessary to ask 'Does it matter?' and if so 'How do I spot a change in depreciation life or method?'.

THE EFFECT ON EARNINGS

To suggest that there is something intrinsically right or wrong in depreciating digital exchanges over ten or 15 years is to miss the point. It is equally difficult and probably irrelevant for us to determine whether unit of usage is a more appropriate method of depreciation for major network developments than the straight-line method.

What is important is to be aware of the impact on profits of a change from one method or period to another. The table below shows Cable & Wireless's five year profits record, adjusted for the change in depreciation policies. The lower pre-tax profits which result from adjusting to reflect the previous depreciation policies would be directly reflected in Earnings per Share since the actual tax charge would be unaffected, as depreciation is not a tax allowable expense. The average growth in profits over the five-year period has been inflated by 2½ per cent p.a. from 14.3 per cent to 16.7 per cent by the depreciation policy changes:

Table 12.2   Cable & Wireless – Adjusting for depreciation charges

Year to 31 March	1985	1986	1987	1988	1989	1990	Five year average growth %
Reported							
Pre-tax profit	245.2	295.0	340.5	356.1	420.5	526.7	+16.7
Tax charge (%)	30	27	22	18	18	18	
EPS (p)	15.8	19.3	22.0	24.0	27.9	31.3	+14.7
Adjustments							
Depreciation							
Actual	92.4	88.0	88.9	99.5	118.7	195.7	
Adjusted	92.4	105.4	116.6	132.7	174.2	250.3	
Difference	–	−17.4	−27.7	−33.2	−55.5	−54.6	
Adjusted pre-tax profit	245.2	277.6	312.8	322.9	365.0	472.1	+14.3

Source: Cable & Wireless Report and Accounts

This is important in assessing the correct rating for the shares – it is just as painful to lose money by buying an overvalued share which falls in price as it is to lose the same amount of money buying shares in a company which fails because of creative accountancy. Moreoever, such accounting charges can create a treadmill effect for a company: if there are no further changes in accounting policy, Cable & Wireless's profits will have to grow 2½ per cent p.a. faster over the next five years to match the *reported* profits growth in 1985-90. The expectation of this profits growth to match the historic performance may well be discounted in the share price, given the dangerous tendency for investment analysts to extrapolate from the past in compiling forecasts, which may prove disappointing if organic profits growth does not move up a gear to replace the impetus previously provided by accounting charges.

How to spot it?

Obviously, close attention to the Accounting Policy notes in the Annual Accounts is necessary to spot changes in depreciation methodology, although it is worth remembering that a change in depreciation method is *not* a change in accounting policy and does not therefore have to be noted as a change in accounting policy notes. Although the new method or period for depreciation will usually be shown in the accounting policy notes, attention may not be drawn to the change by a specific note, so careful attention has to be given to comparing the Accounting Policies with the previous year's notes.

Changes in depreciation policy can also be derived by comparing depreciation with the assets in the business to determine whether the proportion of total assets depreciated each year is changing over time:

Table 12.3 Cable & Wireless – Depreciation over a five-year period

	1985	1986	1987	1988	1989	1990
Depreciation charge (£m) (A)	92	88	89	100	119	196
Average gross assets (£m) (B)	1036	1182	1307	1489	1953	2806
A/B %	8.9	7.4	6.8	6.7	6.1	7.0

Source: Cable & Wireless Report and Accounts

Between 1985 and 1990, Cable & Wireless's depreciation charge fell from 8.9 per cent p.a. of the assets employed to 7.0 per cent. These trends can also be compared with industry competitors to determine whether they represent an industry-wide trend or whether a company's depreciation policy is moving out of line with others in the same business:

Table 12.4   Depreciation/Average Gross Assets (%)

UK	1986	1987	1988	1989	1990
British Telecom	7.5	8.8	9.3	8.9	9.4
Cable & Wireless	7.4	6.8	6.7	6.1	7.0
Racal Telecom	10.5	10.6	11.1	10.0	9.9
USA					
AT&T	9.9	9.4	9.2	8.3	
MCI	10.3	9.3	9.6	10.1	
Sprint	13.7	13.2	11.2	10.9	
United Telecom	7.3	8.3	10.3	8.5	
Ameritech	7.7	7.8	7.3	7.3	
Bell Atlantic	8.6	9.4	8.9	8.5	
Bell South	6.5	7.3	7.1	7.0	
Nynex	7.0	8.5	7.9	7.9	
Pacific Telesis	7.1	7.7	7.7	7.4	
Southwestern Bell	6.5	7.3	7.5	7.5	
US West	6.9	7.4	7.4	6.7	

Source: UBS Phillips & Drew

Intercompany comparisons suffer from some disadvantages, such as the different age profile of the companies' assets, different asset mixes and the fact that the US regional Bell Telephone companies are regulated for the most part by return on assets. Nonetheless there is a clear discrepancy between Cable & Wireless's percentage depreciation/assets at 7.0 per cent and the average for the rest of the industry.

These methods of detecting the impact of changes in depreciation policy are doubly important because policy changes are often implemented *before* completion of major capital expenditure, such as BAA's Stansted terminal, or Cable & Wireless's investment in digital exchanges, so that the impact on profits of a change in policy may not be readily apparent simply from the Accounting Policy change and is only revealed by the sort of calculations shown above.

13

CONVERTIBLES WITH PUT OPTIONS AND AMPS

Just like convertible cars . . . they are fine until it rains

COMPLEX FINANCIAL INSTRUMENTS

In January 1991 the Accounting Standards Board announced its work programme of Financial Reporting Standards (FRS) and Financial Reporting Exposure Drafts (FRED). One important project on which the ASB hoped to have an Exposure Draft within the year was the area of so-called Complex Financial Instruments which had proliferated during the 1980s, some of the most notorious of which are convertibles with put options. The result to date is the 1991 Discussion Paper on Accounting for Capital Instruments.

CONVERTIBLES WITH PUT OPTIONS

Almost all financial instruments issued by companies which can potentially produce dire consequences have one of two characteristics: 1) they are claimed to have the advantages of equity capital but the interest or dividend payment is tax deductible, like interest on debt, and the instrument does not share in the growth in profits or dividends so that ordinary shares are not directly diluted; and/or 2) they provide a method of financing which is cheaper than previously available methods.

Convertibles with put options fall into category 2. They took advantage of the consistent rise in share prices which characterised the bull market in equities which ended in October 1987. This enabled the issuing company to set the conversion terms of the bonds at a significant premium to the current share price in the expectation that this could be reached if share prices kept on rising. To take an example, London International Group issued £50m 4½ per cent Convertible Bonds on 25 March 1981 when the share price stood at 284p with a conversion price of 452p, representing a conversion premium of 59 per cent.

Exibit 13.1 **London International Group – Annual report and accounts 1990**

Note 16. Borrowings

	Group		Holding company	
	1990	1989	1990	1989
	£m	£m	£m	£m
4½% Convertible Bonds 2002	50.0	50.0	50.0	50.0
Bank loans	59.5	57.1	5.7	2.2
Bank overdrafts and acceptances	26.1	18.6	6.6	8.8
Other items	0.5	0.7	–	–
	136.1	126.4	62.3	61.0
The aggregate amounts are repayable as follows:				
More than five years	50.8	51.4	50.0	50.0
Between two and five years	8.6	4.6	4.5	2.0
Between one and two years	33.3	32.6	–	–
	92.7	88.6	54.5	52.0
In one year or less	43.4	37.8	7.8	9.0
	136.1	126.4	62.3	61.0
Borrowings secured on assets of certain subsidiaries	3.0	3.2	–	–
Unsecured borrowings	133.1	123.2	62.3	61.0
	136.1	126.4	62.3	61.0

Borrowings repayable after more than five years, with the exception of the 4½% Convertible bonds, are at interest rates varying from 6½% to 12% and are mainly repayable in annual instalments.

The 4½% Convertible bonds 2002 were issued in October 1987 and the principal terms, including amended terms agreed in May 1989 with the trustee, include:

1. Bondholders may convert their holdings into fully paid ordinary shares at a price of £4.52 per share at any time prior to 18 March 2002.
2. Bondholders may elect to require redemption of the Bonds on 25 March 1992 at a price of 120.70% of the principal amount.
3. Unless previously converted or redeemed Bonds will be redeemed by the Company at their principal amount on 25 March 2002.
4. Bondholders may exercise a put option on 25 March 1997 at a price 155.09% of the principal amount (assuming no supplementary interest) on the same yield as the 1992 put option of 8.53%.

Investors were prepared to buy the bonds with a very high conversion premium and a low interest coupon (UK Base Rate was ten per cent in October 1987 when LIG issued the 4½ per cent Convertible) for one reason: the put option. A put option is a right granted to a holder to sell a security such as a share or bond at a set price, thereby either protecting the investor from a fall in price or, in the case of a put option above the market price, guaranteeing a profit. The bonds carried the right for the holders to sell them back to the issuer at a premium. The combination of the premium and the interest coupon gave a yield to redemption closer to the true rate of borrowing. In the case of LIG, the initial terms of the Bond were amended in May 1989 after the October 1987 Stock Market Crash to give the right to redeem at 120 per cent of the principal amount. Combined with the 4½ per cent coupon, this gave a redemption yield of 8.3 per cent.

Obviously, the companies thought that these put options would never be utilised as share price rises would erode the conversion premium and lead Bond holders to convert into Ordinary shares. Unfortunately the right to convert at £4.52 per share for LIG compared with an actual market share price of 297p on 1 January 1992.

At this point the idea of deriving a cheap source of finance clearly had not entirely worked, but it was still not disastrous – 8.3 per cent yield to redemption including the redemption premium represented a very respectable cost of finance. Problems arose from the way in which companies accounted for this liability, or rather the manner in which they avoided accounting for it.

At least initially, most of the issuers of convertible bonds with put options failed to make any provision in their accounts for the possibility that the bonds would have to be redeemed at a premium. Only the very low coupon was shown in interest payable, which clearly understated the potential cost of the finance and was imprudent. The alternative method is required by US GAAP. This causes a problem if the Bonds are not converted since the whole of the redemption premium would become payable at the expense of the balance sheet, clearly indicating that profits for previous years had been overstated. Moreover, providing alone was not the full answer since actual cash was needed for redemption.

The net result was that a number of the companies involved had to restate their accounts later on a more conservative and realistic basis, and to raise the cash to cover the possibility of redemption:

Exhibit 13.2 London International – Rights Issue document 1991

The rights issue will serve to broaden the company's capital base in advance of March 1992, the first date on which bondholders can require the Company to redeem the £50 million 4½ per cent convertible bond due 2002 (the 'bonds'). The overall yield on the bonds to holders, on the basis that they exercise their first option to require redemption in March 1992, will have been about 8.5 per cent per annum. The bonds were initially issued in 1987 in order to fund substantially the acquisition of Hatu-Ico, a leading condom manufacturer in Italy, together with Hispano-Ico in Spain, at a total cost of almost £60 million.

Despite amendments made in May 1989, in the current market it is likely that the bonds will be redeemed on the first redemption date. However,the Company has benefitted from the low interest costs of bonds since 1987. The Company has sufficient banking facilities at its disposal to meet in full the maximum redemption amount of £60 million in March 1992.

Profit and dividend forecast

As redemption of the bonds now appears likely, the Directors feel it appropriate to make full provision in the accounts to 31 March, 1991 for the accrued supplementary interest which would arise on redemption; an amount of £2.3 million will be included within the interest charge and there will be an exceptional item of £5.8 million, representing a provision for supplementary interest in respect of the period from September 1987 to 31 March 1990.

The LIG rights issue raises another accounting issue related to convertibles with put options. The LIG 4½ per cent Convertible Bond issue proceeds were used to fund acquisitions in Italy and Spain. The profits from these acquisitions had been shown in the profit and loss account since the issue of the Bond, which had been accounted for at a cost of just 4½ per cent p.a.. The income from the Bond proceeds was therefore shown in full, but not the cost, so that the statement of profits was very one-sided. The same effect would be true even if the proceeds of the bonds were simply invested in the money market at ten per cent p.a., which brings us back to the way of spotting financial instruments that can cause problems – there is actually no way of borrowing in sterling at 4½ per cent, when rates are ten per cent. This sort of financial alchemy always has a price, but when that price is hidden by the company accounts, it is not always easy to spot.

LIG was not the only company to issue a convertible with put option or to fail to provide for the full redemption yield although considerably more companies have switched to providing annually for the redemption premium through the profit and loss account recently:

Table 13.1 Companies with convertible bonds with put options

Company	Value	Providing for Put Option?
Argyll	£73m	Yes
Asda	£129m	Yes
Boots	£213m	Yes
Burton	£150m	Yes
Cookson	£86m	Yes
Coats Viyella	£126m	Yes
Hickson	£53m	Yes
Hillsdown	£188m	Yes
Ladbroke	£204m	Yes
London International	£60m	Yes
Next (2 bonds)	£107m	Yes
P&O	£71m	Yes
Ranks Hovis McDougall	£50m	Yes
Ratners	£59m	Yes
Slough Estates	£150m	Yes
Smith & Nephew	£120m	No
Thorn EMI	£103m	No
United Biscuits	£41m	No

Source: UBS Phillips & Drew

The outcome for some participants was also far worse than for LIG. Many different courses of action were undertaken to correct the problems caused by convertibles with put options.

Saatchi & Saatchi does not appear in the above table, even though it issued £176.5m in Convertible Europreference shares due to be redeemed for £211m in July 1992. This liability would almost certainly have been sufficient to put the company into receivership. Consequently, the Europreference shareholders were offered ordinary shares in exchange so that they ended up with 64 per cent of the enlarged share capital, diluting the interests of the existing ordinary shareholders. The effect of this highly dilutive rescue issue (and the recession in the advertising industry) on Saatchi's existing shareholders was a dramatic share price collapse:

Figure 13.1   Saatchi share price chart 1987–91

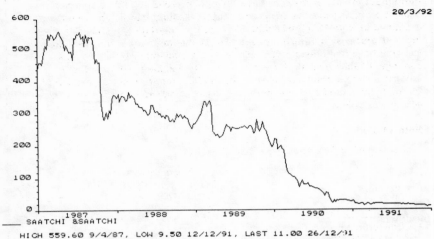

HIGH 559.60 9/4/87, LOW 9.50 12/12/91, LAST 11.00 26/12/91
Source : Datastream

Other firms were forced to sell assets to survive the effects of the creative financing technique of premium puts overlayed on a recessionary trading environment, such as Storehouse and Next which sold its Grattan mail order business for £168m.

One means of postponing the inevitable consequences of a premium put was the rolling put. LIG attempted this solution in May 1989, increasing the put premium from 120.70 per cent in March 1922 to 155.09 per cent in March 1997 to give a redemption yield of 8.53 per cent on the 4½ convertible bonds, and more critically more time for the possibility of conversion to occur. But as we have seen, this did not correct the fundamental flaw of not accounting for the full liability of the put option or having the cash available to meet it, leading to LIG's rights issue in 1991.

The correct way to account for a premium put was demonstrated by Tesco which issued four Convertible Bonds convertible at 174p per share, or redeemable at 127.625 per cent of the principal amount in 1992.

Tesco's profits were struck after allowing for £1.2m p.a. amortisation of the redemption premium; in any event the Tesco issue had a happy ending with the Bondholders converting because of the good share price performance (see Figure 13.2).

Tesco was therefore able to write the unused redemption premium built up into reserves.

Exhibit 13.3   **Tesco – Annual Report and Accounts 1989**

Note 3b) Change of accounting policy

The directors have decided that, on the grounds of prudence and in order to adopt current best accounting practice, the true effective rate of interest throughout the life of the 4% convertible bonds 2002 should be charged against profit, irrespective of whether supplementary interest (more fully explained in Note 13 (c)) will actually be paid. Accordingly interest payable includes a provision of £5.8m of such supplemental interest and the results for last year have been restated to include £5.0m (previously disclosed as a contingent liability) as a prior year charge. The retained profits brought forward for the current year have been similarly reduced, net of taxation of £1.7m. Fully diluted earnings per share are not affected by this change of accounting policy.

Note 13 Creditors

Amounts Falling Due After More than One Year

| | Consolidated | | Tesco PLC | |
| | 1989 | 1988 Restated | 1989 | 1988 Restated |
	£m	£m	£m	£m
9% Convertible unsecured loan stock 2002/2007 (a)	–	16.4	–	16.4
4% Unsecured deep discount loan stock 2006 (b)	64.2	63.0	64.2	63.0
4% Convertible bonds 2002 (c)	115.0	115.0	115.0	115.0
Commercial paper (d)	14.2	17.9	14.2	17.9
Bank loans (e)	–	17.8	–	17.8
Finance leases (Note 15)	–	6.8	–	–
10½% Bonds 2015 (f)	99.6	–	99.6	–
	293.0	236.9	293.0	230.1
Corporate taxation	61.5	52.2	–	–
Other creditors	10.8	5.0	10.8	5.0
	365.3	294.1	303.8	235.1

a) The company has exercised its right compulsorily to convert the 9% convertible unsecured loan stock into fully paid ordinary shares during the year.

b) The 4% unsecured deep discount loan stock is redeemable at par value of £125m in 2006.

c) The 4% convertible bonds are convertible at the holder's option into fully paid ordinary shares of 5p each at a current conversion price of 174p per ordinary share. Alternatively, the bondholder has the option of redeeming such bonds at a redemption price, including supplemental interest, equal to 127.625% of the principal amount thereof in 1992. The bonds may be redeemed at the option of the company at a premium reducing annually until 20th February 1993 and thereafter at par provided that the market price of ordinary shares is at least 226p per share. The supplemental interest on these bonds totalling £10.8m (1988 £5.0m) is shown as other creditors.

Figure 13.2   Tesco share price chart 1987–91

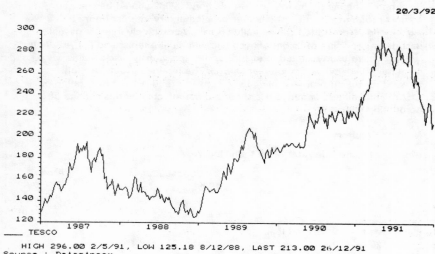

20/3/92

HIGH 296.00 2/5/91, LOW 125.18 8/12/88, LAST 213.00 26/12/91
Source : Datastream

Overall, therefore, it is worth noting that it is not the financing technique which is at fault: convertibles with put options *can* sometimes provide a cheap means of financing. Tesco's ordinary shareholders had the benefit of borrowing money at four per cent p.a. until the Bonds converted. But it is also worth noting that one of the few companies for whom the technique worked as planned was one of the few which accounted prudently from the outset, and that in the end Tesco's balance sheet benefited – this is the obverse of creative accounting – Tesco ended up understating profits by £1.2m p.a. to the benefit of the balance sheet.

Remember the common sense approach: any company which accounts on the basis that it can borrow in sterling at 4½ per cent p.a. and deposit the funds to earn ten per cent should set alarm bells ringing.

AUCTION MARKET PREFERRED STOCK (AMPS)

Another financing technique which has provoked some debate is AMPS, which, it is claimed, has all the advantages of equity without the costs. Sounds familiar?

Auction market preferred stock (AMPS) can have a variety of names. Another is variable rate dividend preference shares. The shares count as equity in the issuing company's balance sheet. They are perpetually in issue like ordinary shares, and can only be redeemed at the option of the issuer.

But the dividend is not a fixed rate – it is reset by an auction process at intervals which can vary from every 28 days to five years.

The buyers of AMPS are other companies with spare cash which can earn a higher rate invested in AMPS than in Treasury Bonds or bank deposits. For the issuer, the AMPS rank behind borrowings in the event of liquidation, but ahead of ordinary shareholders. But the ordinary shareholders escape dilution – the AMPS holders do not share in (hopefully) rising ordinary dividends. AMPS are an American instrument but have nonetheless been issued by a number of UK companies:

Table 13.2 AMPS issues of UK Origin ($m)

Issuer	Amount	Estimated 1991 year end Gearing % AMPS as equity	AMPS as debt
Beazer	101	Hanson takeover	
BET	500	35	155
ECC	400	21	★★69
Elf (UK)	250	–	–
Pioneer	101	–	–
Rank Organisation	200	Refinanced	–
Ratners	★250	45	100
Redland	250	15	30
Tarmac	300	40	52
Thorn EMI	200	60	78
Total	3,333		

★ $50m of this has fixed dividend until October 1994.

★★ Pre-rights issue – 24 per cent post issue.

Source: UBS Phillips & Drew

But problems can arise with AMPS. An example of particular AMPS issue terms which raise problems is the Beazer $101m AMPS issue. Beazer is a construction company which took on substantial gearing to acquire the US aggregate company Koppers. Beazer's issue was backed by a letter of credit from National Westminster Bank, which guaranteed that in a winding-up the AMPS investors would be repaid by NatWest. This would effectively move the AMPS from providing equity capital in a liquidation into the debt category as it would increase Beazer's borrowing from

Exhibit 13.4 Beazer Report and Accounts 1991

Beazer Balance Sheet as at 30 June 1991

	Group		Company	
	1991	*1990*	*1991*	*1990*
	£m	*£m*	*£m*	*£m*
Fixed assets				
Tangible assets	2,063.0	2,095.7	1.8	1.9
Investments	82.1	30.4	789.7	677.4
	2,145.1	2,126.1	791.5	679.3
Current assets				
Tangible assets	140.7	125.2	–	–
Stock	535.7	528.1	–	–
Debtors	382.6	375.8	440.8	47.8
Investments	0.8	2.3	–	0.1
Cash at bank and in hand	210.6	64.3	63.8	0.6
	1,270.4	1,095.7	504.6	48.5
Current liabilities				
Creditor – amounts falling due within one year				
Borrowings	(398.4)	(229.8)	(445.8)	(153.6)
Other creditors	(544.5)	(665.2)	(232.0)	(76.2)
	(942.9)	(895.0)	(687.8)	(229.8)
Net current assets (liabilities)	327.5	200.7	(183.2)	(181.3)
Total assets less current liabilities	2,472.6	2,326.8	608.3	498.0
Creditors – amounts falling due after more than one year				
Borrowings	(836.5)	(751.7)	(188.5)	(54.6)
Other creditors	(228.9)	(275.6)	(20.4)	(53.3)
	(1,065.4)	(1,027.3)	(208.9)	(107.9)
Provisions for liabilities and charges	(188.7)	(202.6)	(9.2)	2.2
Net assets	1,218.5	1,096.9	390.2	392.3
Capital and reserves				
Called up share capital	78.5	78.1	78.5	78.1
Share premium account	249.2	245.6	249.2	245.6
Other reserves	583.0	517.5	61.4	61.4
Profit and loss account	186.9	210.4	1.1	7.2
Shareholders' funds	1,097.6	1,051.6	390.2	392.3
Minority interests				
Preference shares issued by subsidiaries – guaranteed	93.2	28.7	–	–
Other minority interests	27.7	16.6	–	–
	120.9	45.3	–	–
Total capital employed	1,218.5	1,096.9	390.2	392.3

Note 20. Preference shares issued by subsidiaries	1991 £m	1990 £m
50,000,000 7.2% cumulative redeemable preference shares 2000 of US$1.00 each, redeemable at par, (guaranteed by Beazer PLC)	30.9	28.7
101,000 Auction Market Preferred Shares (AMPS) of US$1,000 each redeemable at par at the option of the company	62.3	–
	93.2	28.7

The issue of the US$101m of AMPS, supported by a letter of credit, was completed on 5th September 1990. The letter of credit issued by National Westminster Bank PLC is guaranteed by Beazer PLC.

NatWest when the AMPS holders were repaid. This contradicts one of the main functions of equity capital – to stand behind all other creditors in the event of a liquidation.

Nonetheless the AMPS issue was shown as a minority interest in Beazer's Accounts. But in the end this did not fool anyone: AMPS carry a variable rate which can increase via the auction process if a company gets into difficulties so the burden of the AMPS increases just at a time when the company would not pay a dividend on equity in order to conserve cash – this option is not always available with AMPS. As a result of this, and of course other problems caused by the building recession, Beazer was forced into a rescue takeover by Hanson.

The mechanism of the auction process means that if the rate for AMPS rises at auction this is not an uncontrolled process. There is usually a fall-back rate which gives an upper limit on the rate. If there are insufficient buyers at this rate, the AMPS cost still rises at the worst possible moment for the company.

Other companies which have found that worries about the auction process for AMPS and their financing cause additional problems at a time when there have been worries about their trading income have been BET and Ratners.

14

PENSION FUND ACCOUNTING

The Great Illusion
– title of a book by Norman Angell, 1874 – 1967

How a surplus arises

The last few years in the UK have seen widespread announcements of overfunded pension schemes by UK companies. Of a survey of 100 of the largest companies by market capitalisation in the UK★, the median funding level was 125 per cent of the schemes' liabilities. In a similar survey in November 1990 only six out of 100 companies disclosed a funding level below 100 per cent.

A surplus arises when the actual valuation of a fund produces a figure greater than that required to meet the estimated liabilities to members of the fund. The valuation process by which this funding level is determined is far from straightforward, primarily because the actuary is dealing with pension liabilities which are by their very nature long-term, and he therefore needs to assess the long-term value of the assets held to meet these liabilities.

Moreover, the value of both assets and liabilities will change over time. Liabilities are affected by growth in the wage bill since most pension schemes (or 98 out of the 100 companies surveyed) have defined benefit schemes, where pension payments are linked to an employee's final salary. The company therefore has to ensure that the scheme has sufficient income to make these payments, and the actuary will have to estimate the wage inflation rate for employees of the company up to their date of retirement. Less important, but still a factor in estimating the scheme's liabilities, is the expected rate of inflation or as it is more usually called, indexation of the pensions paid to retired members of the scheme.

On the asset side, the valuation is not the process which most private investors would understand. The actuary does not look up the prices of

★ Bacon & Woodrow, *SSAP 24* Survey of Practice from Published Accounts, September 1991.

shares held by the fund in the *Financial Times* and ask chartered surveyors for valuations of the fund's property assets etc. It is not a realisation value which is being sought, rather the investment return expected on the fund's assets over the same time scale as its liabilities, in order to determine whether those returns are sufficient to cover its liabilities.

The valuation parameters which are usually quoted in the disclosure of actuarial assumptions are the investment return and salary increases (see Table 14.1). In some cases, assumed dividend increases rather than anticipated total investment returns are cited. Also in some cases the expected rate of indexation in pensions is given. In other examples only the difference in growth between investment returns and salary increases is given rather than the absolute figures, since this difference is the critical factor in determining the funding level.

The Bacon & Woodrow survey shows the net investment return (net of expected salary increases) for 91 companies:

Figure 14.1 Frequency chart of assumption for interest net of pay increases

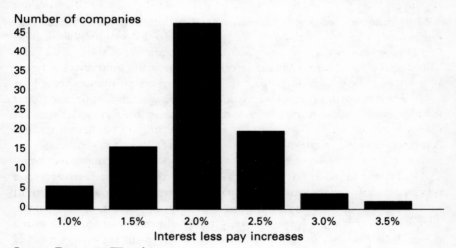

Source: Bacon & Woodron

The net investment return assumptions range from 1 to 3½ per cent, but the majority are around two per cent.

So how do pension fund surpluses arise? 1) Investment returns greater than anticipated, and/or 2) wage increases which are lower than expected. Or, to put it more bluntly, by previous actuarial assumptions on these factors proving to be too pessimistic, so that the contributions which a company has been required to pay into the fund have proved excessive.

In the 1980s in particular, investment returns in UK equities were exceptional during the long bull market, and easily outpaced wage inflation:

Table 14.1   Net investment returns in the 1980s

%	1980	1981	1982	1983	1984	1985	1986	1987	1988	1989	1990	1991
Total return on UK Equities	35.0	13.5	28.9	28.8	31.6	20.6	27.6	8.0	11.6	36.0	−9.7	20.7
Wages & salary inflation	18.6	7.5	6.6	6.8	6.7	8.8	8.7	8.8	11.5	11.3	10.8	5.0

Source: UBS Phillips & Drew

Most funds are revalued triennially, and by the mid 1980s investment returns were clearly outstripping wage inflation so that surpluses were built up. This process was given a big boost at the beginning of the 1980s by the labour shake-out which occurred in UK manufacturing industry during the 1980-81 recession, which helped to produce fund surpluses since it is inflation in the total wage bill which counts in the valuation of the fund, and reductions in headcount clearly relieve this pressure on fund liabilities.

ACCOUNTING FOR A SURPLUS – SSAP 24

SSAP 24 was introduced in May 1988 with the aim of introducing a systematic basis for reporting the impact on companies of the pension fund surpluses which were becoming increasingly important. Prior to the introduction of SSAP 24, the generally accepted practice in the UK was to charge pension costs in the profit and loss account on the basis of actual payments made to the fund i.e. on a cash basis, which obviously caused wide fluctuations in the impact on profits as overfunded schemes arose from triennial valuations and some contributions ceased.

SSAP 24 aimed to spread the charge to profit and loss account for the pension fund contribution over the period in which the company receives benefit from the employee's services i.e. an accruals concept. The Standard explicitly separated this from the funding concept, which is to build up sufficient assets and income in the fund to meet employees' pensions when they are due i.e. a cash flow concept.

SSAP 24 gave companies with a pension fund surplus a choice to account either by recognising the surplus as a balance sheet item and creating a prepayment asset as a prior year item, or by spreading the benefit of the surplus forward in its profit and loss account over the remaining service life of the scheme's members. Since the second of these two methods is by far the most popular method of dealing with a surplus under SSAP 24 we will examine this first.

HOW TO TREAT A SURPLUS

1. *Spreading*

Once a surplus has been identified by one of several actuarial valuation methods, the benefit of the surplus is spread over the remaining service life of the employees. This sounds simple enough, but even the method of spreading can significantly affect disclosed profits. But first, what is the effect of spreading a surplus?

(i) reduced pension fund contributions If spreading of the surplus results in a variation from the regular cash contribution to the fund required by the actuarial valuation of assets and liabilities and projected growth rates. This surplus is credited to the profit and loss acount once it has been spread by one of the several methods (see below) and will result in the reduction or even elimination of the charge for pension fund contributions for a time.

(ii) negative pension cost Where a surplus is large enough, the surplus spread over the remaining service lives may be larger than the regular annual cost, which can result in a credit to the profit and loss account as shown in the WH Smith example (Exhibit 14.1). Smith shows a regular cost of £18.2m for 1991 compared with a variation arising from spreading the pension fund surplus of £29.4m. This obviously made it unnecessary for the regular cost of £18.2m to be debited to profit and loss account in the period, and furthermore the excess of £11.2m was credited to profit and loss account.

These treatments of a pension fund surplus give rise to a number of problems:

(a) Method of spreading a surplus

There is no one accepted method of spreading a surplus, and different methods produce different impacts over time. Spreading over the average service life of the work force requires first an estimate of the *average* length of service remaining until retirement age, taking into account deaths,

---

Exhibit 14.1   WH Smith Annual Report 1991

Note 25. Pension costs

The Group operates a number of pension schemes. The major schemes, which cover over 90% of members, are of the defined benefit type and are contracted-in to the State Earnings Related Pension scheme ('SERPS'). The assets of the schemes are held in separate funds administered by trustees.

The most recent formal actuarial valuations of the schemes were undertaken as at 31 March 1988 adopting the attained age method. The market value of the assets of the UK schemes was £311.8m and the actuarial value of the assets was sufficient at that date to cover 129% of the benefits that had accrued to members after allowing for expected future increases in earnings. The principal actuarial assumptions used for the valuations were as follows:

Investment return	9.0% pa compound
General increase in earnings	7.5% pa compound
Pensions increase	4.0% pa compound

The surplus of the actuarial valuation of assets over the benefits accrued to members is being eliminated by a reduction in employer contributions.

The pension cost relating to the UK schemes has been assessed in accordance with the advice of a qualified actuary based on the same actuarial valuations, updating them to 1 June 1991. The pension cost charged in the profit and loss account is as follows:

Major UK Schemes	52 weeks to 1 June 1991 £m	52 weeks to 2 June 1990 £m
Regular cost	18.2	15.3
Variation from regular cost	(29.4)	(19.3)
	(11.2)	(4.0)
Other schemes	–	0.3
Credit for the period	(11.2)	(3.7)

The variation from regular cost for the period represents the amortisation of the estimated surplus at the beginning of the period spreading it by equal instalments of capital and reducing elements of interest over the estimated service lives of the existing members taken as 9 years. The pension costs relating to overseas schemes are immaterial.

The social security costs shown in note 24 above include SERPS contributions of approximately £3.5m (1990 – £3.2m).

---

retirements, resignations and redundancies. This average will usually be shorter than most people imagine. As the accompanying table shows, it can vary from about six to 15 years.

Once this estimate is established, a method of spreading the surplus over this period must be applied. Three commonly applied methods are: 1) the straight line method, 2) the mortgage or fixed amount method and 3) the percentage of pensionable pay method.

Take the example of a fund with a surplus of £7m spread over eight years. An estimated investment return of nine per cent and payroll inflation of eight per cent would produce the following variation in annual surplus:

Table 14.2 Methods of spreading a surplus

Year	Straight line £	Fixed amount £	Percentage of pay £
1	1385	1160	930
2	1310	1160	1000
3	1235	1160	1065
4	1165	1160	1145
5	1090	1160	1220
6	1020	1160	1310
7	945	1160	1400
8	875	1160	1500
Total	9025	9280	9570

Source: UBS Phillips & Drew

The straight line method is calculated by dividing the surplus of £7m by the number of years service to give a level capital amount per annum of £875,000. Interest is added to the unamortised balance each year to give the total charge. In common with the other methods, this produces a total figure which exceeds the original surplus because of the necessity to include an interest element, since the actuarial surplus itself is a discounted amount or net present value of future flows.

The mortgage or fixed amount method calculates a fixed annuity which would provide the surplus of £7m plus interest in line with the investment return of nine per cent p.a. in the fund. As in mortgage repayments, the annual surplus can be regarded as comprising mainly interest with a small capital element at the outset and vice-versa in later years.

The percentage of pay method is calculated by taking a stream of payments increasing each year at the same rate as the estimated rate of payroll inflation used in valuing the fund (seven per cent).

It can be seen that the methods produce very different impacts upon the profit and loss account, with the straight line method taking the bulk of the benefit of the surplus 'up front' and the percentage of pay method reversing this. This problem is compounded by the fact that companies are not disclosing the method of spreading utilised so that it is impossible to draw comparisons even between two companies with exactly the same pension surplus situation.

b) How should earnings from pension fund surpluses be valued?

Using a pension fund surplus to reduce or eliminate employer's contribution to a pension fund is an increase in earnings since it reduces or eliminates the regular charge in the profit and loss account. But how should this source of earnings be valued? This can be a significant question: the WH Smith pension fund surplus in 1991 eliminated a regular cost of £18.2m. Even ignoring the surplus over and above this amount also credited to profit and loss account of £11.2m, this will have boosted pre-tax profits by 25.7 per cent to £89.0m, plus a further 18.8 per cent for the amount of negative pension cost credited to profit and loss account. Combined this represents nearly a 50 per cent increase in Smith's profits excluding these items.

The most obvious problem with earnings generated from this source is their sustainability. It must be accepted that earnings from this source cannot be guaranteed because future triennial revaluations could throw up deficits rather than surpluses. This happened in the 1970s when wage inflation last outstripped investment returns. Indeed, in a sense the current surpluses only arose in part at least because past actuarial valuations were too pessimistic about investment returns versus wage inflation, including the inability to predict the massive headcount cuts which helped to produce surpluses. Why is it impossible that current valuations are too optimistic?

Moreover, the benefit of the surplus will diminish, the rate depending on the method of spreading used. But clearly a company using the straight line method will have a lower benefit in later years. A simple way of looking at this is to ask what PER would a company attract if its only earnings were these annual pension fund reductions in regular cost? Pretty low, I would suggest, if the benefit diminishes over time, and even lower given that the surplus could disappear completely or be transformed into a deficit at the next triennial valuation.

Without further upward revision in the surplus, a pension fund surplus credit to profit and loss account will naturally reverse in due course, and the company will revert to charging the full annual cost to profit and loss acount. If the surplus is amortised over eight years, then in year nine the company will revert to charging the full regular cost in the profit and loss account which will cause a quantum leap in costs for a company with the size of annual surplus reduction of WH Smith.

Table 14.3   Estimated rundown of WH Smith pension fund credit

Year £m	1	2	3	4	5	6	7	8	9	10
Amortisation of surpluses										
– capital	16	16	16	16	16	16	16	16	16	–
– interest	13.4	11.6	10.2	8.7	7.3	5.9	4.4	3.0	1.5	–
Less:	29.4	27.6	26.2	24.7	23.3	21.9	20.4	19.0	17.3	–
Regular cost	(18.1)	(19.7)	(21.6)	(23.7)	(26.0)	(28.5)	(31.3)	(34.3)	(37.6)	(41.2)
P&L credit (debit)	11.2	7.9	4.6	1.0	(2.7)	(6.6)	(10.9)	(15.3)	(20.1)	(41.2)

Source: UBS Phillips & Drew

To illustrate the point, Table 14.3 above gives an estimate of the run down in the effect of WH Smith's pension fund surplus. The notes to the Accounts indicate that it has been spread using the mortgage method, as shown above. The assumptions are: an investment return of nine per cent p.a. on the fund in line with the actuarial assumptions, wage growth of seven per cent p.a. (ditto) and two per cent p.a. growth in staff numbers in line with the physical expansion of Smith's operations. The surplus is amortised over nine years, in line with Smith's practice.

The result is interesting. By year five the credit to profit and loss account has reverted to being a charge, and there is a leap in this charge in year ten as the surplus has been fully utilised. Any investor who placed the same multiple on Smith's profit and loss credit in year one from the pension fund as on its other earnings would have a nasty shock later.

c) Negative pension cost

The WH Smith example has already shown a fund in which spreading the surplus produces a negative pension cost i.e. a credit to profit and loss account, in the first year. This arises where the amortised surplus exceeds the regular cost. This could occur, for example, where the pension fund surplus is so large that it cannot be eliminated over the average working life of the scheme members by reducing the profit and loss account charge to zero, or where a company is using a front-end loaded method of spreading the surplus such as the straight line method.

There is no reason within SSAP 24 why this 'negative cost' should not be recognised. It does of course give rise to a prepayment asset in the balance sheet. But it is necessary to be aware of the nature of this item. It is a non-cash element of profits i.e. the pension fund does not pay the company anything to match this negative cost so that counting it as part of normal earnings can give a misleading impression of the company's cash generation. And the balance sheet asset formed by this credit has limited usefulness – it can be used to increase employees' pension fund rights but is not freely available for use in the business.

This reflects the fact that despite the philosophy of SSAP 24, which is that a defined benefit pension fund is a vehicle for the company and that any surplus is regarded as a company asset, and any shortfall in provision of the defined benefits would have to be made up by the company, there are very few cases of companies succeeding in getting a cash repayment from an overfunded scheme. Hanson tried and failed with the Imperial Group scheme, although this was complicated by the fact that Hanson had disposed of most of the operating businesses covered by the scheme. Probably the most significant success recorded is Lucas' cash refund of £90m from a £560m surplus.

But all these examples are rare – generally a pension fund credit to profit and loss account which exceeds the regular cost is a non-cash credit and should be treated accordingly. Whether or not a surplus can be realised by the company in cash depends on the exact terms of the trust deed under which the scheme is run, but examples are rare.

2. Prior year adjustment

In the year of implementation of SSAP 24 the Standard permits an alternative method to that of spreading a surplus (or deficit) across the average working lives of the members of the scheme: the incorporation of the surplus or deficit into the balance sheet by a prior year adjustment, creating a prepayment asset (if a surplus) or an accrual (if a deficit). This is a different treatment to an asset which may be created because a pension fund surplus spread over the life of schemes' members exceeds the regular annual cost, thereby causing a 'negative cost' or credit in the profit and loss account, which will give rise to a prepayment asset in the balance sheet. In addition, some prepayments may arise in a company's balance sheet simply because the company has paid into the pension fund earlier than required. An example is given by Marks & Spencer:

Exhibit 14.2 **Marks & Spencer 1990 Annual Report**				
Note 16. Debtors	*Group*		*Company*	
	1990	*1989*	*1990*	*1989*
	£m	*£m*	*£m*	*£m*
Amounts falling due within one year:				
Trade debtors	47.9	47.1	19.4	22.6
Amounts owed by Group companies	–	–	472.2	293.3
Group funds utilised in financial services (see note 14)	46.3	–	–	–
Other debtors	43.4	35.7	37.2	26.6
Prepayments and accrued income	81.9	81.1	71.2	70.0
	219.5	163.9	600.0	412.5
Amounts falling due after more than one year:				
Advance corporation tax recoverable on the proposed final dividend	40.9	34.7	40.9	34.7
Deferred taxation provision arising on short-term timing differences	(21.6)	(23.1)	(18.4)	(20.1)
	19.3	11.6	22.5	14.6
Other debtors	17.9	17.1	17.8	16.7
	37.2	28.7	40.3	31.3
	256.7	192.6	640.3	443.8

Trade debtors include advances to suppliers of £6.7 million (last year £12.4 million) against bills of exchange drawn on the Company in respect of merchandise to be delivered between April and September 1990.

Other debtors include loans to employees, the majority of which are connected with house purchases. These include a loan to an officer of the Company, the balance of which amounted to £8,112 at 31 March 1990 (at date of appointment £9,120). Transactions with directors are set out in note 26 on page 74.

Prepayments and accrued income include £50.6 million in respect of the UK pension scheme for 1990/91 (last year £52.1m in respect of 1989/90).

The decrease in the Group's provision for deferred taxation of £1.5 million (last year increase of £1.5 million) is represented by a credit to the profit and loss account of £2.1 million (last year charge of £0.6 million) and exchange movements of £0.6 million (last year nil).

Although creation of a prepayment asset for a pension fund surplus is within SSAP 24's terms, investors need to be aware of its existence and the effect on key financial ratios:

Exhibit 14.3 **Williams Holdings Report and Accounts 1990**

Note 18. DEBTORS

	Group		Company	
	1990	*1989*	*1990*	*1989*
	£000	*£000*	*£000*	*£000*
Trade debtors	90,744	139,624	173	104
Pension fund repayment (note 28)	72,820	76,465	–	–
Amounts owed by subsidiary companies	–	–	224,552	280,064
Other debtors	16,900	18,199	670	1,818
Prepayments and accrued income	6,050	8,697	462	1,033
Corporation tax net recoverable	37,982	30,376	48,800	29,931
	224,586	273,361	274,657	312,950

Note 28. PENSIONS

The group operates pension schemes for the majority of employees in Europe and North America. The larger schemes are of the defined benefit type, and costs are assessed with the advice of a qualified actuary using the projected unit method. For the purposes of assessing excess funding and contributions, the principal actuarial assumptions are based upon an investment return of 10% per annum, pay growth of 7% per annum and dividend growth of 5.5% per annum. These assumptions have been used to standardise the basis of pension costing throughout the group and may differ from those used by trustees of individual schemes. The resulting net excess funding of **£72,820,000** (1989 £76,465,000) has been included in debtors and the profit and loss account credit for £3,338,000 (1989 £1,514,000) is net of interest accrued on the surplus. The change in the net excess funding in the main arises from the Crown Berger disposal.

In Europe, the latest actuarial assessments of the defined benefit schemes were at various dates between 1 January 1988 and 31 August 1988. The total market value of the assets at the valuation dates was £229 million (1989 £229 million). The combined actuarial value of the assets was 164% (1989 164%) of the combined value of accrued benefits, after allowing for expected future increases in earnings. These are no deficiencies on a current funding level basis.

In North America, the total market value of the assets of the major schemes at the last valuation dates was £6.4 million (1989 £5.8 million). The combined actuarial value of the assets was 89% (1989 97%) of the combined value of accrued benefits after allowing for expected future increases in earnings. There are no deficiencies on a current funding level basis. There are also post-retirement welfare benefit plans, which are expensed as benefits become payable. The £2.4 million (1989 £4.1 million) unfunded actuarial liability for these plans as at 31 December 1990 has been recognised in the group balance sheet as a deduction from debtors.

Exhibit 14.4 **Williams Holdings**

CONSOLIDATED BALANCE SHEET at 31 December 1990

	1990 £000	1989 £000
FIXED ASSETS		
Tangible assets	218,095	267,658
Investments	22,721	41
	240,816	267,699
CURRENT ASSETS		
Stocks	122,608	165,234
Debtors	**224,586**	273,361
Investments and other assets for sale	12,280	46,367
Cash	11,385	15,682
	370,859	500,644
CREDITORS: amounts falling due within one year		
Borrowings and finance leases	(10,115)	(71,836)
Other creditors	(254,022)	(300,597)
NET CURRENT ASSETS	106,722	128,211
TOTAL ASSETS LESS CURRENT LIABILITIES	347,538	395,910
CREDITORS: amounts falling due after more than one year		
Borrowings and finance leases	(5,897)	(106,875)
Other creditors	(997)	(1,816)
PROVISIONS FOR LIABILITIES AND CHARGES	(11,246)	(17,731)
	(18,140)	(126,422
NET ASSETS	329,398	269,488
CAPITAL AND RESERVES		
Share capital	145,770	148,846
Reserves	183,628	120,642
TOTAL FUNDS	329,398	269,488

Williams Holdings showed a surplus of £72.8m in 1990 included within debtors of £225m. The inclusion of this surplus has the following effect on Williams' ratios:

Table 14.4   Williams Holdings

	As reported including surplus	Excluding pension surplus
Net Asset Value (£m)	329.4	256.6
Net Asset Value – per share (p)	106.6	83.0
Current Ratio	1.4	1.1
(Current Assets/Current Liabilities)		

Source: Williams Holdings Report and Accounts

Williams' capital gearing debt/equity calculation would also be affected by the inclusion of the pension fund prepayment asset, although this has not been shown as Williams was already lowly geared in 1990 so the effect was small. But even without the effect it is clear that the prepayment asset boosted stated Net Asset Value from 83p to 107p per share – a 28 per cent increase – and flattered the current ratio.

Why is this important to note? Referring back to earlier sections it is important to appreciate that a significant part of Williams' net assets and current assets is: 1) not realisable, unlike other assets, in that it cannot be turned into cash if needed by the company, 2) outside the control of management – it arises from a valuation by independent actuaries and 3) could disappear as readily as it appeared – a change in investment experience or assumptions for the fund, or in Williams' wage bill inflation could turn the surplus into a deficit at the next triennial valuation.

Whether a surplus can be controlled by a company's management is doubtful given the ability of outside agencies and legal changes to alter the position of the fund. Two recent examples are the Social Security Act 1990 and the Barber case. The Social Security Act introduced a mandatory requirement for indexation of pensions in payment by the annual increase in the Retail Price Index up to a maximum of five per cent p.a. The cost of implementing this requirement for past service could be as high as 50 per cent of disclosed pension fund liabilities, which would significantly erode surpluses. Obviously the cost for future service would not be as high.

The Barber judgement refers to a case before the European Court of Justice, which found that providing different pension benefits for men and women can be viewed as discriminatory. Most schemes have in the past provided for retirement by women at age 60 and men at age 65. It is not clear if this applies to past service rights (i.e. those already 'earned' by members) or future service only, but it has been viewed seriously enough for a provision of £67m to be raised prior to the privatisation of National Power to cover the potential liability for past service:

Exhibit 14.5 **National Power and Powergen Main Prospectus**

Note 19. Pension arrangements

The Group participates in the industry-wide scheme, the Electricity Supply Pension Scheme, for the majority of its employees. This scheme is of the defined benefit type with assets invested in separate trustee administered funds.

In the six months ended 30 September 1990, the pension cost relating to the scheme amounted to £20 million and was assessed in accordance with the advice of a qualified actuary using the attained age method. An actuarial valuation of the scheme is carried out every three years by a qualified actuary, who recommends the rates of contribution payable by each group participating in the scheme. In intervening years the actuary reviews the continuing appropriateness of the rates. The latest actuarial assessment was at 31 March 1989. The assumptions which have the most significant effect on the results of the valuation are those relating to the rate of return on investments and the rates of increase in salaries and pensions. It was assumed that, over the long term, the annual rate of return on investments would be 2 per cent higher than the annual increase in salaries and 3.5 per cent higher than the annual increase in pensions.

At the date of the last actuarial valuation, the market value of the assets of the scheme that relate to the Group was £1,270 million and the actuarial value of those assets covered 101 per cent of the benefits that had accrued to members, after allowing for expected future increases in earnings.

In May 1990, the European Court of Justice decided that the practice of providing different pension benefits for men and women is discriminatory in certain circumstances. Whilst it is not yet certain whether the judgement applies to the past service rights of pension scheme members, a provision of £67 million was made at 31 March 1990 to reflect the probability of an additional past service liability arising.

There are also examples of companies reacting to this judgement.

Exhibit 14.6 **The Boots Company Report and Accounts 1991**

22. PENSIONS

The group operates pension schemes throughout the world, most of which are final salary (defined benefit) schemes, and are fully funded.

The principal UK pension scheme is Boots Pension Scheme, the cost for which is determined by Bacon & Woodrow, consulting actuaries. The pension cost for Boots Pension Scheme was £8.7m for the period to 1 November 1989, from which date it was reduced to zero on the availability of the results of the 1 April 1989 valuation. The zero charge arises as a result of amortisation of surplus being recognised over 12 years, the expected average remaining service life of members, after benefit improvements. Recent benefit improvements to the scheme have anticipated the requirements of the Social Security Act 1990 regarding pension increases and the expected requirements for the equal provision for men and women following the judgement of the European Court of Justice in the case of Barber vs GRE Assurance Group. Allowance for these improvements was made in calculating the zero pension cost.

Given that both statute and case law are capable of affecting a company's pension fund liabilities, including case law from a supranational court, it seems that pension fund surpluses should not be ascribed quite the same certainty as some other assets.

But Williams is far from the most extreme example of the effect on a company's balance sheet from the creation of a prepayment asset representing a pension fund surplus.

Babcock's pension fund prepayment asset of £33.3m has the following affect on its ratios:

Table 14.5 Babcock International 1991

	As reported including surplus	Excluding pension surplus
Net Asset Value (£m)	70.2	36.9
Net Asset Value per share (p)	14.9	7.8
Current ratio	1.1	1.0

Of course, neither Williams' nor Babcock's share rating may be particularly dependent upon asset values – Babcock is primarily an engineering contractor, and contractors tend to fund their operations from prepayments and stage payments on contracts rather than from their own capital, but it is still worth noting that nearly half Babcock's asset value results from capitalisation of a pension fund surplus.

Exhibit 14.7 **Babcock International Group Annual Report and Accounts 1991**

Note 14. DEBTORS

	Group		Company	
	1991 £000	1990 £000	1991 £000	1990 £000
Trade debtors	81,066	85,011	–	–
Amounts recoverable on contracts	48,580	32,873	–	–
Amounts owed by subsidiary undertakings	–	–	1,873	2,000
Amounts owed by associated undertakings	105	166	–	–
Prepayments and accrued income	3,218	1,062	–	–
Pension fund surpluses	**33,266**	**34,366**	–	–
Other debtors	12,035	10,019	7,479	213
	178,270	163,497	9,352	2,213

Included in debtors are the following amounts which are due after more than one year:

Trade debtors	7,832	6,392	–	–
Pension fund surpluses	31,366	33,366	–	–
Other debtors	2,951	98	2,828	–
	42,149	39,856	2,828	–

Note 20. PENSION FUNDING

The group operates a number of different pension arrangements throughout the world, according to local requirements of each country. The total pension costs of the group were as follows:

18 July 1989 to 31 March 1990 £000		Year to 31 March 1991 £000	Year to 31 March 1990 £000
8,432	UK schemes	12,335	11,428
410	Overseas schemes	1,877	710
8,842		14,212	12,138

The three major schemes, which cover 56% of all group employees, are in the UK and South Africa and are of the defined benefit type. In each case the scheme is funded by payments to separate trustee administered funds and the pension cost is assessed in accordance with the advice of independent, qualified actuaries. The details of the latest valuation of these schemes are as follows:

	UK schemes		
	Babcock Thorn	Babcock Group	South Africa
Number of employees	5,023	2,850	755
Date of last valuation	31.3.90	31.3.89	31.3.91
Method of valuation	Attained age	Projected unit	Projected unit
Results of last valuation:			
– market value of assets	£113 million	£279 million	£22 million
– level of funding	100%	113%	125%
Principal valuation assumptions:			
– excess of investment returns over earnings increases	1.50%	2.00%	1.00%
– excess of investment returns over pension increases	3.00%–6.00%	6.00%	5.00%
– annual rate of dividend growth	4.50%	4.25%	4.25%

The surpluses in the Babcock Group UK scheme and the South African scheme are carried as a prepayment in the balance sheet at £33.3 million (1990 £34.3 million), and are being corrected in the short term by a suspension of the group's contributions. An actuarial review of the Babcock Group UK scheme, since the last valuation, has reported investment performance which is significantly in excess of that assumed and recent legislation which is likely to lead to increased pension costs in future years, although neither of these can yet be quantified precisely.

Exhibit 14.8   Babcock International Group Balance Sheet at 31 March 1991

	£000	1991 £000	£000	1990 £000
Fixed assets				
Tangible assets		89,942		63,040
Investments		5,245		6,342
		95,187		69,382
Current assets				
Stocks	39,684		40,715	
Debtors	178,270		163,497	
Cash and bank balances	92,609		87,286	
	310,563		291,498	
Creditors:				
Amounts falling due within one year	(274,072)		(248,386)	
Net current assets		36,491		43,112
Total assets less current liabilities		131,678		112,494
Creditors:				
Amounts falling due after more than one year		(19,363)		(14,435)
Provisions for liabilities and charges		(42,096)		(32,168)
Net assets		70,219		65,891
Capital and reserves				
Called upshare capital		47,130		47,130
Share premium account		10,962		10,962
Profit and loss account		7,954		4,831
		66,046		62,923
Minority interests		4,173		2,968
		70,219		65,891

Certain corresponding amounts in respect of the previous period within the categories of stocks, debtors and creditors have been restated to present better the group's long-term contract-related balances.

OTHER PROBLEMS WITH SSAP 24

1) Interest and Investment Income

When an asset arises in a company's balance sheet because the pension fund cost charged in the profit and loss account differs from the regular cost, SSAP 24 permits notional interest earned on this asset to be credited to the profit and loss account. In the case of Ratners, net interest on the surplus of £1.5m is accrued in determining the annual pension cost of £922,000:

Exhibit 14.9 **Ratners Annual Report and Accounts 1991**

Note 6. PROFIT ON ORDINARY ACTIVITIES BEFORE TAXATION

	1991 £000	1990 £000
Profit on ordinary activities before taxation is stated after charging:		
Share incentive scheme	250	500
Depreciation and amortisation	29,127	22,209
Depreciation on finance lease assets	–	79
Pension costs	**922**	**663**
Auditors' remuneration	418	371
Operating lease rentals:		
Plant and machinery	88	145
Property	80,945	63,554

Note 14. DEBTORS

	1991 Group £000	Company £000	1990 Group £000
Trade debtors	74,006	13,616	38,165
Amounts owed by subsidiary companies	–	63,599	–
Other debtors	11,546	3,084	11,368
Corporation tax recoverable	22,645	6,685	3,459
Prepayments and accrued income	16,125	5,853	10,244
Debtors due within one year	124,322	92,837	63,236
Pension fund prepayment	**16,702**	–	17,012
	141,024	92,837	80,248

Note 23. PENSION FUND COSTS

The Group operates a number of pension schemes in the UK. The majority of the schemes are of the defined benefit type. The assets of the schemes are held in separate trustee administered funds. Contributions to the schemes, which are assessed in accordance with the advice of an independent qualified actuary using the projected unit method of valuation, are charged to the profit and loss account so as to spread the cost of pensions over employees' working lives with the Group.

The most recent actuarial valuation of the main scheme, the H Samuel group pension scheme, was at 6 April 1988. The principal actuarial assumptions adopted in the valuation were that, over the long term, the investment rate of return would be 9% per annum and this would exceed future pensionable earnings increases by 1.5% per annum and increases to present and future pensions in payment by 4% per annum. It was also assumed that dividend increases on the equity portfolio would average 4.5% per annum. The actuarial value of the assets was sufficient to cover 148% of the benefits that had accrued to members at the valuation date, after allowing for expected future increases in earnings and pensions. The market value of the scheme's assets at 6 April 1988 was £49.6 million.

The surplus relating to the Group's UK pension arrangements at 2 February 1991 of £16,702,000 has been reflected in the balance sheet. The movement in the surplus of £310,000 is stated in the net interest of £1,456,000 accrued during the year on the prepayment, and is included in the Group charge of £922,000 in note 6.

This is intended to reflect the return which this prepayment asset is earning as part of the pension fund. Once again, this represents the investment return which is building up on that part of the pension fund representing the surplus – but it is not interest or investment income available in cash to the company.

A practice which can also lead to potentially misleading financial ratios is crediting the surplus when it is spread over the average life of scheme members against interest payable since this can produce a potentially dangerous misconception about the level of interest cover:

Exhibit 14.10 **Courtaulds Textiles Report and Accounts 1990**

Note 2. INTEREST PAYABLE NET OF INTEREST INCOME	1990 £m	1989 £m
Interest element of finance lease payments	0.9	1.0
Interest on bank and other borrowings fully repayable within five years	17.1	15.9
Interest payable on long-term borrowings	0.4	0.7
Interest payable	18.4	17.6
Inerest receivable	(6.6)	(5.2)
	11.8	12.4

The interest charges for 1989 are proforma, details are provided in note 22

Note 20. PENSION COMMITMENTS

The Group participates in a number of pension schemes around the world. The major schemes are of the defined benefit type with assets held in separate trustee administered funds.

Before demerger from Courtaulds plc, Courtaulds Textiles participated in the Courtaulds plc UK Pension Scheme. This scheme was reviewed by consulting actuaries, as at 31 March 1990, using the projected unit method, to determine the proportion of the Fund to be transferred to the Courtaulds Textiles Pension Scheme. The principal actuarial assumptions were that over the long term, the annual rate of return in investments would be 1.5% higher than the annual increase in total pensionable remuneration and 4.5% higher than the annual increase in present and future pension payments. The actuarial value of the assets was sufficient to cover 169% of the benefits which had accrued to members, after allowing for benefit improvements announced in 1989 and expected future increases in pensionable remuneration. On the recommendation of the actuaries no company contributions have been made to the scheme since 1 January 1990 and this will continue for a period of five years, subject to the next actuarial valuation expected to be as at 31 March 1992.

Exhibit 14.10 (contd.) **Courtaulds Textiles Report and Accounts 1990-91**

SSAP 24 requires the Fund to be valued on a reasonable best estimate basis rather than with the very prudent assumptions used by the Trustees in funding the Scheme, which are referred to above. In accounting for pension costs under SSAP 24, the principal actuarial assumptions were that the rate of return on investments would be 2% higher than the annual increase in total pensionable remuneration and 5% higher than the increase in pensions. On this basis the Fund of the new Courtaulds Textiles Pension Scheme was calculated to have an excess of assets over liabilities of £95m and the actuarial value of the assets was sufficient to cover 193% of the benefits which had accrued to members. The market value of the assets at 31 March 1990 was £171.3m. The surplus is being spread over the 11 year average remaining service lives of the current UK employees. The effect of this is a net pension credit to profit before taxation in 1990 of £4.4m (1989 £3.0m) which represents the benefit, in excess of the regular pension cost, arising from the pension fund surplus. In 1990 this credit has reduced interest payable by £4.4m (1989 £4.0m) with a nil (1989 £1.0m) charge to operating profit. As noted above, no company contributions have been paid since 1 January 1990; during 1989 the Company paid pension contributions of £5.0m. The effect of introducing SSAP 24 in 1989 was a benefit of £8.0m.

The actuarial value of the assets of pension schemes abroad approximates to the benefits which have accrued to members, after allowing for expected future increases in pensionable remuneration.

Note 2. Interest payable net of investment income

	1991 £m	1990 £m
Interest element of finance lease payments	3.2	3.0
Interest on bank and other borrowings fully repayable within five years	39.2	51.8
Interest payable on long-term borrowings	1.7	5.7
Interest payable	44.1	60.5
Other interest receivable	(39.2)	(52.5)
	4.9	8.0

Note 27. Pensions commitments

In accounting for pension costs under SSAP 24, the rate of return on investments has been assumed to be 2% higher than the increase in pensionable remuneration and 5% higher in pensions. On this basis the actuarial value of the assets was sufficient to cover 138% of the benefits that have accrued to members after allowing for benefit improvements announced in 1989 and expected future increases in pensionable remuneration. The share of this actuarial surplus is being spread over the 12 year average remaining service life of current Courtaulds employees.

The actuarial value of the assets of pension schemes abroad approximated to the benefits that had accrued to members, after allowing for expected future increases in pensionable remuneration. The Group's US subsidiary undertakings have no significant health and medical plans providing post-retirement benefits.

The pension credit arising from the application of SSAP 24 increased operating profit by £4.3m (1990 £13.8m) and reduced interest payable net of investment income by £14.4m (1990 £15.5m). A prepayment of £42.0m (1990 £23.3m) is included in debtors representing the excess of the pension credit to the profit and loss account over the amounts funded and excludes credits transferred to Courtaulds Textiles.

Table 14.6 Effect on interest cover

| | Year to 31 December 1990 | |
	Courtaulds	Courtaulds Textiles
Reported		
Operating profit	187.4	51.7
Net interest payable	(4.9)	(11.8)
Interest cover (times)	38.2	4.4
less Pension Fund credit		
Net interest payable less pension credit	(19.3)	(16.2)
Revised interest cover	9.7	3.2

In neither case would the Courtauld companies interest cover slip to a dangerous level if the pension fund credit is deducted. But it is as well to perform the calculation – bankers are only interested in whether their interest charge is covered by actual cash received, and an amortised pension fund surplus certainly does not fall into this category. In the case of Courtaulds plc the interest earned by the fund surplus has been included in interest income.

15

CURRENCY MISMATCHING

Business? It's quite simple. It's other people's money
Alexander Dumas fils

WHY MISMATCH?

The advantages of currency mismatching lie in the boost which it can provide to profits, often at the expense of the balance sheet. To take an example, during the first half of 1991, UK interest rates were significantly higher than US dollar rates: average sterling LIBOR was 12.8 per cent versus an average US Prime Rate of 8.9 per cent. Borrowing funds in US dollars and depositing in sterling would on a simple basis seem to produce a positive interest margin of nearly four per cent which could be credited to profit and loss account.

Simple, isn't it? At the time of writing, this interest rate differential has opened further, with short-term US rates at 3.5 per cent versus 10 per cent in the UK.

CURRENCY TRANSLATION

But interest rate differentials between currencies exist for reasons other than to provide companies with net interest income from mismatching borrowings in one currency and deposits in another. They are intended to reflect differing inflationary expectations in the economies concerned and to express differences in the expected movements between currencies – so that potentially hard currencies carry lower interest rates, and softer currencies which are expected to depreciate on the exchanges carry higher rates to compensate for this. Consequently, the interest gain from currency mismatching can be more than wiped out by exchange losses.

Take the example of a company which at the end of 1990 decided to take advantage of the difference in UK and US rates by borrowing $193m, translating this into £100m at the ruling exchange rate of £/$1.93. How would it have fared in the first half of 1990?

Table 15.1 Mismatching: gain on the savings, lose on the roundabouts

	As at 31.12.90 £/$1.93	As at 30.6.91 £/$1.62
Deposit		£100m £100m = $162m
Borrowing	$193 = £100m	$193m

The company should have earned a four per cent interest differential for six months, so that the effect of net interest income on its profit and loss account will be:

Interest income £100 @ 12.8% for 6 months =	£6.4
Interest payable $193m @ 8.9% translated @ $1.78*	£4.8
	£1.6m

*Average exchange rate

Not bad, £1.6m of net interest income for a company which had no cash of its own on deposit. The problems set in when the company goes to unwind the transaction and repay the borrowing from the deposit. Because the dollar has strengthened (there were only 1.62 dollars to the pound by 30 June versus 1.93 dollars six months earlier), the £100m deposit would translate into only $162m but the company has to repay $193m borrowing leaving it with a capital loss of $31m. Not such a good deal!

Of course the company may need to repay the loan at that point, but still translation of the balance sheet assets and liabilities including the deposit and loan will produce the same unrealised loss which is taken to reserves. But herein lies the rub: the net interest income goes through the profit and loss account, but the exchange loss is taken through the balance sheet in accordance with SSAP 20, as shown by BP's accounting policy notes and movements in reserve (see Exhibit 15.1).

Exhibit 15.1   **BP Annual Report and Accounts 1989**

Foreign Currencies

On consolidation, assets and liabilities of subsidiary companies are translated into sterling at closing rates of exchange. Income and source and application of funds statements are translated at average rates of exchange.

Exchange differences resulting from the translation at closing rates of net investments in subsidiary and related companies together with differences between income statements translated at average rates and at closing rates, are dealt with in reserves.

Exchange gains and losses arising on long-term foreign currency borrowings used to finance the group's foreign currency investments are also dealt with in reserves.

All other exchange gains and losses on settlement or translation at closing rates of exchange of monetary assets and liabilities are included in the determination of profit for the year.

Note 28. Reserves

Group reserves include undistributable reserves attributable to:

	£ million	
	1989	1988
Parent company	10	10
Subsidiary companies	2,019	1,626
Related companies	392	414
	2,421	2,050

Included in group reserves are amounts retained by overseas subsidiary and related companies which may be liable to taxation if distributed.

Exchange adjustments for the year include unrealised losses of £15 million (£5 million profit) on long-term foreign currency borrowings.

As a consolidated income statement is presented a separate income statement for the parent company is not required. The profit for the year of the group dealt with by the parent company and the reserves of the parent company are as follows:

	£ million	
	1989	1988
At 1 January	2,601	2,234
1987 final dividend to former Britoil shareholders	–	(9)
Shares purchased from KIO	(2,423)	–
Profit for the year	2,105	1,199
Distribution to shareholders	(795)	(823)
At 31 December	1,488	2,601

POLLY PECK INTERNATIONAL

Polly Peck reported a net interest credit in its accounts to December 1989 despite having begun and ended the year with significant net debt. The figures are shown in the table below:

Table 15.2   Polly Peck – Net borrowings/interest

£m	1989 Beginning	End	Average*	Interest	Implied rate %
Borrowings	377	1106	742	(55.6)	7.5
Bank deposits	124	300	212	68.1	32.1
Net debt	253	806	530	12.5	2.3

*This is the average of the year start and end debt figure, not necessarily the true average debt/cash for the year.

As the balance sheet only shows net debt at start of the year and the end and the group did not give an average net debt figure, we have estimated this by taking the average of these two figures. Polly Peck acquired Del Monte for £557m in December 1989 of which £280m was funded by a rights issue. If the net cash cost of Del Monte is taken off the year end debt figure of £530m, the implied interest rate on the debt of about £200m increases to around 9.2 per cent.

The difference between the interest rate achieved on deposits and that paid on debt can be caused by a number of factors:

1. The group had fixed low rate debt while cash was in deposits at variable rates which were currently high. In Polly Peck's case, the 1989 balance sheet showed guaranteed bonds (Swiss Francs and Dm) of £217.5m at rates between 5.75 and 6.25 per cent.

2. Significant swings in cash flow during the year which can result in the year end figure being substantially different from the average. Supermarkets, for instance, tend to have a regular cash inflow from customers, but pay their suppliers on a particular day of the month. Some businesses have a highly seasonal pattern, such as most retailers with a strong Christmas trade which gives them plenty of cash in a 31 December balance sheet.

3. A difference in the international spread of debt and deposits where deposits are made in soft currencies at high interest rates, but borrowings are made in hard currencies at low rates.

The last factor is potentially very dangerous as, in the long run, soft currencies tend to depreciate against hard currencies resulting in currency losses. In Polly Peck's case, the 1989 accounts stated that a £10.5m provision was made in the Profit and Loss Account in respect of unrealised currency losses. In addition, the group made adjustments direct to reserves of £44.7m in 1989 and £170.3m in 1988 in respect of 'exchange variances on net investments overseas' – this item may have been affected by the international debt/cash position.

MATCHING CURRENCY AND ASSET LIABILITIES

There are circumstances in which no overall loss to a company, realised or unrealised, occurs – primarily where foreign currency borrowings are used to acquire assets in the same currency. In this case the appreciation in the value of the currency borrowing against sterling is equalled and cancelled out by the appreciation in the sterling value of the currency assets acquired.

But this does not mean to say that all companies which finance overseas assets with currency borrowings are exempt from the balance sheet effect of currency mismatching. Often a company concerned will use overseas operations to take on larger debt in the currency than its local assets in order to gain mismatch advantages. Probably one of the best examples recently is Beazer, which had US dollar borrowings representing 96 per cent of net debt based upon its Koppers acquisition. The adverse exchange movements on this debt in the first half of 1991 was one of the reasons which forced Beazer firstly to propose floating its European operations, and then into accepting a rescue takeover bid from Hanson.

THE 'DOUBLE WAMMY' – GEARING AND GOODWILL

For a company which has mismatched currency in an effort to secure an interest income advantage an adverse currency movement can have knock-on effects. It not only produces a debit to reserves equal to the increase in the loan value in excess of the deposit value, but since the value of the loan has risen and reserves have fallen, gearing will rise.

A further interesting effect is where borrowing in a foreign currency such as US dollars is used to finance a local acquisition which involves significant goodwill. If this is capitalised rather than written off to reserves, appreciation of the foreign currency produces a higher sterling value for the debt *and* the goodwill which reduces *tangible* net asset value, so raising capital gearing again.

Movement of Reckitt & Colman's gearing computation (net borrowings to tangible net asset value) were affected by many factors, but the currency translation effect inflated borrowings in sterling and also increased goodwill in foreign acquisitions:

Table 15.3   Reckitt & Colman

| | Year to end December | |
| | 1988 | 1989 |
	£m	£m
Shareholders' funds	519.9	591.6
Minorities	9.6	9.1
	529.5	600.7
Intangibles	(135.2)	(163.5)
	394.3	437.2
Loans and overdrafts net of cash	45.6	68.3
Gearing	11.6	15.6

Exhibit 15.2   **Reckitt & Colman Annual Report 1988**

Note 13. INTANGIBLE ASSETS

	Trade marks £m
Cost:	
At beginning of year	135.21
Additions during the year	11.18
Exchange adjustments	17.10
At 30 December 1989	163.49

Reckitt & Colman Annual Report 1989

Note 13. INTANGIBLE ASSETS

	Trade marks £m
Cost:	
At beginning of year	126.84
Additions during the year	8.00
Disposals during the year	(2.84)
Exchange adjustments	3.21
At 31 December 1988	35.21

Obviously, gearing was not troublesome at 16 per cent, but part of the deterioration is induced by currency movements, including those relating to goodwill carried on the balance sheet.

HOW TO SPOT IT

How can an investor detect when a company may be mismatching currencies? The simplest method is to undertake the calculation shown above for Polly Peck – compare net interest income/expense with average deposits/ borrowings shown in the balance sheet. If this produces an implied rate of interest which looks peculiar then the company *may* be mismatching (see, for example, Exhibit 15.3).

Exhibit 15.3 **Fisons Annual Report and Accounts 1989**

Note 3. Finance income

	1989 £m	1988 £m
Interest payable in respect of loans and overdrafts:		
Wholly repayable within five years	(16.1)	(12.1)
Other	(3.2)	(2.3)
Interest receivable	21.3	17.4
Exchange gains	–	5.4
	2.0	8.4

Note 15. Creditors – amounts falling due after one year

	1989 £m	1988 £m
Notes:		
(1) The aggregate amount repayable by instalments any of which are repayable beyond five years	2.3	2.0
(2) Details of loans other than from banks are:		
Repayable beyond five years		
Parent Company		
5⅞% Unsecured Loan Stock 2004-09	4.3	4.3
Fisons Finance Netherlands BV		
5¼% Guaranteed Convertible Bonds 2001: US$31,690,000		
(1988 – US$46,545,000)	21.9	25.7
	26.2	30.0
Repayable between two and five years:		
Fisons Finance Netherlands BV		
9% Guaranteed Notes 1994		
Kuwaiti Dinars 15,000,000	31.9	–

Included in prepayments is an amount of £0.6m (1988 £0.9m) in respect of bond issue expenses not yet written off.

£m	Net borrowings 1988	1989
6½% Debenture stock	6.2	–
Banks loans and overdrafts	50.0	33.7
Loans other than from banks	116.0	138.3
Finance leases	1.5	1.4
Loans and leases – amount due after one year	44.6	131.0
	218.3	304.4
Less: cash	151.8	189.9
Net borrowing	66.5	114.5

Average net borrowing £90.5m ((£66.5m + £114.5m) divided by 2).

Fisons' net interest income of £2m squares strangely with simple average net debt for the year of £90.5m. Obviously, this calculation carries all the normal caveats about using the balance sheets which only give a snapshot of opening and closing debt, but the implication of earning net interest *income* whilst carrying net *debt* poses some interesting questions, which may be partly answered by the glimpse of Fison's financing techniques given by Note 15 in the Accounts which shows borrowing in foreign currencies including exotica such as Kuwaiti dinars.

There are other reasons why this calculation can produce apparently impossible rates of interest. Nonetheless, this simple method raises questions which should have been sufficient to steer a wary investor clear of Polly Peck.

As a 'screen' this is an effective method of raising questions about currency mismatching:

Table 15.4   1991 Net interest paid
$$\overline{\text{Average net debt}^\star}$$

Company	Interest** paid £m	Interest received £m	Net interest £m	Average net debt £m	Implied† interest rate %
Grand Met	(305)	107	(198)	2748	(7.2)
Fisons	(361)	26	(10)	144	(6.9)
Hazlewood Foods	(16.6)	9.5	(7.1)	103.1	(6.9)
RTZ	(158)	108	(50)	739	(6.8)
Reed Intl	(65.3)	39.2	(26.1)	402.8	(6.5)
Blue Circle	(60.0)	37.0	(23.0)	373.5	(6.2)
Christian Salvesen	(3.0)	–	(3.0)	48.5	(6.2)
Ocean Group	(13.0)	10.0	(3.0)	54.5	(5.5)
Scottish & Newcastle	(36.0)	22.5	(13.5)	290.8	(4.6)
Shell T&T	(678)	630	(48)	1092.5	(4.4)
Smith & Nephew	(35)	32	(3)	75.5	(4.0)
British Gas	(224)	125	(99)	2997.5	(3.3)
Hays	(0.6)	–	(0.6)	21.5	(2.8)
Courtaulds	(44)	39	(5)	221.5	(2.3)
Vickers	(12.4)	12.0	(0.4)	22.0	(1.8)
Redland	(50)	51	1	238.2	0.4
Lasmo	(113)	116	3	800.5	0.4
Bowater	(57)	58	1	196	0.5
Storehouse	(15.7)	16.2	0.5	20.0	2.5
Marks & Spencer	(34.2)	47.5	13.3	351.5	3.8
Cables & Wireless	(53.0)	59.2	6.2	81.5	7.6
Johnson Matthey	–	3.4	3.4	40.0	8.5

Notes: *Average of year opening and year end debt. Convertible loan stocks treated as debt.
   **Including interest capitalised.
   †A cut off rate of approximately 7.0% implied rate paid has been taken.
   ( )Implies interest rate paid.

Table 15.5   1991 Net interest income
Average net cash

Company	Interest paid £m	Interest received £m	Net interest income £m	Average net cash £m	Implied* interest rate %
Northumbrian Water	(7.0)	21.0	14.0	89.0	15.7
Glaxo	(75.0)	254.0	179.0	1124.5	15.9
Kwik Save	–	3.0	3.0	18.5	16.2
British Steel	(23.0)	104.0	81.0	496.5	16.3
Albert Fisher	(15.0)	29.0	14.0	83.0	16.9
Smiths Industries	–	18.0	18.0	96.5	18.7
Severn Trent	(4.8)	56.3	51.5	276.0	18.7
Welsh Water	(2.5)	35.7	33.2	171.0	19.4
Christies	–	7.9	7.9	36.1	21.9
ABF	(45.7)	134.7	89.0	385.0	23.1
Bowthorpe	(3.0)	5.0	2.0	7.7	26.0
Rugby Group	(8.0)	13.0	4.0	15.0	26.6
Wellcome	(20.0)	28.0	8.0	27.5	29.1
Tompkins	(18.5)	27.2	8.7	27.0	32.2
GEC	(55.0)	159.0	104.0	286.0	36.4
Hanson	(751.0)	929	178	454.5	39.2
North West Water	(18.1)	46.0	27.9	70.0	39.9
Southern Water	(2.4)	9.0	6.6	15.5	42.6
TI Group	(15.0)	23.0	8.0	6.5	123.0

Note: *A minimum cut off rate of 15% has been taken.

The companies in Table 15.4 were all apparently paying 7 per cent or less on their average net debt, or actually receiving net interest income despite having net debt. Those in Table 15.5 have an apparently high return on net cash (above 15 per cent p.a.). In both cases this evidence is enough to raise questions. The significant presence in the list of a number of companies with large US operations (Hanson, Grand Met, Reckitt & Colman, Smith & Nephew), or dollar-denominated businesses (oil companies, pharmaceutical companies, Rolls Royce) is noteworthy, whereas the retailers, for example, are probably accounted for by seasonality of cash flows.

Exhibit 15.4 **Hanson – 1991 Accounts**

Consolidated Balance Sheet

at 30 September 1991	1991 £m	1990 £m
Fixed assets		
Tangible	6,199	5,057
Investments	429	704
	6,628	5,751
Current assets		
Stocks	992	984
Debtors	1,192	1,126
Listed investments	6	5
Cash at bank	**7,765**	6,878
	9,955	8,993
Creditors: due within one year		
Debenture loans	1,725	20
Bank loans and overdrafts	810	2,041
Trade creditors	507	501
Other creditors	1,332	1,309
Dividend	377	355
	4,751	4,226
Net current assets	5,204	4,767
Total assets less current liabilities	11,832	10,528
Creditors: due after one year		
Convertible loans	500	–
Debenture loans	579	420
Bank loans	3,801	3,828
	4,880	4,258
Provisions for liabilities	3,627	3,436
Capital and reserves		
Called up share capital	1,202	1,199
Share premium account	1,153	1,155
Revaluation reserve	163	163
Profit and loss account	807	317
	3,325	2,834
	11,832	10,528

15.4 (contd.) Hanson – 1991 Accounts (contd.)

Assets and Liabilities by Currency
at 30 September 1991

	Sterling £m	US Dollars £m	Total £m
Fixed assets			
Tangible	1,387	4,812	6,199
Investments	269	160	429
	1,656	4,972	6,628
Current assets			
Stocks	439	553	992
Debtors	587	605	1,192
Listed investments	1	5	6
Cash at bank	7,532	233	7,765
	8,559	1,396	9,955
Creditors: due within one year			
Debenture loans	358	1,367	1,725
Bank loans and overdrafts	639	171	810
Creditors and taxation	1,128	711	1,839
Dividend	377	–	377
	2,502	2,249	4,751
Net current assets	6,057	(853)	5,204
Total assets less current liabilities	7,713	4,119	11,832
Creditors: due after one year			
Convertible loans	500	–	500
Debenture loans	199	380	579
Bank loans	2,765	1,036	3,801
	3,464	1,416	4,880
Provisions for liabilities	710	2,917	3,627
	4,174	4,333	8,507
Shareholders' funds	3,539	**(214)**	3,325
	7,713	4,119	11,832

An easier guide to potential currency mismatching is simply to look for substantial *gross* short-term borrowings and deposits in the balance sheet even if the net debt or cash position is low. Although holding companies sometimes run borrowings in some subsidiaries and credit balances in others for reasons of local management autonomy, or because the balances are in different countries and provide a currency hedge by financing local assets, it is not always logical treasury management for a group to operate indefinitely with substantial borrowings and credit balances since it is then in essence borrowing its own funds back from the banking system with which they are deposited, and paying a margin for the privilege of doing so.

Hanson, which is high in the table (15.5) of net interest income/expense to average net debt shows: 1) cash at bank £7765m, and borrowings of £7415m at the end of 1991 (Exhibit 15.4), and 2) in the breakdown of assets and liabilities by currency, the US dollar assets and liabilities have net borrowings of £2721m and negative shareholders' funds of £214m to suggest overborrowing in this currency, and sterling operations show net cash of £3.71bn. And of course this is a snapshot so that the mismatching may be greater between balance sheet dates. Net interest income of £188m in 1991 represented 14 per cent of pre-tax profits.

Exhibit 15.5 **Hanson Report and Accounts 1991**

Note 3. Costs and overheads less other income

	1991 £m	1990 £m
Changes in stocks of finished goods and work in progress	86	1
Raw materials and consumables	3,689	3,572
Employment costs (note 4)	1,216	1,107
Depreciation	210	172
Depreciation of finance leases	6	8
Profit on disposal of fixed assets	(22)	(11)
Other operating charges	1,565	1,349
Share of profit on associated undertakings	(20)	(43)
Profit on disposal of natural resources assets	(170)	(101)
Interest receivable	**(929)**	**(824)**
Interest payable (note 5)	**741**	**638**
	6,372	**5,868**

Other operating charges include hire of computers, plant and machinery £71m (£73m), remuneration of auditors £4m (£4m) and expenditure on research and development of £34m (£34m). Income from listed investments amounted to £12m (£32m).

Part IV

16

MAJOR COMPANIES ACCOUNTING
HEALTH CHECK

The list below shows the UK's major quoted companies together with a
checklist (or 'the blob guide' as it has become known) showing which of the
accounting/financing techniques described in the previous section they are
using. Unfortunately no objective and consistent method of ranking the
companies' use of each technique could be found so it is necessary to consult
their Accounts, using the methods illustrated in Parts II and III –
Accounting techniques. But this does not appear to have rendered the
checklist any less useful. Since the original list appeared in the UBS Phillips
& Drew publication at the beginning of 1991, the share price performance of
shares with a high 'blob' count (out of a potential 11 categories on the
original checklist) has been startling:

Table 16.1 Share price performance of high scorers in *Accounting for Growth* checklist

	Number of 'blobs'	Relative share price performance in 1991%
LEP	5	−90
Maxwell	7	−100 (suspended)
ASDA	5	−66
British Aerospace	7	−44
Burton	7	−43
Ultramar	5	−16
Blue Circle	5	−10
Cable & Wireless	6	−5
Granada	5	−4
Sears	5	−4
Laporte	5	+6
Dixons	6	+40
Next	5	+234

The current updated checklist covers over 200 of the largest quoted companies in the UK measured by their market capitalisation at the beginning of 1992. However, inclusion in the list for any particular technique does *not* automatically mean that the company is indulging in creative accounting – reference needs to be made to the individual company accounts to reach a final conclusion.

Technique	Definition
Pre-Acquisition Write Down	Creation and use of provisions including those to cover fair value adjustments in respect of acquisitions
Disposals 1) Above the line	1) Disposal profits on sale of assets or businesses taken 'above the line'.
2) Deconsolidation	2) Deconsolidation of subsidiaries and treatment of associates as trade investments in anticipation of sale.
Deferred Consideration	Earn-out commitments on acquisitions.
Extraordinary & Exceptional items	As defined by SSAP6. Unfortunately no attempt can be easily made in a single table to rank the relative significance of these items.
Off balance sheet finance	Use of quasi-subsidiaries, sale and repurchase of assets and joint ventures.
Contingent liabilities	Liabilities outside the 'normal course of business' e.g. bonds, guarantees of subsidiary overdrafts etc.
Capitalisation of costs	Capitalisation of interest and other costs e.g. R&D
Brand Accounting	Capitalisation of brands in the balance sheet
Changes in depreciation policy	Changes in depreciation life or method.
Convertibles with puts & AMPS	Outstanding issues of convertibles with premium put options or variable rate preferred stocks.
Pension fund surplus	A pension fund surplus which is used to reduce the regular annual charge or to create a prepayment asset.
Currency mismatching	Mismatches between the currency of borrowing and deposits.

Identifying a company as a user of a particular technique still requires some subjective judgements – for example an entry in the Extraordinary and Exceptional items column should not be taken as implying anything detrimental (nor should an entry in any column *per se*) since the inclusion of a gain in Extraordinary items may represent a more conservative treatment than the average, for example. The issue of significance is also difficult to resolve – when is the use of a technique significant in the context of a company's operations?

KEY TO ACCOUNTING HEALTH CHECK TABLE

1. Pre-Acquisition Write Down
2. Disposals 1) Above the line
    2) Deconsolidation
3. Deferred Consideration
4. Extraordinary & Exceptional items
5. Off balance sheet finance
6. Contingent liabilities
7. Capitalisation of costs
8. Brand Accounting
9. Changes in depreciation policy
10. Convertibles with puts & AMPS
11. Pension fund surplus
12. Currency mismatching

FT ACTUARIES SECTOR
Company

	1	2	3	4	5	6	7	8	9	10	11	12
BUILDING MATERIALS												
Blue Circle				•							•	•
BPB												
CRH												
Hepworth											•	
Marley	•			•	•						•	
Meyer International	•	•		•							•	
Pilkington				•		•					•	
Redland			•							•		•
RMC				•		•					•	
Steetley				•								

	1	2	3	4	5	6	7	8	9	10	11	12
Tarmac				●						●		
Rugby Group												
Wolseley	●					●					●	
CONTRACTING & CONSTRUCTION												
AMEC				●	●							
George Wimpey		●		●							●	
Taylor Woodrow		●		●	●		●					
ELECTRICALS												
BICC	●	●	●	●	●		●					
Delta	●		●									
ELECTRONICS												
Electrocomponents		●	●	●			●					
General Electric	●			●		●						●
Racal Electronics	●			●		●						●
ENGINEERING – AEROSPACE												
British Aerospace	●	●		●	●	●	●				●	
Dowty Group	●	●		●			●				●	
Rolls-Royce	●			●			●				●	
Smiths Industries	●			●							●	
ENGINEERING – GENERAL												
APV	●	●		●							●	
IMI	●			●							●	
Siebe	●	●		●						●	●	●
TI Group	●	●									●	
Vickers	●	●	●	●		●					●	
METALS & METAL FORMING												
British Steel	●											
Glynwed	●	●	●	●							●	
Johnson Matthey	●	●		●		●					●	
MOTORS												
BBA				●							●	
GKN		●		●	●		●				●	
Lucas Industries		●		●			●				●	
T&N	●			●		●					●	

	1	2	3	4	5	6	7	8	9	10	11	12
OTHER INDUSTRIAL MATERIALS												
BTR	●	●		●		●						
Charter Consolidated				●		●						
Cookson Group	●		●	●		●						
ECC Group	●			●		●	●			●		
Morgan Crucible	●	●		●		●						
RTZ	●	●		●		●	●					●
Tompkins	●					●						
William Holdings	●	●		●		●					●	
BREWERIES & DISTILLERS												
Allied-Lyons	●	●		●		●	●				●	
Bass	●	●		●		●	●				●	
Grand Metropolitan	●	●		●	●	●	●	●			●	●
Guinness	●		●	●				●			●	
Highland Distilleries									●			
Scottish & Newcastle		●		●					●		●	●
Whitbread	●	●		●		●	●					●
FOOD MANUFACTURING												
AB Foods		●		●							●	
Booker	●	●		●							●	
Cadbury Schweppes	●					●		●			●	
Christian Salvesen				●					●			
Dalgety	●	●		●		●					●	
Hazlewood Foods	●			●					●			
Hillsdown Holdings	●	●		●					●	●		
Northern Foods	●											
Ranks Hovis		●		●				●		●		
Tate & Lyle	●								●	●		
Unigate	●	●		●							●	
Unilever	●	●		●		●						
United Biscuits	●	●		●				●		●		
FOOD RETAILING												
Albert Fisher	●	●	●	●		●				●		●
Argyll Group		●					●			●		
ASDA Group				●			●			●		

	1	2	3	4	5	6	7	8	9	10	11	12
Kwik Save Group	●	●										
Sainsbury J		●					●					
Tesco		●					●					
HEALTH & HOUSEHOLD												
Fisons				●							●	●
Glaxo Holdings												
London International				●				●		●	●	
Medeva												●
Reckitt & Colman								●			●	●
Smith & Nephew				●						●	●	●
SmithKline Beecham											●	●
Wellcome											●	
HOTELS & LEISURE												
Forte		●			●		●					
Granada Group	●	●		●		●	●		●		●	
Ladbroke	●	●		●	●		●	●	●	●		
Queens Moat Houses	●		●	●			●					●
Rank Organisation	●	●		●	●		●			●		●
Thorn EMI	●	●	●	●			●			●		
MEDIA												
Carlton Communications				●			●					
Daily Mail Trust		●		●			●	●		●		
EMAP			●	●				●				
Mirror Group News		●		●				●			●	
Pearson			●	●		●					●	●
Reed International	●		●	●				●			●	●
Reuters Holdings							●		●			
United Newspapers		●	●	●				●		●	●	
PACKAGING, PAPER & PRINTING												
Argjo Wiggins Appleton	●			●		●	●					
Bowater	●			●		●	●					
Bunzl				●		●					●	
CMB Packaging		●		●		●						
De La Rue		●		●		●	●					

	1	2	3	4	5	6	7	8	9	10	11	12
STORES												
Argos				●								
Boots	●	●		●						●		
Burton Group		●		●			●			●		
Dixons		●					●				●	
Great Universal		●										
Kingfisher		●		●			●				●	
Marks & Spencer				●								●
Ratners	●	●		●		●	●			●	●	
Sears		●		●			●				●	
Storehouse				●						●	●	
WH Smith	●			●		●					●	
TEXTILES												
Baird, William			●	●								
Coats Viyella	●	●		●						●	●	
Courtaulds Textiles				●							●	●
Dawson International				●								
BUSINESS SERVICES												
ADT		●								●		
BET	●			●						●		
Hays PLC												
Inchcape												
Rentokil												
CHEMICALS												
Allied Colliods						●	●					
BOC Group		●	●	●		●	●				●	
British Vita							●					
Courtaulds	●					●					●	
ICI	●	●		●		●						
Laporte	●		●	●	●	●					●	
CONGLOMERATES												
Hanson	●	●		●		●			●			●
Harrisons & Crosfield		●		●		●						
Lonrho	●	●		●		●	●				●	
Trafalgar House	●	●	●	●	●	●	●				●	

	1	2	3	4	5	6	7	8	9	10	11	12
SHIPPING & TRANSPORT												
AB Ports		●		●	●		●				●	
BAA							●		●			
British Airways		●			●				●		●	
Eurotunnel							●		●			
NFC		●		●							●	
Ocean Group		●		●							●	
P&O	●				●		●					
Tiphook	●	●		●		●						
Transport Development				●								
ELECTRICITY												
East Midlands Elect				●								
Eastern Electricity				●								
London Electricity				●								
Manweb				●								
Midlands Electricity				●								
National Power				●								
Nothern Electric				●								
Norweb				●								
Powergen				●								
Scottish Hydro Elect				●								
Scottish Power				●								
Seeboard				●								
South Wales Elect				●								
South Western Elect				●								
Southern Electric				●								
Yorkshire Electric				●								
TELEPHONE NETWORKS												
British Telecom	●				●		●				●	
Cable & Wireless	●				●		●		●			
Securicor Security Services			●			●	●					
Vodafone			●	●								
WATER												
Anglian Water		●	●				●		●		●	
Northumbrian Water		●	●				●		●		●	

	1	2	3	4	5	6	7	8	9	10	11	12
NorthWest Water		●					●		●		●	
Severn Trent		●		●			●		●		●	
South West Water		●	●				●		●		●	
Southern Water		●		●			●		●		●	
Thames Water		●					●		●		●	
Welsh Water		●	●				●		●		●	
Wessex Water		●					●		●		●	
Yorkshire Water		●					●		●		●	
MISCELLANEOUS												
BAT Industries		●		●								
Rothmans												
OILS & GAS												
British Gas							●					
British Petroleum		●		●			●					
Burmah Castrol	●		●	●		●						
Calor Group				●								
Enterprise Oil		●					●					●
Lasmo		●					●					●
Shell T&T							●					
BANKS												
Abbey National											●	
Bank of Scotland											●	
Barclays		●									●	
Lloyds Bank											●	
Midland Bank			●								●	
National Westminster			●								●	
Royal Bank of Scotland											●	
Standard Chartered											●	
TSB		●									●	
INSURANCE – LIFE												
Brittanic Assurance												
Legal & General		●	●	●								
Lloyds Abbey Life						●						
London & Manchester			●	●		●						
Prudential Corp		●										
Refuge Group				●		●						

	1	2	3	4	5	6	7	8	9	10	11	12
INSURANCE – COMPOSITE												
Commercial Union						●						
General Accident												
Guardian Royal												
Royal Insurance												
Sun Alliance												
INSURANCE – BROKERS												
Sedgwick				●								
Willis Corroon	●	●		●								
MERCHANT BANKS												
Hambros												
Kleinwort Benson				●								
Schroders												
SG Warburg												
PROPERTY												
British Land							●					
Great Portland Estates						●						
Hammerson Props				●		●	●					
Land Securities										●		
MEPC							●					
Slough Estates				●			●			●		

SURVIVAL TECHNIQUES IN THE ACCOUNTING JUNGLE

Cutting through the jungle with a golden track
N. Vachel Lindsay, 1879–1931, referring to the Congo River

ACCOUNTING FOR GROWTH

We have seen how such 'profitable' enterprises as Coloroll, British & Commonwealth, Polly Peck and Maxwell Communications can go bust taking your money with them if you invest in the shares, and we have looked at a dozen techniques by which companies can massage their accounts to produce growth in the 'magic' Earnings per Share number, and make the balance sheet appear less geared than it actually is.

But imagine that you are faced with your first set of Annual Report and Accounts. How in practice should you go about avoiding the pitfalls of creative accounting?

1. Read the Accounts Backwards

Most public company Annual Report and Accounts are prepared by experts: finance directors, accountants and public relations consultants and the order in which the information appears within them is no accident. True, some of the statutory information required by the Companies Acts and the Stock Exchange listing requirements appears in a particular order, but aside from this the Annual Report and Accounts is set out so as to impress you – the potential or actual investor.

If you start at the front you will encounter the often glossy cover, the Chairman's Statement, the Review of Operations and the Director's Report not to mention the series of glossy photographs before you get to the all important Accounts, the Notes on which are often last of all. Avoid all this 'gloss'. When did you last see a Chairman's Statement that described the performance of the business in less than glowing terms?

Starting from the back of the Annual Report and Accounts and reading forwards is often more instructive. There is a lot of useful information at the back of an Annual Report. Often it contains the resolutions for the Annual General Meeting, which can provide some interesting insights into the powers the Directors want in order to allot shares etc. The last Note to the Accounts is often the Contingent Liabilities Note – a potential killer, as we have seen. Are there any guarantees to businesses sold etc?

Work towards the front through items such as the Notes, if any, on Pension Funding, noting whether the surplus has given rise to any credits in the profit and loss account or prepayment assets in the balance sheet.

Perform calculations as you go: if there is a pension fund prepayment asset, what proportion of Net Asset Value does it represent, what proportion of profits results from amortising a pension fund surplus? If pension fund credits are credited to interest and investment income what would interest cover be if they were excluded?

The Note on Interest payable or received should also be carefully scrutinised. Has interest been capitalised? If so, what would interest cover (operating profit divided by net interest paid) be if interest capitalised is included in interest payable? And so on, searching for each of the creative accounting techniques which we have described.

By the time you reach the Profit and Loss Account and Consolidated Balance Sheet, you should already have cross-referenced to them several times to make calculations which will give you a clearer picture of the company's financial health than the Chairman's Statement will.

2. Read the Accounting Policies – and compare

The Accounting Policies Note which is usually placed just before or after the Profit and Loss Account and Balance Sheet is vital and must be read carefully. If there are any changes in accounting policy it is not sufficient in assessing the company as a potential investment just to ensure that the new policies fall within Generally Accepted Accounting Practice (GAAP). This is assured if the Auditors Report is 'clean' i.e. does not contain any qualifications, but simply states that the accounts present a 'true and fair view'. All of the techniques described in Parts II and III on Accounting Techniques fall within UK GAAP and would not have led to a qualified Auditors Report. In any case, you cannot rely upon the Auditors – you are on your own. In a 'true and fair' statement view the key word is 'view' – it is just someone's opinion.

Any change in Accounting Policy must be considered in the light of the effect which it will have on profits. If it increases the profits by, for example, cutting the depreciation charge, is this reflected in the market rating of the shares compared with similar companies? What is the practice of competitors?

Nor is it sufficient just to read the current year's Accounting Policies Note – read the previous year's since some changes, such as depreciation lives, do not count as a change in Accounting Policy and do not need to be disclosed. But they can be detected by comparing policies in one year with another.

3. 'Screen' the Accounts using various 'filters'

Accounts provide many figures which can be used to screen a company's performance so as to raise questions which can be directed to the company's management, or a stockbroking research analyst, or simply to avoid investment in the company if you don't like the answer. Probably the best example of a screen from Part III on Accounting Techniques is comparing net interest income/expense with the average net cash/debt derived by averaging the figures in the company's opening and closing balance sheets. This test has many pitfalls – seasonal cash flows can make a nonsense of the calculation. *But it is only intended to pose questions, not to provide answers.* And it is worth questioning how a company such as Hanson derives net income of £178m on average net cash in 1990-91 Accounts of £454.5m (see Table 15.5). The answer may lie in seasonal cash flows, or the impact of acquisitions, but the question is a valid one.

Another simple screen which is provided for us by an outside agency is the tax charge. The Inland Revenue has a great deal more information about a business than an investor can obtain from the Annual Report and Accounts. Taxable profits are different from accounting profits so that the tax computation is aiming for a different sort of answer, but where the tax rate varies significantly from the statutory rate, the Inland Revenue is in effect stating that it has a different view of the taxable profit of that business to the profit shown in the Accounts.

A good example is the LEP sale of the St Pauls's Vista property to an off-balance sheet vehicle (see Chapter 8). Although a profit was booked on the sale, the Inland Revenue regarded this as an intra-group transaction i.e. the property never left the Lep Group for tax purposes, so that the profit realised was not taxable. And indeed this was the reality – the property has now been taken back on balance sheet and Lep is in difficulties.

For this reason a low tax charge is another good 'screen' to use for provoking the question: why does the revenue view the company's profits as lower than the figure in the accounts?

Table 17.1 Low Tax Charge Companies★

	%
Stakis	(6.5)
Costain	(3.6)
Storehouse	10.0
Queens Moat House	16.9
CRH	18.7
Cable & Wireless	19.7
Rolls-Royce	20.5
Courtaulds	21.5
Hillsdown	21.8
Booker	22.1
Whitbread	24.4
Hanson	24.4
NFC	24.7
Polly Peck	14.0

★ last available accounts

25 per cent is taken as a cut-off for a 'low' tax charge given a current UK Corporation Tax rate of 33 per cent. As ever, there are plenty of innocent explanations for a low tax charge: timing differences due to capital allowances on capital expenditure exceeding the depreciation charge may reduce taxable profits below the reported pre-tax profits. A company may have substantial overseas operations in areas where the tax rate is below that in the UK, such as Cable & Wireless's Hong Kong Telecom subsidiary. But there are some interesting casualties of the recession in the above list, such as Polly Peck, which could have been avoided on this simple basis alone.

Another useful 'screen' for changes in depreciation lives and policies is to check the percentage of assets which are depreciated each year over a series of years to see if there is any change in the proportion of assets being depreciated. MTM provides a good example:

Table 17.2 MTM – Years to 31 December

	1986 £m	1987 £m	1988 £m	1989 £m	1990 £m
Tangible gross assets	17130	13653	23168	51407	131259
(of which freehold property)	(2592)	(4438)	(3496)	(6764)	(27573)
Depreciation charge for tangible assets	1057	1617	1145	1943	3377
(of which freehold property)	(51)	(55)	(36)	(52)	(162)
Depreciation/Gross Assets %	6.2	11.8	4.9	3.8	2.6
(excluding property)	(6.9)	(17.0)	(5.6)	(4.2)	(3.1)

Apart from 1987, when the figures were distorted by an acquisition, MTM's depreciation as a proportion of gross assets shows a continuous downhill trend to the point where in 1990, depreciation charged was 2½ per cent of gross assets i.e. depreciating the assets at this rate would take an average of 40 years to write down to their residual value on a straight line basis.

Depreciation of tangible assets was not the direct cause of MTM's problems, which were actually in the area of capitalising development costs to create intangible assets, but a review of the company's depreciation policies such as the calculation above would certainly have revealed an interesting trend in the accounting treatment of fixed assets and the capitalisation of costs should also have been picked up as another creative technique.

The result for MTM shareholders of the auditors' final disagreement over accounting for development costs has been the resignation of the Chairman and Chief Executive and a catastrophic fall in the share price:

Figure 17.1 MTM Share price chart 1991-92

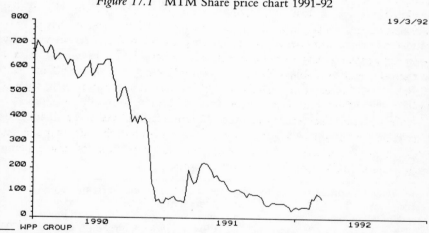

19/3/92

HIGH 712.00 8/1/90, LOW 31.00 23/12/91, LAST 80.00 16/3/92
Source : Datastream

4. *Watch out for transfers between balance sheet and profit and loss account*

Because of the attention given to Earnings per Share by the investment community, companies are apt to pursue techniques which enhance reported profits at the expense of the balance sheet, all of which are potentially dangerous.

Examples include the switching of assets between categories prior to a write-down, especially from development properties to investment properties, so that the write-down is taken direct to reserves such as the Ladbroke example. Currency mismatching can produce a net interest income boost to profits at the expense of currency translation debits taken direct into reserves.

Ladbroke's 1990 Accounts have already been mentioned in Chapter 7 on Extraordinary and Exceptional items. The Accounts show a transfer of £67.9m from dealing properties, which need to be stated at the *lower* of cost or realisable value with any write-downs taken though the profit and loss account (as it would for any type of stock held by a business), to investment properties for which any write-down is taken direct to reserves:

Exhibit 17.1 **Ladbroke Group – 1990 Annual Report and Accounts**

Note 12. Investment Properties

Held for development, third party renting and capital appreciation	Total	Freehold cost or valuation	Long leashold cost or valuation	Short leashold valuation
	£m	£m	£m	£m
At 31st December 1989	757.7	695.8	61.6	0.3
Exchange rate movements	(58.0)	(56.2)	(1.8)	–
Net additions (c)	118.7	93.9	25.0	(0.2)
Revaluation surplus	(105.9)	(97.8)	(8.1)	–
At 31st December 1990	**712.5**	**635.7**	**76.7**	**0.1**
Representing assets stated at:				
Valuation (a)	646.3	575.4	70.8	0.1
Cost (b)	66.2	60.3	5.9	–
At 31st December 1990	**712.5**	**635.7**	**76.7**	**0.1**

(a) Valued by property division directors or a professional executive of the company, following consultation with external professional advisers, or by independent external valuers, on an open market basis. The property division directors were J Anderson, AP Grant, H Harris or PG Martin FRICS and the executive was JD Broughton ARICS.

(b) At cost in the course of development, the current value being estimated by the directors to be not less than the book amount.

(c) Net additions comprise additions of £205.1m including a transfer of £67.9m from dealing properties, freehold disposals of £86.2m and short leasehold disposals of £0.2m.

(d) The amount of investment properties determined according to the historical cost accounting rules, as at 31st December 1990, is £670.7m (1989 £566.2m) which includes capitalised interest of £113.6m (1989 £88.4m).

(e) Investment properties are accounted for in accordance with SSAP19. Where the requirements of SSAP19 conflict with those of the Companies Act 1985, SSAP19 has been followed as the directors believe this is necessary in order to present a true and fair view.

There was also a revaluation write-down on investment properties of £105.9m in 1990. Whilst it is not possible to show that this write-down was on the same properties as those transferred, to the extent that it was, the write-down missed the profit and loss account and was taken through Reserves in the balance sheet.

Similarly, currency mismatching can produce a net interest income boost to profits at the expense of currency translation debits taken direct into reserves.

The use of acquisition provisions is another example of generating profits at the expense of the balance sheet. The provisions are taken direct to the balance sheet in writing down the value of assets acquired and providing for reorganisation expenses, so that when those expenses arise they are debited against the provision in the balance sheet rather than in the profit and loss account.

A good way to check this is to use the ten year record in the Annual Report and Accounts to calculate the movement in Net Asset Value (NAV) per share by dividing the Shareholders' Funds by the number of shares in issue each year. If NAV is static or moves down whilst profits forge ahead, some of these techniques are probably in use. Look out for them.

The ASB has provided some considerable assistance here. In its Exposure Draft on the structure of Financial Statements it proposes a new statement of total recognised gains and losses. This new statement will show all movements in reserves and therefore the change in the net worth of the company.

As an example, Fisons shows EPS of 26.3p for 1990 whereas the new statement of recognised gains and losses shows recognised *losses* of 21p per share before dividends. Most of the difference is from goodwill written off to reserves, plus currency translation losses and asset revaluations producing deficits:

Table 17.3 Fisons 1990

	1990 £m
Attributable Profit	169.0
Goodwill written off to Reserves	(284.4)
Intangible assets written off	(118.9)
Accounts realised on properties	(0.3)
Exchange losses	(8.1)
Total recognised gains and losses	(142.7)
Dividends	(51.5)
Net decrease in shareholders' funds	(194.2)
Total recognised loss per share	(21.0p)

Obviously the goodwill write-off of £284.4m on Fison's acquisition of VG Instruments is the main reason for the difference between Earnings per share of 26.3p and a total loss per share of 21p, but even if this were excluded, the total gain per share would be only 9.8p.

5. Cash is King!

It must be obvious by now that profits can be manufactured by creative accounting, but creating cash is impossible. Moreover, *profits are someone's opinion (or 'true and fair view') whereas cash is a fact*. And cash is more important than profits – it pays the dividends, and lack of sufficient cash is the reason businesses fail, not lack of profits, which takes us back to the Brentford Nylons example with which this book began.

But computing cash flow is not always straightforward. A simple calculation frequently used is attributable profit net of tax, minorities and dividends, but with depreciation added back since this is a non-cash debit to profit and loss account. This is a woefully inadequate measure of cash flow since it ignores all kinds of items. True depreciation is a non-cash debit and should be added back to profits in the computation of cash flow, but capital expenditure should be subtracted since it is the expenditure of cash on fixed assets and therefore the mirror image of depreciation. Working capital is also ignored. If working capital requirements rise faster than profits there will be a cash outflow from a business contrary to the simple indication given by rising profits in this calculation. Conversely a business may show falling profits but may still generate an inflow of cash if it is able to reduce working capital requirements faster than profits are falling. For these reasons any measure of cash flow based simply on profit plus depreciation is virtually useless.

Nor was the Sources and Applications of Funds statement required under SSAP 10 of much help. These funds flow statements usually show movements in net borrowings, which is of little help in tracing events such as Polly Peck's mismatching of hard currency bonds and Turkish lire bank deposits. Most companies do not show provisions made under Sources of Funds and the use of provisions under Applications of Funds. When a provision is made it is just that – an estimate of how much to set aside against future expenditure – it does not provide funds for the expenditure of cash when the costs actually arise. But when a balance sheet provision is utilised to cover an expense – even an expense which was foreseen when the provision was raised – it does not prevent the expense being paid out in cash. Consequently, provisions utilised should be shown as an Application of Funds since their use has inflated the profit figure shown in the Sources of Funds and overstated the cash generated as part of profits.

Exhibit 17.2 Bass Cash Flow Statement

	1991 £m	1991 £m	1990 £m	1990 £m
For the year ended 30 September 1991				
Net cash inflow from operating activities		**676**		**782**
Returns on investments and servicing of finance				
Interest paid	(151)		(182)	
Dividends paid to shareholders	(115)		(101)	
Interest received	44		44	
Dividends paid to minority shareholders	(3)		(2)	
Net cash outflow from returns on investments and servicing of finance		(225)		(241)
Taxation				
UK corporation tax paid	(144)		(231)	
Overseas tax paid	(1)		–	
Tax paid		(145)		(231)
Investing activities				
Subsidiary undertakings acquired* (note 11)	(139)		(65)	
Tangible fixed assets acquired	(334)		(366)	
Trade loans advanced and other investments acquired	(63)		(119)	
Short-term investments acquired	(143)		–	
Short-term investments sold	40		–	
Trade loans repaid and other investments sold	130		66	
Tangible fixed assets sold	193		465	
Subsidiary undertakings sold*	45		12	
Net cash outflow from investing activities		(271)		(7)
Net cash inflow before financing		35		303
Financing				
Issue of ordinary share capital	596		16	
Rights issue costs	(12)		–	
Net borrowings**	1277		924	
Borrowings repaid	(1183)		(1162)	
Net cash inflow/(outflow) from financing		678		(722)
Increase/(decrease) in cash and cash equivalents		713		(419)

* Net of cash and cash equivalents
** The net movements of Commercial Paper issued and repaid is included in new borrowings

(i) Reconciliation of trading profit to net cash inflow from operating activities

	1991 £m	1992 £m
Trading profit	616	673
Depreciation	172	150
Surplus on disposal of fixed assets	(49)	(42)
Decrease in stocks	17	35
(Increase)/decrease in debtors	(90)	38
Increase/(decrease) in creditors	46	(54)
Amortisation of and provisions against investments	7	1
Exceptional items	55	–
Provisions expended:		
DTI compliance	(56)	(11)
Acquisition	(42)	(8)
	676	782

But help is at hand in the form of the new Cash Flow statement required by Financial Reporting Standard (FRS) 1. This is much more comprehensive, including all inflows and outflows of cash and cash equivalents, including provisions, and separating cash flow into 1) operating activities, 2) investing activities – including capital expenditure, acquisitions and disposals, and 3) financing activities – including share issues, new borrowing and repayments. By this means it is possible to see the company's cash flow from operations, how much it is generating or expending on capital expenditure, acquisitions and disposals.

Going through the example reproduced from the Bass 1991 Annual Report shows immediately how misleading profit plus depreciation can be as a rough-and-ready measure of cash flow. There are so many other items affecting cash flow just within the operating activities. In 1991, Bass Trading Profit plus depreciation toalled £788m.

But there were also changes in working capital: stocks were decreased by £17m which is a cash inflow (they were sold), but debtors also increased by £90m which is a cash outflow (presumably some of the stock was sold to customers who have yet to pay and so have become debtors), but Bass also increased its creditors by £46m – taking goods from them which it has yet to pay for. The net effect of changes in Bass's working capital on cash flow was therefore:

£m	Cash Inflow (Outflow)
Decrease in stocks	17
Increase in debtors	(90)
Increase in creditors	46
Cash (Outflow)	(27)

Overall therefore Bass working capital movements led to a cash outflow of £27m in 1991.

Provisions expended (or utilised) cost Bass £98m in 1991 and represent a cash outflow. Presumably cash was paid to meet the cost of the DTI compliance (the 'Beer Orders' requiring the untying of certain pubs) and acquisitions for which the provisions had previously been raised. Therefore utilising these provisions from the balance sheet 'removed' a cash outflow which would otherwise have cropped up in the profit and loss account, albeit quite legitimately, but the apparent cash flow from profits is still affected.

Exhibit 17.3 Bass Annual Report 1991

Note 18. Provisions for liabilities and charges

	Reorganisation provisions £m	DTI Compliance provisions £m	Group Acquisition provisions £m	Deferred tax £m	Total £m	Company deferred tax £m
At 30 September 1990	–	97	86	2	185	(31)
Acquisitions (note 11)	–	–	18	(4)	14	–
Acquisition adjustments (note 23)	–	–	52	(22)	30	–
Companies sold	–	–	–	(6)	(6)	–
Profit and loss account	54	9	–	36	99	2
Expenditure	–	(56)	(43)	–	(99)	–
ACT transfers to corporation tax	–	–	–	28	28	28
ACT recoverable	–	–	–	(37)	(37)	(37)
Exchange and other adjustments	–	–	7	1	8	–
Transfer to debtors (note 14)	–	–	–	2	2	38
	54	50	120	–	224	–

The potential tax liability arising principally from accelerated capital allowances for which provision has not been made and which is not expected to crystallise at 30 September 1991 amounts to £202 million (1990 £172 million).

Adjustments to provisional fair value estimates made at 30 September 1990 in respect of Holiday Corporation, acquired on 7 February 1990, have been made in the light of more accurate information now available. These adjustments, less related deferred tax, have been treated as an adjustment to goodwill and eliminated against distributable reserves.

Investing activities include capital expenditure in fixed assets (£334m) and disposal of fixed assets (£193m) to give 'net' capital expenditure of £141m. In summary, Bass Cash Flow Statement for 1990–91 looks like this:

Table 17.4   Bass 1990–91

Year to 30 September	Cash Flow Statement 1990 £m	1991 £m
Inflow from operations	782	676
Outflow from financing	(241)	(225)
Taxation	(231)	(145)
Net	310	306
Investing activities including capex	(7)	(271)
Net cash flow before financing	303	35
Financing	(722)	678
Increase/(Decrease) in cash	(419)	713

Bass's operating cash flows fell in 1991, as did profits, but the movement after taking into account investing activities including capital expenditure is much more dramatic, with cash flow before financing falling from £303m to £35m. This readily explains the reasons for the rights issue which raised £569m and gave a positive inflow from financing and contrasts with the simple cash flow estimate of £788m from Trading Profit plus depreciation. Calculating operating cash flow per share and cash flow after financing will also give a different picture of a company from its profits, particularly over the longer term when some businesses appear to have strong profits generation but continually have rights issues such as the banks. It also makes it easier to work out per share figures to compare with earnings:

Table 17.5   Bass cash flow and earnings per share

Year to 30 September	1990	1991
Cashflow from operations	£310m	£306m
Weighted average shares in issue (m)	359m	397m
Cash from operations per share	86.4p	77.1p
Cashflow from operations and capex	£409m	£165m
Per share	**113.9p**	**41.6p**
Earnings per share	107.0p	92.7p

The much lower cash flow from operations after deducting capital expenditure on fixed assets in 1991 compared with 1990 is immediately evident whereas with cash flow from operations and after capex of 41.6p in 1991 versus 113.9p in 1990s. But this is not discernible from the trend in earnings per share, which were 92.7p in 1991 – only 13 per cent down on 1990.

Making these calculations of cash flow per share will be easier with the new Cash Flow Statements and will reveal more about a company's cash generation including movements in working capital, provisions and capital expenditure to give a comparison with earnings so that it is possible to see over time whether a company's reported earnings are being converted into cash.

It is also interesting to note that the Accounting Health Check ('blob guide') appears to give some indication of where a company is not generating sufficient cash. Table 17.6 shows companies at the top of the blob guide in the original *Accounting for Growth* publication which needed to raise cash through rights issues in 1991:

Table 17.6   Rights issues in 1991

	Amount raised £m	Capitalisation* £m	%
Burton	161	490	33
British Aerospace	432	1180	37
Granada	163	770	21
ASDA	357	890	40
Total	1113	3330	33

*capitalisation after rights issue

A comparison with Table 16.1 is instinctive!

And remember – Cash is a fact and Cash is King!

6. If in doubt, don't invest

It should by now be evident that you as an investor are on your own. None of the techniques which have been described are in breach of UK GAAP so that the auditors will not warn you about them. Investors who believe that the way to prevent their losses from corporate collapses and creative accountancy piling up is to tighten standards of auditing would appear to be sadly mistaken given the evidence to date!

How about help from the analytical community? Most stockbroking analysis would seem to have focused upon the 'magic' Earnings per Share figure and ignored the wider issues of creative accounting used to generate that figure. Once again, historical precedent at least would suggest that in general investors will not get much help from this quarter.

The investor must perform his own analysis. Much of the analysis I have described in this book will lead to questions rather than answers. These questions should be posed directly to the company. Institutional investors have many opportunities for this, but small investors can ask questions at the AGM, write to the Finance Director or ask their stockbroker the questions. If the answer is not satisfactory in terms of allaying the investor's concern that creative accounting is in use then the best solution is not to invest. This is your only effective sanction, not writing to your M.P. about standards of auditing.

Professional punters in other areas of investment have long realised this is their only solution:

> Not to bet until the odds be considered fair, reasonable or completely in the favour of the backer is an advantage which must never be surrendered. The bookmaker has to lay odds all the time for each and every race – but the backer can choose if and when to bet. (*Braddocks Complete Guide to Horse Race Selection and Betting.*)

APPENDIX I

COLOROLL

Coloroll came to the market in mid-1985 with sales of £37m and profits of a little under £4m. Over the next four years growth was dramatic, with sales reaching £565m and profits £56m. However, in mid-1990 administrative receivers were appointed. The shares, originally issued at 135p, soared to 385p in 1987 but were suspended at under 10p just five years after flotation. At its peak the group's stock market value was £424m.

The main cause of failure was the over-rapid expansion of the group, particularly the massive acquisition programme. As the table shows, in just four years and starting with a market value of £37m, Coloroll acquired companies costing over £400m (around £270m net of disposals).

Coloroll: The main deals

Date	Deals	Value £m	Sales turnover £m
1985 April	Flotation	37	37
1986 June	Acq of Worley (wallcoverings)	2	4
June	Acq of Biltons (ceramics)	5	9
July	Acq of Alexander Drew (fabric printing)	3	4
July	Rights Issue	13	–
August	Acq of Staffordshire Potteries	14	25
1987 Feb	Acq of Fogarty (home furnishings)	31	40
March	Acq of Cartwright & Edwards (ceramics)	3	6
March	Acq of Wallpapers Inc	10	23
March	Acq of Wallbridge Carpets	9	18
May	Acq of Crown House (glass & tableware)	87	207
June	Sale of Packaging Div	6	n/a
Sept	Sale of Crown House Engineering	36	150
1988 June	Acq of John Crowther Group	215	358
Aug	Sale Crowther Cloth & clothing	93	159
Sept	Acq of William Barrett (furniture)	15	24
Sept	Acq of Texture Tex (carpet yarns)	4	13
1989 Jan	Acq of Burlington (wall coverings)	7	11

It is likely that the main problems came with the £215m purchase of Crowther in June 1988. However, even before this there were signs that acquisition and merger accounting techniques were being exploited by Coloroll to enhance profits to the detriment of its balance sheet.

Goodwill and acquisition provisions

Coloroll wasted no time in issuing its newly quoted shares. In the year to March 1987 the accounts show that £78m (largely in shares) was spent on acquisitions and £57m was written off as goodwill. The largest of these deals was Fogarty which cost £31m. Fogarty's published accounts showed net assets in excess of £12m, suggesting goodwill of £19m. However, Coloroll's accounts show goodwill relating to this purchase of £26m. For Staffordshire Potteries, which cost £14m with published net assets of £7m, Coloroll wrote-off £11m as goodwill.

These differences are likely to be explained by heavy provisioning on acquisition. Indeed the 1987 Coloroll accounts show for the first time £11m 'other provisions' arising on acquisitions, none of which was charged to the P&L. £2m of these were utilised during the year. By comparison, Coloroll's reported profits were £10m. These 'other provisions' were subsequently (in 1988 accounts) identified as 'costs of reorganisation of subsidiaries acquired and business segments closures'.

In 1988 goodwill write-offs and acquisition provisions were again a prominent and worrying feature of the accounts. £77m goodwill was written off reserves of which £69m related to the purchase of Crown House. This was a surprisingly large sum given that the original cost of Crown House of some £84–90m was reduced by around to £35m by disposals of some of Crown's businesses during the year (i.e. the cost net of disposals was only some £50m). Coloroll made £22m 'other provisions' on acquisition: only £1m was charged to the P&L and £22m was utilised during 1987/88. By comparison declared profits were £26m. The following table shows these provisions' movements over the two years. While the exact nature of these is unknown, it is likely that at least some of the costs and writedowns would have been charged to the P&L under a more conservative accounting régime.

Coloroll: Provisions & profits

£m	Other provisions+	Declared pre-tax profit
Opening March 1986	Nil	
Arising on acquisition	11	
Charged to P&L	–	
Utilised in year	–2	10
Opening March 1987	9	
Arising on acquisition	22	
Charged to P&L	1	
Utilised in year	–22	26
Opening March 1988	10	

+ Provisions 'comprise costs of reorganisation of subsidiaries acquired & business segments closures'.

The John Crowther acquisition

Although there were doubts over the quality of profits in 1986/87 and 1987/88, the balance sheet at March 1988 was still relatively healthy with debt/equity of some 20 per cent (34 per cent if finance leases were included). Trading conditions were in general buoyant, acquisitions had been made largely with shares (the price of which soared in 1986 and early 1987) and substantial disposals had been made for cash. However, the Crowther deal, partly because of its sheer size, had a marked impact on the balance sheet. The main problems arose from the following:

- The history of Crowther

- Continued exploitation of acquisition accounting

- Consolidation of acquired debt

- Off balance sheet debt and guarantees

An unstable acquisition?

Crowther was itself the product of mass acquisition with some 25 deals taking sales from £7m to £350m over the four years to 1987. It is likely that neither management structures nor reporting controls had been fully established in all the subsidiaries – or at least tested in a recession. The size in turnover terms and the cost (£215m) were large in relation to Coloroll and posed significant risks in the event of a downturn in trading.

Further use of acquisition accounting

The accounting treatment of the acquisition of Crowther was remarkable. Crowther was acquired for £215m in cash and shares but by the time the assets appeared to Coloroll's accounts a total of £224m – more than the original cost – had been written off as goodwill.

The documents issued in April 1988 indicate that immediately before acquisition, Crowther had net assets of around £70m, suggesting in normal circumstances goodwill of £215m minus £70m = £145m. However, by the time Coloroll's next set of accounts was published (for the year to March 1989) the total cost of the deal had effectively been raised by £75m to £290m through 'incidental' costs, stock and debtor write offs, redundancy and reorganisation costs and other items. These costs and adjustments are shown in the table:

Coloroll: Crowther acquisition cost adjustments

	£m
Original cost	215
'Incidental' costs	11
Stock & debtor write downs	10
Redundancy & relocation costs	20
Loss on disposals	10
Other write downs & payments	24
	290
Net assets of Crowther	66
Goodwill written off	224

Write downs of stock and debtors in this way easily enhance reported profits. Redundancy and relocation costs should normally be charged to pre-tax profits as exceptional items, rather than extraordinary items, where they relate to businesses which are ongoing.

In 1989 Coloroll established provisions of £56m relating to acquisitions, most of which were part of the £75m 'extra' goodwill noted above. Of these £52m were utilised during 1988/89 thereby effectively reducing costs which would otherwise be seen in the P&L account (probably as exceptional or extraordinary items). This compares with the total group's pre-tax profits of just £56m that Coloroll declared for the year.

Assumed debt

As a result of its acquisitions over 1988/89, of which Crowther was the largest, not only did Coloroll pay out cash of £39m but it also had to assume debt of some £96m. The need to assume this level of debt was far from obvious for Coloroll – or Crowther – shareholders at the time of the proposed deal in the first half of 1988.

£96m was considerably larger than the £26m debt shown for Crowther alone in the statement of proforma combined net assets in Coloroll's listing particulars dated April 1988. This used Crowther's December 1987 balance sheet. By March 1988 notes in the same document suggested that Crowther's debt had risen to £67m and seasonal influences would have played a significant part in this increase. However, it is likely that the 1987 Crowther accounts included two recent acquisitions, McCalls (US) and Homfray Carpets (Australia) as 'investments' for balance sheet purposes thereby not consolidating debt of £35m. Crowther, through an ingenious structure, held only 50 per cent of the common stock and units of these two very highly geared companies (hence qualifying for non-consolidation of balance sheets) but did have 100 per cent of the 'partially participating preferred' stock and units for P&L purposes.

All this and its implications might have been divined by the earnest reader of the listing particulars, but it would not have been easy. The 60-page complex document included not only information on Coloroll and Crowther, but was further complicated by information on Crown House, acquired by Coloroll almost a year earlier.

The status of McCalls under Coloroll was never clearly indicated – it filed for voluntary protection under Chapter 11 of the US bankruptcy code in December 1988. There was however no recourse to Coloroll in this case. Homfray Carpets (Australia) almost certainly became a true subsidiary of Coloroll but was to cause further unease later on.

The effect of the consolidation of the acquired debt, together with the goodwill write-offs and the cash element of the extra costs of Crowther acquisition, had a marked impact on Coloroll's balance sheet. Despite disposals with a beneficial cash effect of some £90m during 1988/89, Coloroll's net debt soared to £85m and debt/equity at March 1989 rose to around 100 per cent. (This includes finance leases as debt but excludes convertible preference from equity and debt.) Trading conditions would become progressively more difficult over the next year: Coloroll was ill equipped in balance sheet terms to cope with this.

Contingent liabilities & guarantees

In the second half of 1988, in an attempt to reduce borrowings, Coloroll agreed to dispose of the cloth and clothing divisions of Crowther. The divisions were sold to a management buy-out for a total £93m. The consideration was a complex mixture of £53m cash, £21m of debt being sold on by Coloroll, the issue to Coloroll as vendor of £8m nominal redeemable preference shares, £10m of subordinated loan notes and £1m of shares of the MBO equity called the Response Group.

The redeemable preference shares and the loan notes carried a yield of 12 per cent, although this was payable by way of a premium on redemption. Coloroll sold on these securities to realise cash of approximately £18m, but the sale was 'subject to recourse to Coloroll in certain circumstances'. This liability appeared as a note in the March 1989 Coloroll accounts as a contingent liability, totalling by then £22m.

When the MBO got into financial difficulties in January 1990 the recourse conditions were triggered and Coloroll was obliged to make good the losses to the debt holders. A press release in January 1990 indicated that this particular exposure had risen further to £26m.

Another disposal which did not isolate Coloroll from the underlying debt was that of Homfray Carpets (Australia). This sale, again to a management buy-out, was approved in late April 1989 but was reflected as complete in Coloroll's March 1989 balance sheet. The A$42m deal was structured in a complex but by now familiar way: A$19m repayment of intercompany debt, the issue to the vendors of a A$7m loan note and only A$16m of direct cash. Additionally, a 26 per cent stake in the MBO was retained by Coloroll.

Moreoever, Coloroll had guaranteed 'borrowings and other bank facilities' of Homfray with a note in the 1989 accounts indicating that these were equivalent to £15m at the time.

Coloroll also guaranteed borrowings of over £4m of a purchaser of land from the group during 1988/89.

Window dressing

By March 1989 the group's gearing had increased substantially, but the formal consolidated balance sheet was presented in such a way as to suggest on initial reading that debt was around £67m and capital plus reserves was around £102m. This was a high – but not excessive – ratio.

Further detailed examination of the notes to the accounts showed that this debt figure excluded short-term debentures (issued for payment of an acquisition) and finance leases, both of which unlike bank loans had not been separated out of 'other creditors'. Moreover, bills of exchange had increased from almost nil to £6m. Capital included for the first time 'guaranteed redeemable convertible cumulative preference stock' repayable in 1997 at a premium if not converted. Moreover, equity reserves had been boosted by an asset revaluation in the year – something that would have normally been carried out during 'fair value' adjustments on consolidation of acquisitions.

The balance sheet for March 1989 could be redrafted to suggest debt/equity over 100 per cent before any consideration of contingent liabilities as shown in the table.

Coloroll: Restatement of debt & equity for March 1989

	Debt £m		Capital & reserves £m
Net bank debt as shown	67	Capital & reserves as shown	102
Add debentures	7	Less convertible pref	18
Add finance leases	11	Less revaluation surplus	9
Total debt	*85		75

*Excludes contingent liabilities, mainly debt guarantees, of £40m.

The final stage

The crystallisation of the contingent liabilities associated with some of the disposals was probably one of the key events leading to the downfall of the entire group.

Trading conditions deteriorated rapidly through 1989. The interim results showed profit halved and a trading statement in January 1990 warned of second half profits materially below the first. Debt had risen to around £150m by January 1990 with the group bearing the costs of restructuring and integration of acquisitions – and much higher working capital. The contingent liabilities – mainly associated with the guarantees of loans to the Response Group and Homfray Carpets (Australia) – were now £40m. The appointment of a receiver at the Response Group and deteriorating conditions in Australia meant that total potential debt was thus heading towards £200m, while the true equity base after further write-offs was probably lower than the £80m in March 1989 accounts. (These accounts were showing Coloroll's residual holdings in Response and Homfray at £9m.)

The preference dividend was passed in March 1990.

Refinancing proposals were discussed through May but were unsuccessful. Administrative receivers were appointed in the following month.

APPENDIX II

BRITISH & COMMONWEALTH

British & Commonwealth has yet to be finally buried, largely because the mess at Atlantic Computers, which brought the group down in May 1990, has still to be sorted out. When it is, B&Cs various classes of stockholders will be left with nothing or very little to show for their investment. Although Atlantic was the final nail in the coffin, and is often referred to as a 'deal too far', B&C would have been a pretty sickly mess, even without the massive liability bequeathed by Atlantic.

At its peak in 1987 B&C was capitalised at just under £2bn and was the 46th largest FTSE–100 stock.

Personality cult

The personality of John Gunn was very much at the heart of B&C. Small in stature, but with a strong and colourful personality, he was very much a product of Thatcher's Britain and was rarely out of the business sections of the Press. Starting his business career as a foreign exchange trader at Barclays, he made his name at Exco, the moneybroking empire he built from a £5.2m management buyout in 1979 and of which he was chief executive until he resigned in September 1985. By this time Exco was worth £510m, having been floated on the Stock Exchange in 1981 for £56m. The buyout had been backed by the original British & Commonwealth Shipping Company who also backed Gunn in the build–up of Telerate in which Exco had a 52 per cent stake. From an investment at minimal cost, Exco sold its stake in Telerate for £360m and it was over the question of what to do with the proceeds of this sale that Gunn resigned from Exco.

Nevertheless, it was the success of Exco, whose pre–tax profits rose from £9m in 1981 to £21.6m in 1985, and the Telerate deal in particular, which endowed Gunn with a King Midas reputation. This is very important to the understanding of future events at B&C which Gunn joined as an executive director after he resigned from Exco in September 1985. He then became chairman at the end of 1986. The announcement of both events had the effect of boosting B&C's share price significantly in anticipation of great things ahead. In the end it took just three years to turn an asset-rich if sleepy commercial services conglomerate into a rag-bag of financial services companies supported by a balance sheet with borrowings of £1.8bn and a net tangible deficit of £300m in the last published accounts at the end of 1989. The excesses which led to this situation were clearly encouraged by the raging bull market prior to October 1987. But long afterwards, the questions of the goodwill and level of debt on B&C's balance sheet were never given the attention they should have received, until it was too late.

The major deals

It was perhaps John Gunn's reputation that led the market to give B&C the benefit of the doubt whenever there was any. Because the group had a venture capital arm which took stakes in a whole range of companies from Anglia Secure Homes to Midland and Scottish Resources, B&C gave the impression of being more hyperactive than it actually was. The list of deals is nonetheless a fairly staggering one over such a short space of time and in itself says much about the corporate excesses of the 1980s.

B&C's major deals

Date	Deal	Company	%	Consideration £m
Nov 85	Sale	Exco	22	109
Nov 86	Bid	Exco	100	637
Dec 86	Bid	Steel Bros	55	45
Jun 87	Purchase	B&C shares	27	427
Aug 87	Sale	Country & New Town	44	45
Aug 87	Bid	Mercantile House	100	567
Jan 88	Bid	Abaco	100	188
Jun 88	Sale	Bricom	78	348
Jul 88	Bid	Atlantic Computers	100	410
Aug 89	Sale	Marshalls	100	160
Aug 89	Sale	Woodchester	31	67
Nov 89	Sale	Gartmore	100	155
Dec 89	Sale	Woodchester	29	49

Before looking at some of B&C's deals individually, it is worth quoting from B&C's strategy statement in January 1987. This said that 'Funding of subsidiaries and associates will be more centralised with greater emphasis on regular reporting of P&L, cash flow and balance sheets'. Hindsight permits a wry smile at this statement but in fact there appears to have been little central control. Instead, there appears to have been an obsession for doing the next deal and very little day-to-day control of the operating businesses from the centre. Indeed, it is worth repeating the point made in the introduction that B&C might just have survived the Atlantic debacle had all the previous deals been soundly based and if B&C had adhered to its own strategy statement. It should be remembered that B&C paid £416m for Atlantic in July 1988. The previous December B&C's accounts showed shareholders' funds of £1.34bn, so although the demise of Atlantic would have been extremely painful, it would not necessarily have been fatal had everything else been well. But it wasn't.

The Exco acquisition

John Gunn's first major deal was well received and gave little hint of the problems ahead apart from one aspect which was completely ignored at the time.

The £637m B&C paid for Exco was equivalent to 265p a share. Exco then owned London Forfaiting and had a cash pile of £322m, thanks to the sale of the Telerate stake. In 1987 moneybroking made pre-tax profits of £44.7m and London Forfaiting £16.5m. Thus, on a 35 per cent tax charge and after allowing for the £322m cash pile, B&C paid £315m for net profits of just under £30m in 1987 – a reasonable P/E of around 10. So far, so good. B&C had acquired a strong cash flow and Exco's cashpile provided the ammunition to develop the group into a financial services conglomerate.

The only aspect of the deal that might have caused concern was that when Gunn joined the B&C board in September 1985, the first move thereafter was the sale by B&C of its 21.6 per cent in Exco held as a result of backing the 1979 buyout. The stake was sold at 215p a share, 50p below the price at which B&C launched their bid for the whole of Exco only 13 months later. The inference here is a lack of long-term strategic thinking. There may also have been a hint of an addiction to deal-making as an end itself which could have been levelled at B&C with more justification a year or two later.

The Caledonia share buy-in

In June 1987 the next deal came from an unexpected source when B&C announced that it was to buy in for cancellation 90m shares representing 26 per cent of the total for £427m, equivalent to 475p a share. The shares were part of the 32 per cent stake held by Caledonia Investments, the vehicle through which the Cayzer family had exercised effective control over the old B&C for years. B&C paid Caledonia £100m in cash and issued £327m preference shares which were to be repaid in equal instalments from 1988 to 1991 covered by a bank guarantee, but one which carried a rising coupon which would cost B&C £14m a year.

For the Cayzers, this was an excellent deal; the way it was structured enabled them to cash in the majority of their investment in B&C free of capital gains tax and their capital repayments were guaranteed by Barclays Bank. For B&C, the benefits were less clear. The commitment to pay £105m (including ACT) a year for four years in capital redemption plus £14m p.a. interest on the new preference shares helped to complete the deadly triangle when Atlantic's profits proved to be illusory and the disposal programme failed to go according to plan. At the time, no-one paid much attention to the cash-flow implications of the deal, which was viewed as welcome because it removed the influence of the Cayzers whose significant minority might have slowed down the transition of B&C into a financial services group. Also, despite paying out £100m in cash, B&C still had £350m of cash or near cash with which to develop the group.

Mercantile House

In July 1987, B&C announced an agreed £490m bid for Mercantile House, Exco's main moneybroking rival which also owned Alexanders Laing & Cruickshank (ALC) and Oppenheimer, the US fund manager which managed $10bn of funds (ten per cent in UK unit trusts). It was Oppenheimer that attracted B&C because it was complementary to Gartmore, its existing UK fund management operation. B&C had already agreed to sell ALC to Credit Lyonnais and in due course planned to sell the operations of Marshalls (moneybrokers) and Williams Street (US government bond brokers).

A potential rival bid from Quadrex forced B&C to increase the value of its bid to £567m in August 1987 and the offer went unconditional a few weeks before the stock market crash. Consideration was via the issue of new shares and convertible preference shares. As part of the revised bid, Quadrex had apparently agreed to buy Marshalls and William Street for £280m, but after the crash it failed to complete the agreement (the resulting litigation has yet to be concluded). Marshalls was eventually sold to the management for £160m, William Street proved unsaleable, and after deducting the £36m paid for ALC, B&C ended up paying a net £371m for $10bn (£6.4bn) of funds under management or a very pricey 5.8 per cent of funds. B&C's administrators will now be lucky to get £120m for Oppenheimer.

As well as the question of price, there was the matter of goodwill which represented most of the purchase price and still amounted to around £350m after the sale of Marshalls and nearly £600m when the Exco acquisition was taken into account. Although B&C opted to write off the goodwill in a straight line over 25 years (the 1988 amortisation charge was £41.9m) this method clearly overstated the worth of B&C's assets, particularly when the price paid reflected the inflated pre-crash market.

Abaco

The acquisition of Abaco was B&C's next move and further stoked up the goodwill carried on B&C's balance sheet. Abaco had been a 26 per cent associate of B&C since 1986 and was engaged primarily in insurance broking, loss adjusting and estate agency – all 'people businesses'. B&C's offer in December 1987 for the remainder of the share capital at 69p a share valued Abaco at £186m, yet as at 30 June 1987, Abaco had shareholders' funds of only £507,000 and EPS in the year to June 1987 were only 2.3p a share. It is not surprising that after the acquisition, B&C injected £30m of new capital into Abaco. This, plus the cash element of the bid removed £106m from B&C's cash pile.

Abaco's pre-tax profit in 1987 was £6.5m but the offer document stated that the results did 'not reflect the earnings capacity of the business as (then) constituted because of the large number of significant acquisitions completed during the year and since the year end'. Abaco's own accounts would make an interesting case study, but suffice it to say that the subsequent collapse of the housing market meant the earnings capacity was never realised, leaving B&C with another £150m of pretty useless goodwill on its balance sheet.

The Bricom buyout

B&C's balance sheet problems were compounded by the sale of a majority stake in Bricom to the management in July 1988 for £398m. Bricom contained the commercial and service activities of the old B&C. Apart from property worth in the region of £100m, Bricom represented virtually all the tangible assets of B&C. On the surface, the P/E of 19.6 looked a good deal for B&C, but the £30.5m pre-tax profits reported in 1987 really did understate the earnings potential of the group and the conservative accounting used over the years for what had been the heart of British & Commonwealth under the Cayzer family's management had also understated the asset value of the group. At Bristow Helicopters, for example, one of Bricom's subsidiaries, the fleet was depreciated over eight years against a typical life of 25 years – hardly accounting for growth!

B&C retained a 22 per cent stake in Bricom. Using its cash flow and disposal proceeds, Bricom repaid over half its acquisition loan within 18 months and the 1990 medium-term loan was repaid a year early. When, 20 months after the buyout, B&C sold most of its residual stake to Bricom's other institutional shareholders for £21.6m, B&C proudly announced the value of its investment had doubled. What a pity it only held 22 per cent of the equity! The ultimate twist came just before the final demise of B&C when Bricom, now debt free, was sold to a Swedish buyer for £338m.

Atlantic Computers

Meanwhile, B&C had made what proved to be its fifth major acquisition having also built up a 60 per cent interest in Woodchester Investments, the Irish leasing company, through market purchases and capital injections for a total cost of around £35m. The agreed £416m bid for Atlantic was announced barely a month after the Bricom deal and added another £350m of goodwill to the balance sheet, bringing the total to around £1.5bn which exceeded shareholders' funds by around £300m at the end of 1988. Thus, with a net tangible deficit of £300m and total borrowings of £1.8bn at the end of 1988, B&C never really had a chance once its operating profits began to be hit by the downturn in financial services. The accounting treatment of Atlantic's profits was found to have exaggerated them hugely, as discussed in Chapter 9 on Contingent Liabilities. The bottom line here was that B&C had to write off £550m against the £416m acquisition cost of Atlantic less than two years after it was made. B&C's administrators are still wrestling with Atlantic's liabilities and the final bill is still unquantified.

Holed below the water line

However, as referred to earlier, B&C's balance sheet was already in a sickly state before Atlantic went under. There was no question of dubious accounting here because all this was in the balance sheet as outlined below. What is not clear is that the goodwill carried from B&C's acquisitions was far too high in relation to the then current worth of the businesses. We have outlined these major acquisitions earlier and whereas the Exco deal was a good one in price terms and strategic logic, B&C paid far too much with the benefit of hindsight for Mercantile House, Abaco and Atlantic. The errors were compounded by the sale of Bricom at what turned out to be something of a bargain price for the buyers.

British & Commonwealth debt position

31 December	1988 £m	1988 £m	1989 est £m	1989 est £m
Debt repayable within one year				
Bank overdrafts and loans	−472.0		−102	
Cash	272.4			
Caledonia Pref shares	−81.9		−81.9	
Debt repayable after more than one year		−281.5		−183.9
Fixed loans and overdrafts	−621.1		−621.1	
7.75% CULS	−320.5		−320.5	
10.5% unsecured loan stock 23012	−231.4		−231.4	
Other	−96.4		−96.4	
Caledonia Pref shares	−245.6		−163.7	
	−1515.0		−1413.1	
Total borrowings		−1796.5		−1617.0
Less liquid investments		265.9		160.0
Total net debt		−1530.6		−1453.0

1989 cash in		1989 cash out	
Marshalls sale	£160m	Caledonia pref (inc ACT)	£105m
Woodchester sale	£67m	ESOP	£50m
Portfolio sales	£120m est	Dividend payments	£34m
		Advance to BCMB	£60m
	£347m		£249m

Without Atlantic, B&C could have made around £60m pre-tax in 1990, but after tax, preference dividends and minorities this would have left attributable profits of only £18m. Thus, if the group had maintained the dividend at 9.25p at a cost of £33m, the 1990 Caledonia preference share repayment of £105m would have led to a cash outflow of around £120m. On top of the existing debt mountain this means that B&C would have had no option but to start selling the family silver such as Gartmore. Once this started to occur, there really was no future for B&C.

Ignoring the warning signs

It cannot be said that the market entirely ignored B&C's problems because the shares fell from a peak of 565p in 1987 to well below 100p before the final disaster occurred. However, a number of commentators were seeking to explain away B&C's debt despite it being clearly exposed in the accounts, and few people seriously questioned the value of B&C's goodwill or considered the cash–flow implications of the Caledonia deal and the interest bill on the mounting debt.

It was cash flow as much as anything which killed B&C; but we must finish with Atlantic and the signal which proved to be the thin end of the accounting wedge. In B&C's 1989 interim statement, barely 12 months after Atlantic became a subsidiary of the group, the following paragraph appeared:

> The pattern of investment in computer technology is changing rapidly and Atlantic has responded by further improving its leasing strategy and its lease portfolio management techniques. Accordingly, Atlantic's lease portfolio is being reviewed as part of our assessment of the fair value of the businesses acquired and appropriate provisions will be made as necessary. This review is not expected to have material impact on Atlantic's continuing growth or on the group's 1989 earnings.

In retrospect, this turned out to be the most potent warning of all.

APPENDIX III

POLLY PECK

On 3 September 1990 Polly Peck announced record interim results for the six months to 30 June 1990 and made enthusiastic comments on prospects for the year and beyond. On 20 September 1990 the shares were suspended at 108p following a Serious Fraud Office raid on a private company associated with Polly Peck's Chairman, Chief Executive and 25 per cent shareholder Asil Nadir. After a further month of negotiations with its banks Polly Peck was placed in administration on 25 October 1990.

The rise

In 1980 Asil Nadir took control of a small UK textiles company, Polly Peck, which enjoyed spectacular share price performance following the injection and development of his Cyprus/Turkey assets. While the general direction was up, performance was volatile with both the existence and profitability of the assets under constant question, as was the relationship with other Nadir vehicles. In the mid 1980s the shares suffered a major setback. Profits growth slowed, City expectations were disappointed and after a period of isolation a number of key senior management appointments were made.

At the start of 1989 Polly Peck was capitalised at around £700m and comprised two main business areas, food and electronics, with two smaller operations in leisure and textiles – the former expanding, the latter contracting. Both food and electronics were based in Cyprus and Turkey although a number of acquisitions had been made in Europe, the USA and the Far East in an attempt to expand the geographical spread of the group. This strategy was only partially successful and a stagnant share price was unsettled by a number of management departures.

All this changed in September 1989 when Polly Peck bought Del Monte, the USA fresh food group, for £560m partially funded by a £280m rights issue at 245p, and in October a 51 per cent stake in Sansui, a quoted Japanese electronics company for £69m. Both Del Monte and Sansui operated in activities where Polly Peck had considerable experience and both added strong brand names and international exposure.

Amid widespread talk of synergy benefits the share price performed strongly at the end of 1989 and into 1990 and entered the FTSE 100 with a peak market capitalisation of over £1.5bn. This strength was maintained by anticipation of further corporate activity designed both to reduce debt and to ensure the share price reflected the true value of its underlying businesses, statements formally repeated in the April 1990 report and accounts.

The first restructuring took place in May 1990 when Polly Peck injected its Far Eastern electronics operations into Sansui, taking its stake from 51 per cent to 70 per cent, and floated a minority stake in its Turkish electronics operation, Vestel, on the Istanbul stock exchange. This provided a market valuation for all of the electronics division and in the middle of 1990 the market was tantalised by the expectation of similar proposals for the food division although these were subsequently overtaken by the events of August onwards.

Bankers worry

The interim balance sheet for June 1990 showed net debt of £863m and gearing of 93 per cent, little changed from the full year December 1989 position of £800m of net debt and 95 per cent gearing. Net debt was expected to fall in the near future from a number of corporate disposals resulting from the ongoing restructuring of Polly Peck following the major acquisitions of Del Monte and Sansui in 1989.

It is not totally clear whether the collapse in the share price following the aborted buyout caused the fall in confidence among Polly Peck's bankers or whether events proceeded in parallel. However September saw debts being called and uncommitted bank lines withdrawn, causing a major cash flow problem. On 5 October 1990 Polly Peck made a presentation to its bankers and a steering committee of ten banks was formed to represent the more than 100 lenders to Polly Peck. The committee commissioned a report into the company's financial affairs. However as details emerged of the position in Northern Cyprus the banks' standstill agreement collapsed and the company was placed in administration.

Subsequent revelations showed that of £405m cash balances at the interim stage £300m was deposited with banks in Northern Cyprus and Turkey and apparently unavailable for remittance back to the UK. It also became clear that leisure expenditure in Northern Cyprus was considerably higher than expected, with some £230m apparently committed to a number of unspecified new ventures.

It was ironic but perhaps inevitable that Cyprus and Turkey should result in Polly Peck's downfall. After all the group spent much of the 1980s under suspicion over both the quality and quantity of profits arising from the region. However in 1989, the completion of two major acquisitions, Del Monte and Sanui, offered the prospect of totally transforming the group through extending regional strengths to the international markets.

The fall

August 1990 was the month when Polly Peck began to unravel. Press reports pointed to an Inland Revenue investigation into European–based dealing in Polly Peck shares. This began to destabilise the share price which had started the month at 418p, although this situation was rapidly reversed when Asil Nadir announced that he was considering taking Polly Peck private.

However within a week these intentions were withdrawn following representations from unspecified significant shareholders; the Polly Peck share price began to fall, a fall that was accelerated by an adverse Stock Exchange report into the conduct of Mr Nadir and various other directors of the company during the course of the 'buyout', together with press revelations about well–informed European trading in Polly Peck shares.

It was not until the shares had been suspended that the full details of Polly Peck's problems started to emerge. Firstly it became clear that the share price fall was accelerated by banks selling Polly Peck stock held by them as security for loans to Asil Nadir, notwithstanding further buying by Mr Nadir as the share price fell. Secondly, a full–scale financial crisis developed.

Conclusions

With the benefits of hindsight the market appears to have been misled on two counts: firstly the shares appear to have been manipulated and secondly considerable unexpected capital expenditure appears to have taken place in the leisure division.

It is possible that the blocked Cyprus/Turkey balances also fall into this category although examination of the 1988 and 1989 accounts reveals a number of areas of concern. Interest charges were remarkably low in relation to levels of debt; the cash flow particularly in 1988 showed considerable currency impact and finally the tax charge was well below average. In 1989, however, the currency impact was minimal although cash flow remained negative with funds from operations being more than offset by a sharp rise in working capital.

Even now it is difficult to judge whether Polly Peck failed because of malpractice or from fundamental flaws in currency mismatching, working capital controls or even just the absolute level of debt. Had Polly Peck been able to complete its planned 1990 restructuring it is possible that debt pressures could have fallen sharply. However it is clear that capital commitments in the leisure division were rising sharply which would have once more increased the Cyprus exposure and left the group uncomfortably exposed to the then forthcoming recession.

INDEX